Children in the City

COI‍‍

This timely and thought-provoking book explores children's lives and well-being in contemporary cities. At a time of intense debate about the quality of life in cities, this book examines how they can become good places for children to live. Through contributions from childhood researchers in Europe, Australia and America, the book shows the importance of studying children's lives in cities from a comparative and generational perspective. It also contains fascinating accounts of city living from children themselves and offers practical design solutions.

The authors consider the importance of the city as a social, cultural and material place for children, and explore the connections and boundaries between home, neighbourhood, community and city. Throughout, they stress the importance of engaging with how children see their city in order to reform it within a child-sensitive framework.

This book is invaluable reading for students and academics in the field of anthropology, sociology, social policy and education. It will also be of interest to those working in the field of architecture, urban planning and design.

Pia Christensen is Senior Researcher at the National Institute of Public Health, Copenhagen, Denmark. Her previous publications include *Research with Children: Perspectives and Practices*, Falmer Press (2000).

Margaret O'Brien is a Reader at the Centre for Research on the Child and Family in the School of Social Work and Psychosocial Studies, University of East Anglia, United Kingdom. Her previous publications include *Children in Families: Research and Policy*, Falmer Press (1996).

Future of Childhood Series
Series Editor: Alan Prout

Children in the City
Home, neighbourhood and community

Edited by
Pia Christensen and
Margaret O'Brien

 RoutledgeFalmer
Taylor & Francis Group

LONDON AND NEW YORK

First published 2003 by RoutledgeFalmer
11 New Fetter Lane, London EC4P 4EE

Simultaneously published in the USA and Canada
by RoutledgeFalmer
29 West 35th Street, New York, NY 10001

RoutledgeFalmer is an imprint of the Taylor & Francis Group

© 2003 Pia Christensen and Margaret O'Brien, selection and
editorial matter; individual chapters, the contributors

Typeset in 10.5/12pt Bembo by Graphicraft Limited, Hong Kong
Printed and bound in Great Britain by TJ International Ltd,
Padstow, Cornwall

British Library Cataloguing in Publication Data
A catalogue record for this book is available from the British Library

Library of Congress Cataloging in Publication Data
A catalog record has been requested

ISBN 0-415-25925-8 (PB)
ISBN 0-415-25924-X (HB)

To our children of the city and the country
Josefine, Tobias, Patrick and Rosie

Contents

Figures

Tables

Contributors

Editors

Pia Christensen is Senior Researcher at the National Institute of Public Health, Copenhagen, Denmark, and was formerly Co-director of Centre for the Social Study of Childhood, University of Hull. Her main research interests are in the anthropology of children, medical anthropology, and rural and urban families. She has published widely on children and health, schooling and the family. These publications include *Research with Children: Perspectives and Practices*, co-edited with A. James (Falmer Press, 2000). Her recent research includes studies of children's use and understanding of time (part of the ESRC Research Programme on Children 5–16: Growing into the 21st Century (UK) and the Danish Research Council's 'Children's Living Conditions and Welfare' programme). She is currently carrying out research on children, young people and food.

Margaret O'Brien is a Reader at the Centre for Research on the Child and Family in the Department of Social Work and Psychosocial Studies at the University of East Anglia. Her research interests are in the social relations and community context of family life and childhood and in the position of fathers in families. She is an empirical social science researcher and clinical psychologist. She has published widely, including *Children in Families: Research and Policy*, co-edited with Julia Brannen (Falmer, 1996); and *Muslim Families in Europe: Social Existence and Social Care*, co-authored with Fatima Husain (EU DGV, 1999). Recent research projects include: Childhood, Urban Space and Citizenship: Child-sensitive Urban Regeneration, which is part of the ESRC Research Programme on Children 5–16: Growing into the 21st Century, and Muslim Families in Europe (EU-funded).

Contributors

Claudio Baraldi is Associate Professor in the Department of Language and Culture Sciences at the University of Modena and Reggio Emilia and scientific secretary of LIA (Childhood and Adolescence Research Centre) in the Department of Sociology at the University of Urbino. His studies and research concern cultures of childhood, children's cultures and forms of communication between children and adults, primarily in interventions promoting children's education and social participation. Recently he has edited *I diritti di bambini e degli adolescenti* (Donzelli, 2001), *Il bambino salta il muro* (Junior, 2001), *Una città con i bambini*, with Guido Maggioni (Donzelli, 2000).

Louise Chawla is an Associate Professor at Whitney Young College, Kentucky State University and Associate Faculty in the Environmental Studies Program at Antioch New England Graduate School in New Hampshire. She is a developmental and environmental psychologist whose research and publications focus on children's environmental experience and the development of environmental values and behaviours. She also serves as international coordinator of Growing Up in Cities for the MOST Programme of UNESCO. Her latest publication is *Growing Up in an Urbanising World* (UNESCO/ Earthscan, 2001).

Karen Fog Olwig is a Senior Lecturer in Anthropology at the University of Copenhagen and Professor at the University in Trondheim. She is currently using life-story interviews to research dispersed Caribbean family networks and the socio-cultural meaning of place for family relations. She is also co-editing a volume on children and place as seen from different cross-cultural perspectives. Her publications include *Global Culture, Island Identity* (Harwood, 1993), *Siting Culture*, co-edited with Kirsten Hastrup (Routledge, 1997) and *Migration and Work*, co-edited with Ninna Nyberg Sørensen (Routledge, 2002).

Gunilla Halldén is Professor at the Department of Child Studies, Linköping University. She has carried out research on parental ideas and common-sense psychology and on children's ideas about family life. Her work deals with the construction of childhood and of the 'good parent' in relation to gender issues. Recent publications include: 'Competence and connection; gender and generation in boy's narratives', *Gender and Education* (1997), 'Boyhood and fatherhood: narratives about a future family life', *Childhood* (1998), '"To be or not to be": absurd and humoristic descriptions as a strategy to avoid idyllic life stories – boys write about family life', *Gender and Education* (1999).

Karen Malone is a Senior Lecturer in science and environmental education at Monash University, Australia, and Asia-Pacific Director of the UNESCO-MOST Growing Up in Cities project. Her recent publications include *Researching Youth* (ACYS Press), co-edited with Julie McLeod, co-author of *Case Studies in Environmental Education* (Deakin University Press) and a chapter in *Growing Up in an Urbanising World* (UNESCO/Earthscan, 2001). In 2001 she was invited editor of a special edition of the international journal *Local Environment* on children, youth and sustainable cities (vol. 6 (1), 2001). She was a recent finalist for the prestigious National Eureka Allen Strom Research in Environmental Education Award, for the Australian National Museum, and Australian delegate for the IUCN World Conservation Union Education and Communication committee. Her research interests include narrative inquiry and participatory research, children's environmental literacy, environmental activism and children and sustainable development.

Hugh Matthews is Professor of Geography, Dean of the Graduate School and Director of the Centre for Children and Youth at University College Northampton. His research interests are in the geographies of children – in particular how they make use of place and understand space. Publications include *Making Sense of Place: Children's Understanding of Large-Scale Environments* (1992) and *Children and Community Regeneration* (2001). Hugh is inaugural editor of the new journal *Children's Geographies* (Taylor and Francis, 2003).

Virginia Morrow is a Senior Research Fellow in the Gender Institute, London School of Economics and Political Science. Children and young people's perspectives have been the primary focus of her research activities, about which she has published widely. Her Ph.D was a sociological study of secondary school children's involvement in work. Recent publications include: *Understanding Families: Children's Perspectives* (JRF/York Publishing Services, 1999); *Networks and Neighbourhoods: Children's and Young People's Perspectives* (Health Development Agency, 2001). She has also published papers on ethical and methodological issues related to social research with children.

Kim Rasmussen is a Research-lecturer in the Centre for Institutional Research, Højvangseminariet, Denmark. He is a Cultural Sociologist MA, and his Ph.D is on 'Media Literacy'. He has lectured at the University of Copenhagen, and the Royal Danish School of Educational Studies. He has published widely on modernity, media, photography, learning processes, children, childhood and disabled children, alternative early childhood institutions, reflexive pedagogic and the modernised welfare state. Since 1997 he has been involved in a series of research projects about childhood and childhood institutions. His recent book (with Søren Smidt) is *Spor af børns institutionsliv* [*Traces of the Institutional Lives of Children*] (Hans Reitzels Forlag, 2001).

Søren Smidt is a Researcher at the Centre for Institutional Research Højvangseminariet, Denmark. He is a psychologist (Cand Psych.) and Ph.D. He has written books and articles on modern childhood, institutionalisation in modernity, learning processes and education. He works with narrativity as a tool in child observation and with children as informants and social actors. He is active in developing strategies for democratic change in day-care institutions. His recent book (with Kim Rasmussen) is *Spor af børns institutionsliv* [*Traces of the Institutional Lives of Children*] (Hans Reitzels Forlag, 2001).

Helga Zeiher is a Research Scientist at the Max Planck Institute for Human Development and Education, Berlin, Germany. Until 1999, she was founding chair of the Sociology of Childhood section in the German Association of Sociology, and is now chair of the Working Group 'Children's access to space and use of time' in the European COST Action 19 'Children's Welfare'.

Her main research interests are children's shaping of their daily lives in family and peer relations and intergenerational division of labour. Recent book publications include: H. J. Zeiher and H. Zeiher, *Orte und Zeiten der Kinder: Soziales Leben im Alltag von Grossstadtkindern* [*Children's Places and Times: Everyday Social Life of City Children*] (Juventa, 1994); H. Zeiher, P. Buchner and J. Zinnecker (eds), *Kinder als Aussenseiter? Umbrüche in der gesellschaftlichen Wahrnehmung von Kindern und Kindheit* [*Are Children Outside Society? Changes in Social Perceptions of Children and Childhood*] (Juventa, 1996); and H. Hengst and H. Zeiher (eds), *Die Arbeit der Kinder: Kindheitskonzept und Arbeitsteilung zwischen den Generationen* [*Children's Work: The Concept of Childhood and the Intergenerational Division of Labour*] (Juventa, 2000).

Preface

In their Introduction to *Children in the City*, Pia Christensen and Margaret O'Brien draw attention to the current intense international debate about the future of the city. Half of the world's population, that is over 6 billion people, live in cities. City living presents many advantages because, in principle, it concentrates services, social networks, cultural resources and so on together and enables their efficient provision. However, in practice contemporary cities face many problems. Although there are still many differences of scale and kind between cities in different parts of the world, these issues traverse the distinction between developed and developing countries. For example, poverty flourishes in the midst of prosperity and in many countries the gap between the rich and the poor is widening; social divisions proliferate and new ones are created; people face homelessness and insecure tenure; there are threats to the environment and health; and transport systems face overload and breakdown. Such problems might, it seems, be best approached through new social and political alliances and through forms of inclusive governance that help to make the voices of marginalised groups, including children, better heard. Though this book deals primarily with children of the 'North', it nevertheless brings an international dimension to the discussion, with contributions from Europe, the Americas and Australia.

Children too are concentrated in cities. It is estimated by the UN that 60 per cent of the world's children will live in cities by the year 2025. For millions of children the contours of their everyday life and experience are (in part) shaped by city environments. Many contributors to this volume show the importance of this, for example in their relationships with adults and other children, their mobility and the kinds of experiences that are opened or closed for them. Children experience and use the urban environment in ways that may overlap with but are also different from adults. The problems of contemporary cities impact on them through, for example, crime, traffic, racism and environmental decay and squalor. Not all children are affected in the same way. Relatively affluent children may be insulated and isolated from these problems (although the social division that this maintains and perhaps magnifies is also a problem). For poorer children the street and other public spaces may still be important places. But in their use of them they are often identified as 'out of place' and dangerous. They are also, in fact, exposed to risks that threaten their health and well being precisely because cities seem to have become less 'child-friendly'. However, whilst attention is often focused on the different childhood experiences of the poor and the rich, it is also important that attention is paid to what we must, for want of a better term, call 'ordinary childhoods'. This involves moving beyond ideas of the city as a problem or children as a problem, highlighting how such ordinary city child-hoods are formed, lived and experienced. It is important that this perspective is brought to the study of city life and it is a noticeable and valuable feature of many chapters in *Children in the City*.

Over the last decade the social sciences have seen a tremendous growth of interest in 'space' and 'place'. Not only has their importance been redis-covered as a feature of social relationships but also the concepts themselves have been unpacked and explored in numerous ways. Although children have not been absent from this debate, they are far from being equal figures with adults. This book, therefore, makes an important contribution to a small but growing literature located at the intersection of spatial and generational relationships. *Children in the City* records children's experiences of and per-spectives on the city in many different social and historical circumstances. It critically examines ways in which children's interests might be better represented in the processes through which cities change. It is, therefore, for reasons of both social action and social science that I welcome this new addition to the *Future of Childhood Series*.

Alan Prout
Series Editor

Acknowledgements

We are indebted to the sterling technical and administrative support provided by Julia Warner, of the Centre for Research on the Child and Family at the University of East Anglia, in the production of the final manuscript. We would also like to thank Alan Prout, *The Future of Childhood* series editor, for his intellectual support and helpful advice throughout the life of the book. Pia Christensen would like to thank her family for their keen interest in and support of her work on the social study of children. Finally Margaret O'Brien would like to thank her husband Jon Greenfield for his continual support to her and his enthusiasm for the urban project.

1   Children in the city

Introducing new perspectives

Pia Christensen and Margaret O'Brien

> I don't want a Childhood City. I want a city where children live in the
> same world as I do.
>
> (Ward 1978: 204)

The aim of this book is to explore children's lives in contemporary cities. We
are writing at a time of intense international debate about the quality of life
in cities, and a central theme in this debate has been how cities can become
good enough places for children to live in alongside other generations. Colin
Ward, in his important book *The Child in the City*, from which we have
drawn great inspiration, strongly advocates that cities should be places where
children and adults can live together. However, as many of the chapters in
this book show, the creation and sustaining of cities in such a way involves
a complex and difficult process of negotiation. The sites of negotiation are
multiple, from struggles over where to kick a football or discussions between
parents and children about going out to play to wider debates concerning
land use or planning for the future form of cities.

Three key themes permeate this book. Firstly, the issue of extending
the principle of inclusivity to children in debates about the city is crucial.
We argue that 'a city for all' has to include sensitivity to children both as a
social group, with all its complexities, and to children as individuals. A key
part of this sensitivity involves understanding city life from children's perspectives. Our second theme is an emphasis on the overlapping connections
between home, neighbourhood, community and city. Living in the city is as
much about negotiating relationships with other humans as it is about living
in material places and spaces: there is continual interactivity between the
webs of relationships, places and spaces for children and adults alike. A third
theme concerns the importance of promoting sensitivity to children and an
engagement of children in the processes of change in cities. We argue that an
understanding of how children experience and construct a sense of place is
a foundation for engaging children in changing such places. We need to
know how they see the city in order to reform the city within a child-
sensitive framework. Whilst the successful modern urban child might be
expected to be an active navigator through the multiple settings of modern

cities, the contributors to this collection show that children occupy both complex and contradictory spaces in contemporary cities.

Studying children in cities

Internationally during the last two decades there has been an upsurge of human and social science research from the perspectives of children (Qvortrup *et al.* 1994; James and Prout 1990). Studies of children's lives, circumstances and welfare in contemporary societies have provided empirical evidence for children's agency, experiences and conceptual understandings in a range of different social contexts. This work has produced so much original insight that children have been acknowledged as active social and cultural actors and, as informants and participants in research. Children have emerged as a key source for understanding the dynamics of their everyday lives (Christensen and James 2000a). The paradigm shift within the human and social sciences, in particular, has had wide influence on theoretical thinking, with an impact also on policy and practice. However, childhood research is also a complex field, signified as it is by the coexistence of new and traditional perspectives, a reality that raises important questions about what working with children's perspectives entails. Firstly, this question underlines the necessity for researchers to attend to and carefully work through the implications of seeing children as social actors for research practice. Being reflexive and being systematic seem to be important requirements of researchers, when conventional thinking and routine actions may threaten or undermine genuine endeavours to work with children. Secondly, as is strongly pointed out and discussed by several authors in this volume (Chawla and Malone, Chapter 8; O'Brien, Chapter 9; Morrow, Chapter 10; Baraldi, Chapter 11), when it comes to working together with children to improve and plan their neighbourhood, town or city, it is important that children's insights are carefully considered, interpreted and followed through in action. In their work these authors have been particularly committed to making children's insights accessible and usable for town planners and politicians and, as they emphasise, there are many important lessons to be drawn. It is stressed, for example, that participation must not become a meaningless token. It is important that all bodies involved in the process are willing to let children's perspectives be influential in the design process. Part of the task of involving children therefore is to prepare the ground in this way. For, as Roberts has argued with sensitivity and clarity: 'It is clear that *listening* to children, *hearing* children, and *acting* on what children say are three very different activities, although they are frequently elided as if they were not' (Roberts 2000: 238) (our emphasis).

Child research is a wide interdisciplinary field with many different approaches to the study of children. At present a split between qualitative and quantitative approaches tends to mark the area. In this volume, however, we have brought these different approaches together to show how a rich account of children's lives in contemporary cities can be gained only through drawing on different sources. Much work has to be done to integrate knowledge that is produced in intensive research, such as qualitative and ethnographic investigations, with knowledge produced in extensive research, such as surveys and longitudinal studies. Neither qualitative nor quantitative methods are sufficient in themselves when seeking to understand the complexity of children's lives in the contemporary city. It seems, however, that there is much scope for using a mixed-methods approach, which can draw on the strength of each perspective and at the same time can combine these with more in-depth and sensitive analysis of what life in the city means to children.

In the studies reported in this book a wide range of methods have been employed. These can be grouped around the distinction between children 'seeing' the city and children's use of or 'doing' the city (cf. Augé 1995). To illuminate children's observations, perceptions and views many authors have used children's photographs, drawings and maps. A narrative approach, such as the use of life stories, recollections, and children writing stories and keeping diaries, is favoured by several contributors to this volume because they facilitate children's, and indeed older people's, reflexivity on the immediate and distant past, but also as a way to explore with children their imagined futures. Together with more commonly used methods such as interviews, focus and peer group discussions, participant observation and surveys this book establishes a broad range of methods to study children in cities.

For all contributors, eliciting children's perspectives has been a central commitment. Baraldi (Chapter 11), for example, advocates the necessity for researchers to be imaginative and sensitive in their approach to working with children. It is important to develop ways of involving children that build on their own communicative practices (Clarke and Moss 2001) and engage with their 'cultures of communication' (Christensen and James 2000a) through paying attention to the social actions of children, their use of language and the meanings they put into words, notions and actions.

Children at home in the city

During the nineteenth century in Europe and North America the gradual separation of the work place from the home led to the emergence of the 'home' as a prime physical and spatial location for people's social and emotional lives. The home became a key context for the family, which came to represent 'the modern domestic ideal' of parents and children living together forming a nuclear family (Allan and Crow 1989). This process centres children within the family, nested in bonds of love and care, with the parents responsible for their health and socialisation.

From a contemporary European and North American perspective therefore, children are placed in the family home and this location has become a prominent site for establishing a sense of belonging (Brannen and O'Brien 1996). The family and the home are sites within which togetherness become articulated and established regardless of material, ideological and emotional conditions (Douglas 1991). Douglas argues that homes structure time and memory through their capacity to order the activities of family members spatially, for example through such practices as communal eating, the division of labour, moral obligations and the distribution of resources. Human interactions take place within the physical space of the house, which is, in and through time, transformed into a 'home', the place where identities are worked on (see for example Birdwell-Pheasant and Lawrence-Zúniga 1999).

In addition, as Bachelard's (1958 (1994)) classic account suggests, houses can contain and shape the memories and dreams of their inhabitants as a shelter from an ever-changing outside. In this sense then the home can be seen to form an important base for children. However, the home is often thought of in static terms (Sibley 1995). In contrast it has been suggested that 'home' must also be seen as constituted by the movements – in and out of the house – by family members: 'Children's understanding of themselves and of their family is achieved through the movement in, out and around the home of different family members as much as it is through the "home" as a material space and a fixed locality' (Christensen *et al.* 2000: 143). We suggest that children's understanding of the house and their 'border work' around the inside and the outside forms part of the foundation for children to develop social skills and competencies as navigators and negotiators in the public realm of the neighbourhood and the city.

Throughout this volume the authors demonstrate how what goes on in the domestic life of homes, and what happens in neighbourhoods including the city at large, are closely connected. In their everyday life children regularly move in and between the spaces of the home, street, neighbourhood, town and city. Norms and practices governing space and time in one arena have their impact on the other. For example, changes in the perceived safety of public spaces, generated by concerns about traffic or strangers, re-structure family practices, and in turn affect children's participation in civic life. Also as O'Brien (Chapter 9) argues, the increases in time spent indoors at home by many children in contemporary cities question the aptness of traditional layouts and space standards of conventional social housing. She points to the need for city planners to rethink indoor as well as outdoor space requirements in the move towards child-friendly neighbourhoods.

Children can be seen to share parents' constructions of the world outside the home as a place of risk and danger (Halldén, Chapter 3; O'Brien, Chapter 9; Morrow, Chapter 10) and they hold sometimes strongly ambivalent views about the safety of their city space. Children fear, like their parents, the risk of traffic, stranger danger, risk of drugs or they fear encounters with older teens and young people in the streets (Scott *et al.* 1998; Matthews *et al.* 1999; 2000). The latter exposes, of course, how the morals of the external world prey on the 'innocence' of children as older children are seen as causing trouble and danger for others (James and Jenks 1996).

By contrast, the physical structure of the house shelters the inside from the outside. The home can become a haven where parents can ensure their children's upbringing. They can make sure that they are safe and protected, provided with comfort and care, and safeguarded in their health and well-being. Yet, to some extent, these images are untrue when, for example, risk from the outside world can be recognised as exaggerated and the home is revealed as the primary context for the abuse to children.

The importance of the house as shelter for children and their families is explored through the practical engagement of children in creating their own house. Halldén (Chapter 3) examines the location of the home itself and the negotiation of inside and outside boundaries from children's perspectives. Through their stories of their prospective futures, which she gathered from them, the children also explore their present positions. Halldén carefully discusses through her case examples how, for children, 'the family is created in a house that becomes a home through the caring routines' of family members. In the children's accounts thresholds link the inside with the outside and as such form part of the constitution of home and family. Everyday domestic routines are especially important in children's accounts for creating a sense of place. In contrast, Olwig's oral histories of older people in St Thomas, part of the Danish West Indian islands (Chapter 4), shows how they remember the street as a place that allowed them as children to be 'at home'. As children they had been moved from the island of St John to St Thomas to work as servants. It was through their movements out of the city homes where they worked and into the street that the children were able to maintain a sense of home through meetings and contacts with their family and kin relations. The street allowed the children to be 'at home' with their family and kin and thus sustain a sense of belonging although they did not share the physical surroundings of a house with them. The children were only 'out of place', and in a vulnerable position, when they lost contact with this larger network community and became incorporated as isolated dependants into a city of strangers. Olwig's chapter throws light on the ways in which the city is constructed as place, and as a social and cultural site, in the lives of children. This socio-spatial perspective, she suggests, is important whether researchers are concerned with children 'confined' to urban institutions in Europe or North America, or with children living a life in the street in the developing world.

The street as passageway to neighbourhood and adulthood

In Olwig's account the street appears as an important site and vehicle for children's construction of social and cultural identity. This topic is also central to Matthews's argument (Chapter 7), which draws on data from children and young people in an English town. Matthews suggests that any decline in the use of 'the street' reduces children's opportunities for identity construction as 'the street' is often a site where children can 'separate or engage in the processes of separation' away from the adult gaze. In the street children and young people spend time with their peers. It is through their different uses and occupation of street space, including their encounters with adults, that young and older children, girls and boys, explore and come to understand their own present and prospective social relations and positions. In this way, Matthews argues that the street is important for understanding how children engage with their own growing up, suggesting that experiencing being in the street is a central part of a young person's separation from childhood. The streets in Matthews's account can be seen as providing liminal and fuzzy zones supporting young people in the transition to adulthood. In this way he takes a 'new' stance on the 'problem' of young people in city streets resonating with Addams's (1909 (1972)) classic manifesto. First writing in 1909 in America, she argued against pessimistic adult perspectives which construed children's and young people's presence in the public domain of the city streets as problematic, instead arguing that their presence formed part of their life project and indicated aspirations towards a serious engagement with civic life.

The street can allow children to develop social competencies and to perform or enact their growing maturity through movements in and away from the home and their neighbourhood. In this process of knowing and learning it is important to make a distinction between streets and children's own routes and shortcuts (Christensen, Chapter 2; Morrow, Chapter 10). Routes are ways in which children and young people track their own way through the city. They come to know their local place, and through developing such knowledge they become independent users of the city. Their routes are in and off the streets, using and learning their city through personal and collective routes rather than relying entirely on formal mapping or physical structures.

The loss of key locations such as the street as places to play in many contemporary cities is a theme that emerges in several chapters of this book. The importance of the availability of places and spaces near home is explored by Chawla and Malone (Chapter 8) and O'Brien (Chapter 9), who argue that there is a strong sense in which 'children live in the local' and that the quality of children's immediate environment close to home is crucial. As many studies have shown, when children grow older they also increase their home range and reach out to the public spaces and places just beyond the boundaries of the household (Moore 1986). In this context the spaces outside the apartment or house, such as courtyards, the garden, nearby green space and parks, become central sites of exploration and are important locations for the creation of confidence in being in the public arena for children. In contemporary urban contexts, significant unaccompanied movement out of the domestic home space and its immediate surroundings occurs from the ages of 8 or 9 years, often later for girls, and is greatest when children are in the company of other children (Matthews 1992). However, the incorporation of a regular, routinised outdoor life is most apparent from about the age of

11, when children in many countries move from primary school to the more distant secondary or high school using public transport. In other European countries such as the Nordic countries or Germany, where school finishes earlier in the afternoon, after-school clubs often allow more autonomous movement for children from the age of 11 onwards. Clearly, institutional contexts such as the organisation and structure of the school day, in particular its timing and the school's proximity to home, have significant impacts on children's use of the city and create expectations about their appropriate movement through it.

Several contributors to the book use the concept of institutionalisation to capture the loss of unstructured space free from regulation and supervision apparent in many contemporary societies. Zeiher (Chapter 5) in her study of highly urbanised Berlin, for example, expresses concern that modern children are growing up in an urban context where they tend to be ferried between dislocated 'islands' of activity. She suggests that urban children's life spaces are characterised by a context of insularisation whereby 'most of the children who live in the same neighbourhood spend much time in child-specific institutions'. In her analysis of two boys during the afternoons living in different neighbourhoods in West Berlin she traces their own shaping of their daily lives and its interconnection to physical and structural phenomena in contemporary society. She is also able to show how children themselves and in their everyday lives may resist the loss of spontaneous time and space to play. They do this by using strategies such as failing to turn up on time for organised events or arranging to meet friends on the way to after-school activities. In effect the children's actions meant that several institutions in their particular neighbourhood had to restructure some of their pre-organised schemes to make them more attractive to the children. However, whilst there is reason to be critical of this trend towards segregated play-spaces, recent studies also show that organised leisure centres and after-school clubs can be stimulating places for children (McKendrick *et al.* 2000; Smith and Barker 2000).

Rasmussen and Smidt (Chapter 6) perceive the move towards predetermined social activities as part of the broader process of *institutionalisation* occurring at a neighbourhood level. However, their research highlights the fact that informal locations, such as special hideaway places, offer children a wide range of play settings for autonomous exploration (cf. Hart 1979). In their study of Danish children's perception of their neighbourhoods, Rasmussen and Smidt stress the physicality and bodily nature of children's interactions with their environment. They argue that the realm of the senses is particularly important in understanding how children use their neighbourhoods. It is through bodily and sensory encounters with the physical environment that children come to embody the neighbourhood 'under their skin'. Similarly, Christensen (Chapter 2), drawing on studies carried out in Denmark and in England, shows how children construct an 'emplaced' knowledge of their neighbourhood as a simultaneously social and physical location, through their experiences, movements through it and embodied social interactions in it. Furthermore children through their life course are seen as engaged in constructing and understanding their personal biography in and of particular spatial localities. Her ethnographic account emphasises the collective practices of children as important in this process. Another important aspect, she argues, is the complex negotiation of knowledge of place and space between children and adults.

It is of course the case that because of their size children's sensual experience of the neighbourhood and household will be different from an adult one.

> Obviously the younger the child the closer his eye level to the ground, and this is one of the reasons why the floorscape – the texture and subdivisions of flooring and paving, as well as changes of level in steps and curves . . . is very much more significant for the young.
>
> (Ward 1978: 22)

The 'bigness' of people, furniture, lampposts, and cars to young children becomes real to adults only when a child's eye view is taken. Ward (1978) describes the surprise of architectural students when they created a mock-up of a room two-and-a-half times its actual size to represent a child's eye view. However, it is important to recognise that children's physical size also enables them to interact with the physical environment in ways that adults find difficult. In fieldwork data from an earlier study carried out by Christensen in Copenhagen, children themselves stressed this aspect. In essays where children wrote about 'what can children do that adults cannot do' children described how they could hide and crawl in and out of spaces in ways that were impossible for adults.

Children in cities and children's participation in urban planning

Since the post war period there has been a lively and imaginative body of literature on children's place in the city (McKendrick 2000). Key areas of research have included: cognitive mapping (Lynch 1977; Matthews 1992), the impact of urban traffic on children's mobility (Hillman *et al.* 1990), children's use of recreational and play space (Hart 1997; Moore 1986) and the more recent critical children's geographies (Holloway and Valentine 2000; Philo 2000). This book draws together new empirical enquiry on children in the city, from researchers who have been influenced by the new social studies of childhood perspective.

A rich tapestry of cities is represented in this book showing different levels of population density: from the high levels in London and Berlin to the relatively sparsely populated Nordic cities. Urban theorists such as Castells and Sassen have characterised large cities such as London, New York and Tokyo as global cities with a 'front-yard' of key financial control and command centres and a concentration of knowledge based economies, set against a 'back-yard' of highly polarised social and economic relations (Castells 1989; Sassen 1991). The impact of social and economic polarisation on children's lives in cities is traced in particular by Morrow (Chapter, 10) and O'Brien (Chapter 9), whose field work in urban centres in England, including London, highlights the emergence of no-go areas for children sustained by deteriorating infrastructures, traffic problems, ethnic tensions and enhanced parental anxieties. Fear and loathing of inner-city traffic, pollution, crime, and density have increased the attraction of out-of-town neighbourhoods for some families. For other families, particularly those living in dual-earner or poor households, urban living remains the only viable economic or lifestyle option.

As a consequence of the deteriorating quality of life in cities, making neighbourhoods better places for children and families has become more central in the debate about the state of the city in Europe and North America (Hart 1979; Bartlett *et al.* 1999). In the British context a recent national investigation team, led by the leading architect Sir Richard Rogers (Urban Task Force 1999), noted that the presence of children often changes adults' perceptions of their city:

> In persuading people to re-consider urban living we have to recognise that . . . *the crunch comes with having children.* An urban environment, previously perceived as diverse and stimulating, starts to appear unsafe. Schools and health services become more important.
>
> (Urban Task Force 1999: 35, our emphasis)

The importance of the quality of life for children, a key barometer of the good-enough neighbourhood, city or community is highlighted in Chawla and Malone's chapter which investigates neighbourhood quality through children's eyes. Their work is a part of the important Growing Up in Cities UNESCO programme, initiated in the 1970s by Kevin Lynch (1977). Using participatory action research with 10–15-year-olds living in low- and mixed-income communities across eight nations Chawla and Malone show how young people evaluate their urban environments and collaborate with adults to plan and implement improvements. Despite socio-economic variations in the communities Chawla and Malone found many similarities in how children and young people evaluated their cities as positive or negative places to live. These 'child-based indicators' are presented in the chapter alongside two case studies from Australia.

Similarly Morrow illuminates the importance of taking a holistic perspective of children's social relationships within different place contexts. Indeed in her study of 12–15-year-olds living in a deprived English town, she argues that social relationships take precedence over place in constructing a sense of community for children: 'community' for children appears to be located in a sense of 'belonging' that resides in relationships with other people, rather than in places. She shows that peer friendships as well as relationships within school and with kin are central to building up a sense of trust and security in the children's neighbourhoods and that urban regeneration programmes could facilitate these bonds between children and between the generations. Her chapter contains reflections on how Putman's concept of social capital can be applied to children in neighbourhoods and shows how 'a focus on social capital as a community level attribute has allowed research to prioritise the social context of children's everyday lives, rather than their individual health behaviours'.

The particular contribution children can make to ideas about improving urban neighbourhoods is shown in O'Brien's chapter, where she compares London children's ideas for urban improvement with those of their parents. Children had many useful ideas on neighbourhood renewal. More play space and city maintenance were high priorities, particularly for inner and outer London children. Better lighting was also important for children. Parents were more likely to prioritise enhanced security and traffic safety, showing different generational preoccupations about urban renewal. A more holistic urban regeneration policy approach clearly needs to balance children's needs and desires with parental needs and anxieties. Both O'Brien (Chapter 9) and Baraldi (Chapter 11) show how children can be insightful and creative when asked about their city environments.

In his analysis of the innovative Town of Children project based in Fano, a small coastal Italian town, Baraldi is able to show the importance of the mode of communication used by adults when they work with children in the urban planning process. He argues that a 'testimonial' form of communication between adult planner and children whereby the adult focuses on listening, understanding and discussing the children's perspectives, giving voice to their personal creativity, is a vital component of consultation. Through the analysis of videoed and transcribed group sessions he demonstrates the power of a participative testimonial approach over a more didactic way of working with children.

As Baraldi shows, we need to find ways of enabling children to express their preferences, desires and imagination about planning changes in the city as a way of informing future planning practice both in substance and in process. The practical requirement is to find a space between adult-dominated planning processes which simply ignore children's needs and desires, or which make ungrounded assumptions about them, and on the other hand a naive idealism which assumes that children can straightforwardly take the roles of adult citizens in a planning process. The need is to take account of the unavoidable complexities arising from different levels of maturity and understanding which largely depend on age, whilst nevertheless giving enhanced weight to the life-world of children. Whilst children as a social group do not always speak with one voice, the chapters in this book demonstrate that they show tremendous insight into how we can move towards a more generationally inclusive contemporary city.

References

Addams, J., 1909 (1972), *The Spirit of Youth and the City Streets* (Urbana and Chicago: University of Illinois Press).

Allan, G. and Crow, G. (eds), 1989, *Home and Family: Creating the Domestic Space* (Basingstoke: Macmillan).

Augé, M., 1995, *Non-places: Introduction to an Anthropology of Supermodernity* (London: Verso).

Bachelard, G., 1958 (1994), *The Poetics of Space* (Boston: Beacon Press).

Bartlett, S., Hart, R., Satterthwaite, D., De la Barra, X. and Missair, A., 1999, *Cities for Children: Children's Rights, Poverty and Urban Management* (London: Earthscan).

Birdwell-Pheasant, D. and Lawrence-Zúniga, D. (eds), 1999, *Houselife: Space, Place and Family in Europe* (Oxford: Berg).

Brannen, J. and O'Brien, M., 1996, 'Introduction'. In Brannen and O'Brien (eds), *Children in Families: Research and Policy* (London: Falmer Press).

Castells, M., 1989, *The Informational City* (Oxford: Blackwell Books).

Christensen, P. and James, A. (eds), 2000, *Research with Children: Perspectives and Practices* (London: Falmer Press).

Christensen, P. and James, A., 2000a, 'Researching children and childhood: cultures of communication'. In Christensen and James (eds), *Research with Children: Perspectives and Practices* (London: Falmer Press).

Christensen, P., James, A. and Jenks, C., 2000, 'Home and movement: children constructing "family time"'. In S. L. Holloway and G. Valentine (eds), *Children's Geographies: Playing, Living, Learning* (London: Routledge).

Clarke, A. and Moss, P., 2001, *Listening to Young Children: The MOSAIC Approach* (London: National Children's Bureau and Joseph Rowntree Foundation).

Douglas, M., 1991, 'The idea of home: a kind of space'. *Social Research*, 58 (1), 287–307.

Hart, R., 1979, *Children's Experiences of Place* (New York: Irvington).

Hart, R., 1997, *Children's Participation: From Tokenism to Citizenship* (London: Earthscan/ UNICEF).

Hillman, M., Adams, J. and Whitelegg, J., 1990, *One False Move: A Study of Children's Independent Mobility* (London: PSI).

Holloway, S. and Valentine, G. (eds), 2000, *Children's Geographies: Living, Playing and Transforming Everyday Worlds.* (London: Routledge).

James, A. and Jenks, C., 1996, 'Public perceptions of childhood criminality'. *British Journal of Sociology*, 47 (2), 315–331.

James, A. and Prout, A. (eds), 1990, *Constructing and Reconstructing Childhood: Contemporary Issues in the Sociological Study of Childhood* (London: Falmer Press).

Lynch, K., 1977, *Growing Up in Cities* (Cambridge, MA: MIT Press).

McKendrick, J., 2000, 'The geography of children: an annotated bibliography'. *Childhood* (Special issue on children's geographies), 7 (3), 359–87.

McKendrick, J., Bradford, M. and Fielder, A., 2000, 'Time for a party! Making sense of the commercialisation of leisure space for children'. In S. L. Holloway and G. Valentine (eds), *Children's Geographies: Living, Playing and Transforming Everyday Worlds* (London: Routledge).

Matthews, H., 1992, *Making Sense of Place: Children's Understanding of Large-Scale Environments* (Hemel Hempstead: Harvester Wheatsheaf).

Matthews, H., Limb, M. and Taylor, M., 1999, 'Reclaiming the streets: the discourse of curfew'. *Environment and Planning* A, 31, 10, 1713–30.

Matthews, H., Limb, M. and Taylor, M., 2000 'The street as thirdspace'. In S. L. Holloway and G. Valentine (eds), *Children's Geographies: Playing, Living and Learning*. (London: Routledge), 63–79.

Moore, R., 1986, *Children's Domain: Play and Play Space in Child Development* (London: Croom Helm).

Philo, C., 2000, 'The corner-stones of my world'. *Childhood* (Special issue on children's geographies), 7 (3), 243–56.

Qvortrup, J., 1995, 'Childhood and modern society: a paradoxical relationship'. In J. Brannen and M. O'Brien (eds), *Childhood and Parenthood* (London: Institute of Education).

Qvortrup, J., Bardy, M., Sgritta, G. and Wintersberger, H. (eds), 1994, *Childhood Matters: Social Theory, Practice and Politics* (Aldoshot: Avebury).

Roberts, 2000, 'Listening to children: and hearing them'. In Christensen and James (eds), *Research with Children: Perspectives and Practices* (London: Falmer Press).

Sassen, S., 1991, *The Global City* (Princeton: Princeton University Press).

Scott, S., Jackson, S. and Backett-Milburn, K., 1998, 'Swings and roundabouts: risk anxiety and the everyday worlds of children'. *Sociology*, 32 (4), 689–705.

Sibley, D., 1995, 'Families and domestic routines: constructing the boundaries of childhood'. In S. Pile and N. Thrift (eds), *Mapping the Subject* (London: Routledge).

Smith, F. and Barker, J., 2000, 'Contested spaces: children's experiences of out of school care in England and Wales'. *Childhood* (Special issue on children's geographies), 7 (3), 315–33.

Urban Task Force, 1999, *Towards an Urban Renaissance* (London: DETR).

Ward, C., 1978, *The Child in the City* (London: Architectural Press).

2 Place, space and knowledge

Children in the village and the city

Pia Christensen

> I walked. My mother had given me the freedom of the street as soon as I could say our telephone number. I walked and memorized the neighbourhood. I made a mental map and located myself upon it. At night in bed I rehearsed the small world's scheme and set challenges: Find the store using backyards only. Imagine a route from the school to my friend's house. I mastered chunks of town in one direction only; I ignored the other direction, toward the Catholic church . . . Walking was my project before reading. The text I read was the town; the book I made up was a map.
>
> (Dillard 1987: 424)

This is an account that Annie Dillard gives of her growing up in Pittsburgh, USA, in the 1950s. It is a vivid picture of how as a child she came to know her local area through her independent explorations and increasing mobility. Her account reveals that personal biography is always emplaced. For me, for example, first reading her book evoked memories of my own childhood and experiences of growing up during the same period in Copenhagen. Like Annie Dillard, I remember lying in bed before I went to sleep rehearsing routes, places and newly discovered shortcuts. I would go over playing in the courtyard of the flats I lived in or at friends' houses, in gardens and in the streets. I would linger on my experience of freedom and achieving new bodily skills and as I mastered different physical challenges and environments.

I reflected on my walk to school and how I had been doing in the game that, together with other children, I enjoyed playing on the way. The game involved walking without treading on the cracks between the paving stones. For whole periods this was set as our daily challenge. When someone failed to avoid the cracks, by putting a foot on even a tiny bit of the black line, it meant that he or she had to start again from the corner, the big white house or the lamppost that we had just passed. Only when it was getting really late and we had to run the last bit of the way was the challenge temporarily overturned. Often we played this game as a whole group, together setting the rules we had to obey. At other times I would play the game on my own.

Less pleasurable events also coloured my experience of walking to school. For example, when for some weeks a group of boys was making it a misery by threatening to beat me up or start regular physical fighting. I tried to work out how I could possibly escape them if only there was 'another way'. But the boys had carefully picked a spot where there was no other way to go. They blocked the path leading up to the school and uttered their threats and thus constrained my freedom to walk alone.

Through these kinds of activity I built up detailed knowledge of the local environment, its textures and structures, exploring and sensing it as I moved through it. In this chapter I want to take up these themes in relation to contemporary children, exploring the relationship between children's biography, movement and local knowledge of space and place. However, here I will not adopt the traditional approach, such as that cited above, where adults remember their childhood, although it can give important insights into childhood experiences from the child's point of view (Gullestad, 1996; see also Olwig, Chapter 4, below). Rather I will use material where children and young people themselves and in the present explore connections between their life course, identity and the places of their daily life (Rasmussen and Smidt 2001). In doing so I will draw on fieldwork material that I produced during ethnographic studies of children's understanding and use of time in a village in northern England and with children and young people in the city of Copenhagen, Denmark.[1] However, in this chapter I do not use the material to make a comparative analysis of England and Denmark, nor do I make a comparative analysis of villages and cities, although in my discussion I will draw out some differences and commonalities between them.

In this chapter I will explore the processes through which children gain knowledge about where they live, using material from these two different locations. I am concerned therefore with how children experience a place and how they construct a sense of place. These questions I suggest are fundamental to a broader understanding of children's lives in contemporary cities (as well as other localities).

Central to my exploration is Geertz's statement that 'No one lives in the world in general' (Geertz 1996: 262). My approach is phenomenological. I am concerned therefore with how we may begin to understand children's lives as formed through and out of a processual relationship in which personal biography, generation and growing up are interwoven with the use and meaning of the physical environment. The chapter shows some of the ways that children encounter, traverse, construct and perceive places. During their life course children are engaged in constructing and understanding their personal biography in and of particular spatial localities. In their accounts children both in the English village and in urban Copenhagen mapped their experiences and memories of growing up on to the spaces and places in which they took place. As these spaces came into place so, at the same time, the children themselves came into place.

This chapter demonstrates how children's coming to understand themselves takes place through their experiences, memories and use of the house, streets, neighbourhood, village and the city at large. For example, the children related their experiences and memories of growing up to their changing mobility in and between the house, neighbourhood and their wider environment. Their changing mobility in and between these different spaces was important to how they saw themselves achieving independence, competence and maturity and to how they formed and sustained their social relations with peers. As I will go on to show, in mapping their personal biographies children engage with place as a simultaneously social and physical location, describing how they come to inhabit and belong to a place through their experiences and use of it.

In their accounts the children interwove their personal biography and social relationships with the exploration, use and mastering of place. They saw generational relationships and conflicts as played out in part through the differentiation of places according to their use by different generations. They read generational meaning from this experience. In part this involved a differentiation of generational perspectives on time and place. Children's orientation emphasised the temporal experience of growing up, achieving independence, coming to inhabit the places of their lives through embodied movement and detailed knowledge of them as concrete, local places. The adult generation were also thoroughly placed in certain localities. However, in many of their interactions with children adults could be seen as more future-oriented. Adults were concerned with forms of knowledge that they believed the children would come to need rather than the knowledge that children were developing through their emplaced[2] being. One aspect of this was demonstrated at school where teachers were focused on more generalised forms of knowledge that we can understand as spatial rather than emplaced. The relationship between these forms of knowledge varied. In some cases the children's emplaced knowledge and the adults' spatial knowledge were counterposed. However, as I will go on to show with case examples from Copenhagen, teachers would also engage in the project of connecting children's emplaced knowledge with spatial knowledge.

Place and space

Over the last two decades social theory and contemporary cultural geographies have cast new light on space and place. This has transformed our conceptions of *space* from being either a neutral setting for social action or a determined outcome of material conditions awaiting cartography (Christensen *et al.* 2000). At the same time the importance of honouring and paying close attention to the practical, concrete experience of people's sense of place has emerged as an important theme (Feld and Basso 1996). Echoing Geertz (1996), Casey, for example, writes that: 'To live is to live locally and to know is first of all to know the places one is in.' (Casey 1996: 18).

In this sense the experience of place, he suggests, is not inferior to space, indeed it can be seen as primary. We are always 'emplaced'. Both spaces and sensations are themselves emplaced from the very first moment and at every subsequent moment as well. There is no knowing or sensing a place except by being in that place and being in a position to perceive it.

Following Merleau–Ponty (1962), Casey argues that to *be in place* means that a person becomes consciously aware of his or her sensuous presence in the world. Such perception at its primary level is synaesthetic – an affair of the whole body sensing and moving. Human sensing is not pre-cultural or pre-social: practices and institutions pervade every level of perception from the implicit to the explicit, even when a given perception is preconceptual and prediscursive. The primacy of perception is ultimately a primacy of the lived body and of habitual cultural and social processes. Bodily movement is central to this process: 'Part of the power of place, its very dynamic is found in its encouragement of motion in its midst, its "e-motive" (and often explicitly emotional) thrust' (Casey 1996: 23).

In the understanding that emerges from embodied movement through place, knowledge and perception are not separate: knowledge of place becomes part of the dialectic of perception and place that traverses the whole life course. Knowledge of place accumulates and changes over one's lifetime through inhabiting, being and becoming in a place. It is not an expression of some underlying and primary phenomenon of space. However, emplaced knowledge is frequently thought of in this way, that is as secondary to *objective* space, and thus constituted as in some way inferior to knowledge of space.

Spatial knowledge, then, is more formalised, abstract and generalised knowledge. It strips emplaced knowledge of its local particularities and its social and personal content. It can, however, itself be thought of as a form of specialised knowledge embedded in particular local contexts like mapping and measuring. Although not intrinsically superior to local knowledge, it is often performed as such (Augé 1995). In these circumstances its relation-ship to emplaced knowledge can become highly problematic. It assumes the mantle of a dominating superiority that falsely claims to be able to subsume local knowledge and, as such, it detaches itself from local knowledge thus making connections between spatial and emplaced knowledge difficult to comprehend.

Emplaced children: a walk around Woldsby

From this perspective children construct an emplaced knowledge of their local environment, full of personal and social meaning, built up through their everyday encounters with it. I will illustrate this by first considering the emplaced knowledge of children in Woldsby, the village in northern England where I carried out my ethnographic fieldwork.[3]

By contemporary European urban standards, the children of Woldsby en-joyed a high degree of autonomous mobility. From the age of 7 or 8 they were allowed to move around the village on their own and in groups. It was common, for example, for children who lived in the village to walk to their primary school, located as it was within the village envelope. It is often suggested that such independent mobility on the part of children has been declining in cities (O'Brien *et al.* 2000, and see also Zeiher, Chapter 5, below). However, O'Brien *et al.* conclude that 'there are significant variations in how contemporary children use their public spaces . . . linked to the particular "place" characteristics of the local urban settings' (O'Brien *et al.* 2000: 274). In this sense the experiences of village and city children may well be different but, I suggest, an examination of the experiences of children in Woldsby illuminates how children engage in a relatively unconstrained exploration of their local environment. It shows, in particular, the ways in which they emplace themselves, fusing a sense of local place with the formation of identity and the creation of significant meaning to place. Later I will show how children in Copenhagen were engaged in similar processes, although they also did this in different ways and at a somewhat older age.

First, however, I will give a brief background to the village based on my field notes. Typically for the region, the housing in Woldsby is characterised by traditional stone-built cottages surrounded by gardens growing vegetables, herbs and flowers, and by farmhouses with fields of arable crops, sheep and cattle at the edge of the village. Over the years a couple of small estates had been build on former farmland that had brought new families to the village. At the time of the study a small estate was finished and made ready for housing. A busy trunk road cross-cut the middle of the village connecting the region's market towns. The village was part of the relatively affluent agricultural community in the local area. There was a church, a pub, a shop and a post office, a village hall and a small primary school.

However, the villages must be seen not as bounded units but as communities constituted most importantly through sets of ongoing connections between and among families and businesses scattered across the local regional area. At the school, for example, not only children who lived in Woldsby attended but also children from neighbouring villages or from the farms scattered outside the village. Many adults living in Woldsby were occupied as office workers or in the social services or had a small business in the nearby market town or the larger provincial town. Many also had work that was farm-related or connected to the farming that took place in the wider region. It was not unusual to work in businesses servicing farming, such as for seed companies, machinery and tools companies, car firms, or agricultural clothing supplies for example.

Some families had been settled for only a short time in the village whilst others left for better working opportunities elsewhere. But many villagers maintained a strong sense of belonging to their local area. In conversations with children about their prospective futures, some children emphasised their connection to the village through seeing themselves as continuing to live within the local area when they grew up and had their own families. This sense of belonging locally was most strongly revealed in the farming families, where family members were tied to the farm and the land through the family extending across the generations. In youth and throughout their adult lives these families lived in the farmhouse, having the main responsibility for the land. Eventually the older generation would retire into a bungalow or one of the cottages in the village where sometimes other kin lived. Thus the spatial distribution of land and patterns of residence within the villages offered a graphic representation of the interconnectedness of family, kin and generation.

Children living in and around Woldsby can thus be seen as embedded in a network of emplaced social relationships. This became evident as I walked around the village with a group of children one mid-morning in the summer of 1998. I was sitting with Tom, Bill and Rebecca on a hilltop next to the asphalted playground outside the primary school. They were all feeling fed up. It was two weeks before the end of term, and their last weeks at primary school. After the summer holidays Tom, Bill and Rebecca were to begin secondary school in the market town nearby. I had been carrying out the field study at the school, working closely with four of the six children in Year 6. In addition to the time spent in the classroom, we met every Thursday morning, when I was allowed to take them out of class for an hour or two for interviews and group discussions.

This morning Rebecca suggested that they show me around Woldsby. They were keen to get out of school. The walk around the village became significant because what they presented was a picture of the village, as they knew it. Whilst moving through the village their stories brought my attention to both present experiences and early childhood memories that together formed part of their life in the village. They pieced together experiences and practical knowledge, and through this personal and collective mapping they created a sense of place. Their family and kin, friends and other people living and working there populated the village. Through this generational mapping they also presented to me their own place as children in the village. The picture they created was a social and moral landscape of the place where they lived. The people they knew were linked by their name to their house, by characteristics such as their kin or other relationship to them or by personal idiosyncrasies. The children would guess about the identity and character of those people whom they did not know personally, reading clues from their appearance and behaviour and from stories they had heard about what they might be like. They pointed out the people who were 'good' and to the people with suspicious characters. They took me up streets showing me particular spots. We walked along the main road and took shortcuts. They told about local shopping and drew my attention also to their relations with pets and the local wildlife. They concluded the walk by tasting 'forbidden' cherries from a tree outside the village hall just across from the primary school.

The trip was about sensing, sharing experiences and making explorations around the village. The children made suggestions and discussed among themselves where to go next and which turnings to make. It is their narrative of Woldsby as a place that I aim to convey, illustrating their local, emplaced knowledge of it. On the walk we altogether visited twenty different locations. To give a flavour of this emplaced knowledge I will discuss a few of these.

The first example was our visit to the duck pond, where the children engaged in talking about 'What you can learn from studying the social life of ducks'. The example illustrates how the children used a particular place to explore issues of the life course and belonging as they emerge from a local incident connected with the village duck pond. My field notes recorded our discussion:

> 'Ducks!' Bill exclaimed – to announce our first destination, the village pond. 'There's a little baby one, there at the moment', Bill continued and Rebecca said: 'Yeah, a yellow one. Yeah, little yellow duckling.' 'When we get to the duck pond,' Bill said, affirming this. Then he warned me putting his arm out protectively as we had now reached the main road, 'Yeah, be careful now when you cross the road.' The young ducklings were tiny, all covered in warm yellow down. Bill leaned over the fence surrounding parts of the edge of the pond. 'Where is Waterhead, look there he is,' he shouted pointing towards a group of ducks. 'It's bad I just want to eat it,' Tom said wryly. Rebecca gazed over the pond to look for other inhabitants: 'Erm, there was, there used to be some other ones. Oh, look at these little ducklings.' She chuckled pointing towards the ducklings swimming with a female duck towards us. 'She's trying [to show] him how to swim,' Bill explains pointing at the mother duck. Rebecca then noticed the danger from the big swan approaching steadily through the water: 'She's just getting ready.' Rebecca warned us with details of how dangerous it might be.
>
> We continued to talk about the ducks and swans for some time before the children begin to tell me that there used to be two swans in the pond. Rebecca and Tom tell us that one of them was shot with an air catapult. This was a story that had made it into the local newspaper, *The Woldsby Tatler*, where they had both read about it. This talk about *The Woldsby Tatler* brings on a discussion among the children. They are concerned whether Tom, who lives in a country house outside the village, actually belongs in Woldsby when he does not receive the *Tatler* 'through the post' every week. Tom thinks they *ought* to have one sent and that he still lives in Woldsby even though his house is out in the country. Bill and Rebecca think he does not live in the village because he does not receive the paper. Tom insists that his house is in Woldsby Parish. Rebecca tells us that her parents have to go to another village to vote for the election, but they still belong to Woldsby.

The second example took place a few minutes later in the park, one of the places specifically dedicated to the children living in the village. In particular this example illustrates how the playground formed a scene for the collective life of the boys. My field notes recorded this part of the walk:

> When we reached the park, a large newly refurbished public playground, the children set off running towards the swings. Swinging on the swings they explain to me that the Council made the playground about one year ago. When I ask, 'What do you do here?', Tom almost mechanically says, 'Swing on the swing.' A few minutes later Bill tells us about some earlier events on the playground and I come to understand that going to the playground for him is connected with 'doing things for a laugh'. A few weeks before our visit he had been up there with some friends. The group of boys, some younger and some older than him, had been playing around teasing each other. This culminated when, in turns, they had been standing at the top of the slide and peed down it.
>
> Before we leave Tom points to some letters carved into a wooden pole. It says 'B S'. Bill suggests the letters are put there because 'I'm so popular'. Tom corrects this by stating that it stands for Barry Smith. The boys can leave their mark on a place in more ways than one!

The walk continued, taking in the house of the man who keeps smelly ferrets, the new house of Tom's grandma, the house of the disabled man who has his wheelchair pulled by his dog, the house where Rebecca's mum works as a cleaner, several houses that are admired for being 'massive', a haunted house and the house of the old lady who keeps 'hundreds of cats'.

Each of these locations gives rise to all kinds of comments and discussion. Running through these was a moral evaluation of the people associated with each place. The physical landscape was thus also a moral one, populated by different kinds of people. This became very clear when we passed a lane where one of the girls from the children's year group at school lived. They pointed it out to me but they were all determined not to go down it. Bill said, 'We're not off down where Michelle lives! We don't go in the bit where they actually live because it's all like smoke and everything.' The other children agreed and Tom added, 'Yeah, people that walk past them for school, they throw cigarettes at you and drink.' The walk also took us past Bill's house. He showed us the garden in front of the house and told us about how he used to play there. 'This is the tree I used to climb when I was little,' Bill said, giving the tree trunk a friendly pat. However, Bill has grown and, as we continued our walk, told us regretfully that the tree would no longer take his weight.

Summing up so far, the above material illustrates how children are em-placed: they have a detailed local knowledge of the village built up through their concrete engagement with it and through their mobility in and around it. Their emplaced knowledge is partly biographical and personal but is also collectively produced. The children's inhabitation of the village is done together, and the meaning of places is worked on and produced in collect-ive activity and engagement. The children's movement brings them into relationship with places that are already saturated with social meaning. Some places, such as the pub, are mostly for adults and others, such as the playground, are mostly for children. Some places are known as locations of the work of their parents to which they do not have access, unless it is with their parents, and therefore they know of them only at second hand. In the children's accounts houses are places lived in by other children, friends or 'enemies', but also places to where older people, including grandparents, have moved or retired.

Children in Copenhagen

In Copenhagen I carried out field work among children, young people and families in a local district called Vanløse.[4] This area is considered to be affluent, with many residents being skilled workers, teachers, nurses, clerical workers, small business people and professionals such as doctors, lawyers and architects. Few parents are unemployed or receive social security. In more recent years it has attracted families of the upper middle class and has gradually achieved a distinct character, being distinguished from neighbouring districts, partly through its housing and partly through its economic base. Some main roads with heavy traffic cross-cut parts of the area and also encircle its centre. Many inhabitants captured its 'local spirit' by describing living there as like living in 'a village'.

The school where I focused my field work is situated in a residential area with no heavy traffic. It is close to the local shopping centre, 'the heart' of Vanløse, and near to the railway station and buses. Some housing around the school consists of three- and four-storey apartment blocks, but most of it is detached houses, the majority of which have been built since the 1930s. There are also some large recreational areas and some smaller parks.

The children in Vanløse enjoyed a lower degree of independent mobility around their local neighbourhood when compared to those living in Woldsby.[5] In Vanløse young children were taken to daycare institutions and school by car or on parents' bikes. This continued as they became older, and only when they were aged 10 or 11 did most children begin to walk or cycle to school on their own. At this age they were also allowed by parents to move around the neighbourhood with their friends. In this setting an important source of local knowledge was that gained from and shared with their peers. For example, by walking with friends to each other's houses the 11-year-olds actively engaged in extending the knowledge they had gained when they were younger and were accompanied by their parents or older siblings.

Despite starting to move independently around Vanløse at an older age, the children in this urban environment, nevertheless, engaged with processes of emplacement similar to those of the children in Woldsby. This is shown in the following example. Jimmy and Lars, two 15-year-olds, had lived in the same house with their families in Vanløse since their early childhood. In my conversations with them they independently described the way they learned about their neighbourhood. This was accomplished through the gradual process of knowing one's house, playing outside in the garden, gradually being able to leave the house to play in the street with other children and thus learning about his neighbourhood (and later the city as a whole). Jimmy describes how he got a skateboard when 7 or 8 years old. For him this signified the move from playing in the garden to being allowed outside. Jimmy said:

> At first my dad wouldn't let me out of sight. I remember how he was standing behind the fence leaning over to keep an eye on me. After a bit I was allowed to be on the street on my own but with instructions about how far I was allowed to skate up and down the road. Later I could just be out there and also go down to the park.

Just like the Woldsby children, Lars pointed to how a place becomes familiar and inscribed with memories. He said:

> It's like you know a place very well as part of your childhood really. You walk on the street outside your house and you look at the paving stone where you used to stumble when you were little. And as if you can still see the mark of your knee you greet it and say: 'Oh hello!'

In Vanløse children's independent mobility begins at an older age and is more regulated by parents. This interaction between adult knowledge and children's development of their own emplaced knowledge is illustrated in the next example. It concerns an 11-year-old girl called Mie. She knew her local neighbourhood only through the particular routes she used. She knew the route from home to school and also the route from her house to the local cinema but she did not know the route from school to the cinema. This became an issue for her when a children's film club started up at the cinema every Thursday afternoon just after school ended. Her father, therefore, tried to instruct her about the most direct route she could take from school. On the way to school he stopped at the corner of the main road. He pointed to where the cinema is, along the street by the traffic lights some 500 metres down the main road. However, Mie refused to use this route, insisting that 'I don't know the way.' Her father, pointing out what for him is the significant marker of her destination, explained: 'But can't you see? There, where the lights are and just a little further. There is the cinema.'

He eventually had to give up, as Mie decided to find her way by following the back streets from school. This was a longer way. Her father feared that this was a more complicated route but Mie thought it was better because she could walk some of the way with a friend, whose house is close to the cinema. Eventually other friends who already knew the route walked with her and a few weeks later she could easily walk to the cinema independently using the back streets. At this point she had also worked out that the cinema is located next to the library, which the children frequently visit together with their teacher.

Generationed knowledge: space and place

This example draws attention to a dislocation between children and adults around different forms of knowledge about place and space. For Mie the goal that is the cinema in the far distance is of less importance when weighed against not having knowledge of the route she has to walk to get there on her own. In particular she has not been able to explore the kind of experiences she might encounter on the way and prefers to take the back streets with her friends even though this is a longer route. For her father, however, the length and directness of the route are the most important factors.

The tension between knowledge of place and space is, according to Casey, one between emplaced knowledge and abstract or formal knowledge. Much of adults' knowledge is emplaced. Their understanding of the neighbourhood is also full of social and personal meaning. However, adults also often employ a more abstract knowledge of space. One important aspect is that adults, both parents and teachers, want to introduce and equip children with formal knowledge of space. Children are faced with the difficult task of integrating this spatial knowledge with their developing emplaced knowledge of the neighbourhood. Some of the different ways in which adults and children can engage with each other on this problem can be illustrated with examples drawn from the school life of children in both Woldsby and Vanløse.

My first example comes from Woldsby. In the village school the fifty-six children were separated in two non-age-segregated classes. I spent the time of the study in a class of 7–11-year-olds. For a couple of weeks during the spring term their geography lessons were dedicated to learning about their local area. The lessons centred on the regional capital, Sealford, a large coastal town about twenty miles from where they lived. The project would conclude with a one-day school trip to visit and look around the town and beach. The children were drawing maps, locating the town on maps, pencilling in its size and shape. Most lessons, however, were dedicated to children learning that one can draw out knowledge of a place by using the telephone directory. Through developing their skills in using the index pages and working their way around the different sections of the many-paged book the children were supposed to learn about their village and its region.

For most children this was a rather tedious job. Although they were able to choose whether they wanted to work alone or in pairs, it was often a slow process. The children's task was to make lists of for example how many primary schools there were, how many doctors and dentists and other local services and institutions. The children's records were lists counting the different services. They also checked that the area code of the telephone number was correct and that the address was indeed located in Sealford. Then they had to copy the names of the doctors or dentists on to their paper. There was not much scope for children's own ideas and interests when conducting this task. The most fun the children made out of this task was to giggle about

'What silly names doctors had' or break out in surprise at the number of primary schools in Sealford.

This example may foster the opinion that when a large part of teaching is based on reproduction it does not leave room enough for children's creativity. Nor, however, does the information the children gathered connect very well with the emplaced knowledge that they already had of their village and its region. This is a question of central concern in discussions of the current context of children's learning experiences in England. Changes in educational policy and the introduction of a National Curriculum that is highly prescriptive of the different subject areas to be taught has led to time being an increasingly scarce resource in English schools (Christensen and James 2001). This means, it has been suggested, that there is little time for teachers to connect with children's experiences and explorations. As a consequence of these pressures, then, the project of schooling can be seen to be increasingly under the teacher's, rather than children's, control and authority. This tendency has detrimental effects on children's experiences of their schooling to have the potential to take up a meaningful place in their everyday lives and for their school experience to be seen as part of their personal life project (Christensen and James 2001).

In the above example the generational relationships enacted around place draw on a hierarchical model. The lessons were essentially concerned with knowledge of space in its formal, generalised aspect. This, however, is not the only possibility and I will for the purpose of this chapter contrast this example with some field data from the study I carried out in Vanløse. In the examples I discuss below, the sets of relationships between children and teachers around place can be seen to form a more negotiative practice, both in terms of connecting children's emplaced knowledge with that of formalised space and in terms of the relationships between children and adults.

In Vanløse the approach taken by teachers drew on the idea of children learning about local physical spaces and local geography in a quite literal sense through the body. This was quite different from the previous example in that it connected more closely with children's own practices of exploring their neighbourhood. In part this may be because, as noted above, the children in Vanløse had less opportunity for independent exploration and the teachers were concerned to give them more of this experience. The example concerns the fourth-graders (9–10-year-olds) in a PE (physical education) lesson who were sent on an excursion round their local area. The children were divided into small groups and provided with a sheet of paper listing a range of particular spots together with a map, an enlarged section of the local area. The task of the children was to find their way around the local neighbourhood locating particular spots via the road name and number given on the paper. The questions on the sheet were for example: 'What colour is the gate of 26 Maple Street?' or 'What are the colours of the window frames of 17 Oak Street?'. The questionnaire thus created a circular walk taking the children around a particular part of their local neighbourhood through the streets surrounding the school.

On the way the children walked, ran, jumped up in the air, kicked stones and, along the way, were deeply engaged discussing what they saw. Suddenly finding themselves in front of a friend's house, they called out, 'That's where Emma lives' and 'That's Martin's house'. A barking dog made some children scared and they passed it making a big circle and cautiously kept a safe distance. Others stopped courageously and for a little while discussed whether to tease the dog away, estimating the danger they would face if it suddenly ran loose.

The trip was set up almost as a game. The children explored the local area through active movement and using their senses. As one 10-year-old girl later told me: 'It was because we were to use our muscles and our brains.'

The children used their skills, such as sense of direction and their existing local knowledge, to read the map, sometimes figuring out what would be the best shortcuts on the route. They observed and guessed colours, cracks in walls, bent road signs, flowers and missing road numbers, all details that sometimes had gone unnoticed on earlier visits. They came to explore places they had not been before. They got new experiences and they related these to earlier experiences or to the experiences of other children. In another local school the teacher also sent children from the fifth grade (10–11-year-olds) out on an excursion around the local area but this time into the busier shopping centre. She equipped the children with her mobile phone number and ensured that all groups had at least one child with a mobile phone. In this way she wanted to ensure that the children could get hold of her if they got lost or encountered problems on the way. Teachers would in this way engage with connecting and developing children's local knowledge with their formal knowledge through mastering geographical concepts and tools such as map reading and the measurement of distance and direction.

Conclusion

In this chapter I have used ethnographic material from a village and a neigh-bourhood of a city to explore how children themselves construct emplaced knowledge of their locality. Such an endeavour can be instructive. There are of course differences between village and city locations. In the village children had a higher degree of independent mobility and were able to explore their locality at an earlier age than the children of the city. In the city children were more governed, especially by parents, in their independent mobility. The village formed a denser network of personal and kinship rela-tionships than was to be found in the city neighbourhood where I carried out the study.

Nevertheless there are also important continuities. In both locations children actively explored the area through their independent mobility. In this they built up an emplaced understanding of it through their bodily encounters and using all their senses. This knowledge was rich with personal and social meaning. In both locations children built up their own individual knowledge but this was shared with other children. They engaged in a collective process of making sense of the neighbourhood. In particular the children made meaning of their experiences and understandings through their own collective practices and discussions. The meanings they made in this process were sometimes different from those of older generations. They created a specific emplaced knowledge that was also situated in time.

In both locations children were engaged in an intergenerational exchange with their parents and teachers. This exchange concerned the task of integrating emplaced and spatial knowledge. This is indeed a complex process that does not resolve into a simple dichotomy in which adults have spatial knowledge and children have emplaced knowledge. There are a number of reasons for rejecting such a simple dualism. Many, if not most, adults depend on their own emplaced knowledge of the localities in which they spend their everyday lives. The children and adults who co-inhabit a locality are likely to share, or come to share, some of this emplaced knowledge, even though they give this their own generational content. Furthermore, spatial knowledge cannot be seen just as adult knowledge. Many disparities between spatial and emplaced knowledge do not have a generational form. For example, conflicts between road planners and local people often concern the clash between the planners' logic of spatial knowledge and its transgression of the emplaced meaning of local residents.

However, the relationship between spatial and emplaced knowledge can take, or can be given, a generational aspect. This happens, for example, when knowledge of space is seen as part of the social and cultural capital that a person needs and as something that a growing child has to acquire. This spatial knowledge is indeed a requirement of living in modern societies. For adults it has become an important task to equip children with such cultural capital even if it does not connect very well with their own local, meaningful, emplaced knowledge. In this sense the adults and children of both Woldsby and Copenhagen can be seen to be addressing the same problem.

The point of my two contrasting examples of how the relationship between spatial and emplaced knowledge is handled is not that Danish schools are necessarily more negotiative than ones in the UK. No doubt counterexamples from both Denmark and England could be quite easily found. Schools also change from hierarchical to negotiative orderings and vice versa. Rather, the examples illustrate two different ways of connecting up knowledge of space with children's knowledge of place.

However, both these cases are concerned with the issue of connecting different modes of knowledge. I suggest that in any endeavour to do so it is important to understand how children experience and construct a sense of place. Such understanding and engagement with children is also a foundation for the participation of children in the process of changing the physical environment in which they live. We need to know how they see the city in order to reform it. In short we need to explore how children emplace themselves.

Notes

1 The UK study was carried out together with Allison James and Chris Jenks. This study involved 10-year-old children living in two villages and a provincial city in the north of England. The *Changing Times* project was funded by the ESRC as part of the research programme Children 5–16: Growing into the 21st Century. The Danish data derive from a study *Børn og Tid* on children's time that I carried out with children and young people living in a local district of Copenhagen. This study was funded by the Danish Research Council's research programme Children's Living Conditions and Welfare. I wish to thank both funding bodies for providing financial support for carrying out the research. I am grateful to all the children and young people who participated in the studies.

2 The notion of *emplacement* refers to the process through which consciousness, the body, sensuous presence and place are simultaneously produced and knitted together. Examples of its deployment are found in Casey (1996) and Feld (1996).

3 In north England I was carrying out field studies centred on children in two villages in the eastern part of Yorkshire. However, my knowledge of the local area derives from four years intense field research in four village communities. The data I present in this chapter are from children living in the small village, Woldsby. I use a pseudonym to protect the identity of individuals.

4 My particular knowledge of children and families living in this particular local area of Copenhagen derives from three ethnographic studies centred on different aspects of children's everyday lives that I have been carrying out since 1990. The data presented in this chapter derive from a recent field study carried out in 2000, investigating 10–11-year-old and 14–16-year-old children's use and understanding of time.

5 In the rural area children depended on their parents (in particular mothers) to provide transport to attend after-school activities in the local market town or when visiting their friends living in the countryside. This meant that they, similarly to the children in Vanløse, also had little say over and opportunity to have an independent social life.

References

Augé, M., 1995, *Non-places: Introduction to an Anthropology of Supermodernity* (London: Verso).

Casey, E., 1996, 'How to get from space to place in a fairly short stretch of time: phenomenological prolegomena'. In S. Feld and K. Basso (eds), *Senses of Place*. (Santa Fe: SAR Press).

Christensen, P. and James, A., 2001, 'What are schools for? The temporal experience of schooling'. In L. Alanen and B. Mayall (eds), *Conceptualising Child–Adult Relations* (London: Falmer Press).

Christensen, P., James, A. and Jenks, C., 2000, 'Home and movement: children constructing "family time"'. In S.L. Holloway and G. Valentine (eds), *Children's Geographies: Playing, Living, Learning* (London: Routledge).

Dillard, A., 1987, *An American Childhood* (New York: Harper Perenial).

Feld, S., 1996, 'Waterfalls of song: an acoustemology of place resounding in Bosavi, Papua New Guinea'. In S. Feld and K. Basso (eds), *Senses of Place* (Santa Fe: SAR Press).

Feld, S. and Basso, K. (eds), 1996, *Senses of Place* (Santa Fe: SAR Press).

Geertz, G., 1996, 'Afterword'. In S. Feld and K. Basso (eds), *Senses of Place* (Santa Fe: SAR Press).

Gullestad, M. (ed.), 1996, *Imagined Childhoods* (Oslo: Scandinavian University Press).

Merleau-Ponty, M., 1962, *Phenomenology of Perception* (New York: Humanities Press).

O'Brien, M., Jones, D., Sloan, D. and Rustin, M., 2000, 'Children's independent spatial mobility in the public realm'. *Childhood*, 7 (3), 257–77.

Rasmussen, K. and Smidt, S., 2001, *Spor af børns institutionsliv* (*Traces of the Institutional Lives of Children*) (Copenhagen: Hans Reitzels Forlag).

3 Children's views of family, home and house

Gunilla Halldén

During a study of children's narratives about 'my future family' presented in this chapter, two 13–14-year-old boys wrote about going hunting. In their parallel stories they, as the main characters, go on a hunt, leaving their family at home. The close relationship between the men is contrasted to a more quiescent family life back in the house: in their stories the place of importance for them as grown-up men lies outside the house. One of the boys wrote:

> It's the year 2008. January 21st, minus ten degrees. I'm going out to hunt for rabbits with Anders. We agreed to meet in the woods at 7.30. I guess our old ladies are at home with the kids sleeping, said Anders. Yeah, I guess they are, you know what old ladies are like.

Time and space are interconnected in important ways in this narrative. The two men get up early in the morning while the rest of the family is still in bed sleeping. In establishing the time of the day it appears that they are also separating a male world from a more feminised family world. The place that is important for proving the competence of the men is the woods. They describe it as a familiar place, a place where they will surely find their quarry. Negotiating the boundary between the house, as a family-oriented place of shelter, and the surrounding world emerges as a key theme in the narrative and is a central focus of this chapter. Here I will explore the processes of boundary-making narrated by the children, concentrating in particular on the house, the home and routines that create a domestic place.

Recent discussion on children's agency and childhood from a social perspective has emphasised the importance of place (Holloway and Valentine 2000). Geographies of childhood are beginning to deal with questions such as where children are located, how they negotiate access to specific places and how these places are given meanings. Philo (2000: 245) writes about the importance of taking into account 'diverse spaces (types of settings for interaction), places (specific sites of meaning), environments (surroundings full of nature and humanity) and landscapes (visible scenes and prospects)'. Within this interdisciplinary field children's playing, living and learning are discussed in relation to places. Holloway and Valentine (2000: 16) emphasise that the social construction of childhood in contemporary Britain is highly spatialised. Children's place is in the home and not in the streets. As Matthews *et al.* (2000) have pointed out, the adult world has laid claim to the public domain and declared it out-of-bounds for children and young people. The reason given is that children need to be kept under supervision, for example in supervised playgrounds, or their morals need to be protected, for example by setting age limits for entry to certain places (Matthews *et al.* 2000). Holloway and Valentine (2000) also direct attention to the connection between child-hood and the countryside. Drawing on the work of Jones (1997), they point out that autobiographies about childhood and children's books often contain the theme of a rural childhood idyll where children play outdoors, away from parents' control. In this rural idyll children's 'innocence is reproduced through their closeness with and to nature' (Holloway and Valentine 2000: 17). Whilst nature is often portrayed as idyllic and peaceful, it can also be represented as a grim and unyielding wilderness.

The notion of a rural idyll can be linked to the child-saving movement. During the twentieth century the city was consistently portrayed as a danger-ous place for children. Philanthropic agents mobilised organisations to remove children from the risks of life on the streets, and the global child-saving movement was an attempt to give children a proper childhood by organising their lives (see e.g. Steedman 1990). We could, however, also look upon these arrangements as a way to save the adult population from uncontrollable crowds of children. Sandin (1997) has shown how compulsory schooling in Sweden can be interpreted as a device to keep children off the streets, where they were regarded as a disruptive element. Hendrick (1997) has pointed to the same phenomenon in Britain.

So, to understand why children were put on the agenda by the philanthropic movement, we have to discuss children both as a threat and as vulnerable human beings. At the beginning of the twentieth century, the children of the poor were the subject of discussion both as a humanitarian issue and as a potential threat to society. According to the philanthropic view, these chil-dren had to be *saved*, for their own good as well as for the good of society. Public interest in the child, which seems to have increased rapidly during this time, was reflected in legislation and in the inauguration of a number of privately initiated programmes for children. There was a strong emphasis on childhood and the well-being of children, and many organisations were engaged in the effort. As historical research has shown, children's homes, holiday camps, kindergartens and afternoon schools were, at least in part, endeavours to arrange places for children to keep them off the streets, protect them from bad influences and train them in handicraft (see e.g. De Conick-Smith *et al.* 1997). This could be seen as a way to discipline and control working-class children, but it could also be seen as an ideology and as one of the cultural meanings of children and childhood; that is, as a manifestation of the best interest of the child. As Woodhead (1990: 73) has pointed out, children's needs must be discussed as cultural constructions, not in the sense that they are not real, rather that their needs are closely related to the culture in which they live.

Child-nature and child-home: the Swedish context

My interest in this chapter is the house, the home and the relation between indoors and outdoors as it is accounted for in children's narratives. Before exploring the narratives, however, I will place the analysis in a Swedish context with its emphasis on nature and children: the importance of the healthy outdoors and of the protected home environment. If we wish to reflect on the relationship between children and place, we must take into consideration the deeply rooted Swedish tradition of associating children with nature.

There has been considerable research in Sweden about changes in the meaning of childhood and its interplay with philanthropy, the welfare state and family life (see e.g. Munger 2000; Olsson 1999; Sandin 1992; Söderlind 1999; Weiner 1995). An important issue when discussing children living in the cities concerns the ideology about nature and outdoor life that was widespread in the beginning of the twentieth century, and is still persistent today. In Munger's (2000) study of holiday camps in Sweden from when they were first established in the late nineteenth century to the middle of the twentieth century, she attempts to grasp the underlying ideology and the lived life within these camps. The holiday camp movement communicated what was considered to be a new awareness of time and place with respect to working-class children. Of special importance was the teaching of wholesome and healthy habits. Both the child's body and soul were to receive care, and children were to assimilate a healthy lifestyle. Besides teaching good habits of physical hygiene, holiday camps were to stimulate an interest in healthy food, fresh air and exercising control over the body.

Urban areas are regarded as more dangerous than rural ones, and being outside in the fresh air and the benefits of playing outdoors are ideological tenets representing essential elements of a good childhood. Eckert (2001) has shown that Swedish parents attach great importance to children's outdoor play; this is part of a framework that Eckert has labelled the cultural meaning of an idyllic childhood. Welles-Nyström *et al.* (1994) have found the same strong tendency among Swedish parents to expose their children to fresh air in order to toughen them to adapt to a harsh climate, in contrast to the American and especially Italian parents of their study. In Norway, Gullestad (1997) has also underscored this strong connection between childhood and nature. In many Nordic countries 'love of nature' is regarded as an important part of nationalism and is meant to be learned during childhood. Karin Johannesson (2001) has written on 'nostalgia', a concept that during the eighteenth and nineteenth century was translated into homesickness. She refers to Dorothee Neff (1956 in Johannesson 2001) who ascertained that home has different connotations in different countries. In France home is associated with the language, in Russia with the earth, in America with the family and in Scandinavia with nature. So we can note the connection between home and nature as well as the connection between children and nature.

The idyllic childhood spent in close contact with nature is, however, threatened by the dangers that can lurk outside. The parents whom Eckert (2001) interviewed could be seen to shift between images of the robust child whose body is strengthened by fresh air and the vulnerable child who needs protection. The home is looked upon as a shelter for children, but life outside the home underscores the connection between children and nature, and parents are caught in a dilemma between contrasting ideologies.

The welfare system in Scandinavia allows women to combine being gainfully employed with having a family, and today women make up a large part of the workforce. As a result children's lives are being increasingly institutionalised. Today, most parents work outside the home and leave their children to be cared for in institutional settings under the supervision of professionals. Then, at home, many children have their own rooms in housing which, from a global perspective, is spacious (Swedish Official Reports 2001: 55). Thus, on the one hand children spend much of their time in an institutionalised collective and, on the other, they have a large space all to themselves at home. This phenomenon can be discussed as a situation where children, at least the younger ones, are controlled by adults and have little time for activities other than those monitored by adults. It also means that children are not obliged to spend much of their time outside the home, or are perhaps not allowed to. The ideology that connects children to nature may in practice often turn out to be problematic.

In an article about children in the local community, Fog Olwig (2000) discusses the process by which a place acquires special meaning. She bases her discussion on anthropological research exploring the links between belonging and the social organisation of a community (see Cohen 1982). Her point of departure is that a community is constituted by the people living there and the many ways in which they are interconnected with each other. She refers to Appadurai's (1995) idea of 'the production of locality' where locality is not merely a geographic area but is also a place where people can acquire a sense of solidarity. The Swedish social psychologist Johan Asplund (1983) writes about place as a geographical area that opens up for participation, in contrast to what he calls 'placelessness'. A place that has this capacity is a geographical area that is 'colonised' by a group of people. Colonising is the process whereby people give meaning to a place and make it part of their self-identity. The meaning of a place is created by the people, who attach themselves to that place. This process can be studied in narratives where groups of people describe places that are important to them. Because borders are important for identifying a place, we can borrow the concept 'border work' from Thorne (1993) to describe what children do to make a place inclusive or exclusive, thereby also creating the conditions for belonging and social organisation in particular kinship. Children are dependent, but they also create an autonomy within the frames set by parents and professionals. What I wish to emphasise here, however, is not children's lives as controlled by parents and professionals, nor the cultural meaning of children and childhood, but rather how children describe house and home as a domestic place and a central child-space. When children describe this area, they depict a place of importance that is identified partly by its borders. The description of the house can be looked upon as a way to explore this distinction between inside and outside and the border between.

In the introductory part of this chapter, a story about a hunting game was quoted. Inside/outside was an important issue in this narrative, where inside was associated with the family, wife and children. The contrast was established between the warm indoors and the coldness of the outdoors. The children seem to belong to the inside domain whereas the men who went hunting could manage the coldness of the woods. In characterising the Swedish context I have emphasised the association between children and nature. The 'theme of healthy outdoors' plays a prominent role in how parents talk about their children (Eckert 2001). Children's connection to nature is part of the rural idyll, and the love of nature is an important part of nationalism in the Nordic countries (Gullestad 1997). When children write about a future family, however, the strongest link is between children and the home. This does not imply that children do not include the rural childhood idyll in their ideas about what characterises a good childhood, but when it comes to relating children to family the important place seems to be the home.

The study

The study on which I base this chapter was carried out in schools in three towns.[1] Two age groups took part: one group of 32 children (18 girls and 14 boys) 8 to 10 years of age, and one group of 141 children (73 girls and 68 boys) 13 to 14 years of age. The younger children came from a middle-sized town in Sweden of about a hundred thousand inhabitants and lived in a housing area consisting of blocks of flats. Some of the children were living in nuclear families and others with single mothers. Some came from immigrant families, but most were from Swedish families. The older age group came from two schools in two other towns. One group came from a town of approximately the same size as that from which the younger children came. Their school was located in a suburb reputed to have quite a few families with social problems; many of these pupils came from immigrant families. Some of the pupils lived in this suburb, but several lived in more affluent parts of the town and came to the school only to attend a music class. The other group of 13–14-year-olds came from a small town located in a rural area surrounded by farmland and small villages. In all three groups there was broad socio-economic variation. Some of the pupils came from relatively impoverished circumstances, others were from the more well-to-do middle class. However, this sample was not drawn for the purpose of analysing difference between the variables of age, cultural identity or degree of urbanisation but instead to ensure enough variation was present to capture the diverse experiences of the children's lives. The analysis is a qualitative one concerned with in-depth interpretation of children's drawings and stories.

All the children were contacted via their teachers, who had agreed to include as part of the ordinary school work the assignment to write about 'My future family'. The theme was introduced in the same way to all the children. They were asked to think about a possible future life, to draw a picture of a make-believe family and of the house they could imagine themselves living in when grown up. The pupils were then asked to write a story about their fictitious families. The teachers avoided stressing the concept of *family*; instead, they asked the children to express their thoughts on the future, to imagine how they would live and with whom, if they would have children or if they would be living on their own. The children wrote on the theme intermittently throughout a two-month period; their drawings of their future home became the cover illustrations for each child's personal book of narratives. The project produced a rich material, some of which has already been published in other contexts (Halldén 1994a, 1994b, 1997, 1998, 1999, 2001; Grewin 2001). Here, I want to draw especially on two of the younger children's stories.

The house as a place for caring and for constructing the inside/outside boundary

In this chapter my focus is on children's ways of producing locality and colonising a place (see also Christensen, Chapter 2, above). In particular I will discuss the house as a symbol of the family and an intimate place for children. In the narratives the children described their future family, using as a starting-point the creation of a place or a house, which the children saw as a prerequisite for a good life. The house creates opportunities for everyday life and is a key site for 'belonging' and for creating and maintaining social ties and relationships, a shelter for children and their families. The two narratives I draw on were produced by a girl and a boy. Both children described the house as a domestic scene, a place for reproduction where intimate relationships are formed, but in their stories they use different ways to mark the relationship with the outside world. In this chapter I will focus on the house as an important factor in the construction of inside and outside, and 'the well-known' versus 'the strange'. The border is not only a physical demarcation, it is also a symbol of the demarcation between public and private, as I will show, a line where important changes of social life take place.

The narratives on which I base my discussion were written by Barbara and Bill (both names are fictitious), two 9-year-olds living in a medium-sized town in Sweden. They wrote about their future family over a two-month period. Bill produced thirteen pages, which was the average length of the boys' narratives. The girls generally wrote somewhat longer stories, some of them considerably so. Barbara produced the longest story, sixty-four pages. Barbara's and Bill's stories have 'care' as the underlying theme and both place the important events that occur at the border between inside and outside.

To use Bakhtin's concept of chronotope (Bakhtin 1937 (1981)), we can say that the threshold chronotope is used in the narrative to locate important events. 'We will give the name chronotope (literally, "time space") to the intrinsic connectedness of temporal and spatial relationships that are artistic-ally expressed in literature' (Bakhtin 1937 (1981): 84). The chronotopes are characterised by their meaning for the narrative. 'They are the organizing centres for the fundamental narrative events of the novel. The chronotope is the place where the knots of the narrative are tied and untied. It can be said without qualification that to them belongs the meaning that shapes the narra-tive' (Bakhtin 1937 (1981): 250). Bakhtin distinguished between different chronotopes, one of which is the threshold chronotope. In Bakhtin's words the chronotope of threshold is highly charged with emotion and value:

> It can be combined with the motif of encounter, but its most fundamental instance is as the chronotope of *crises* and *break* in a life. The word 'thre-shold' itself already has a metaphorical meaning in everyday usage (together with its literal meaning), and is connected with the breaking point in a life, the moment of crisis, the decision that changes life (or indecisiveness that fails to change life, the fear of stepping over the threshold).
>
> (Bakhtin 1937 (1981): 248)

On the threshold significant changes take place. Bakhtin's interest is to describe the reciprocity between time and place in narratives in different genres. In doing this he locates parts which, in his terminology, have chronotopic value. These parts are used to emphasise a turning point in the narrative, and different genres have different ways of doing this. The threshold chronotope is used in idyllic family novels to underscore the division between the well-known parts of family life and the outside world, but also the possibility of crossing the border between them.

The stories analysed here use very different styles, and the border markings also differ. Barbara writes a kind of canonised story where nothing is omitted from the text, whereas Bill's story is written in a highly condensed form. In Barbara's story we meet a woman who bears the main responsibility, who takes care of the family and establishes the rituals for making the transition from night to day, and whose primary aim is to establish order. Bill writes about himself living alone with a dog who in the course of the story gives birth to puppies. The important theme in both stories is reproduction, both in the sense of feeding and cleaning (to reproduce the home) and in the sense of giving birth. The main character describes the house where life is lived and in doing so a border is marked. The border marks the inside from the outside, and the contact between these two worlds is maintained when someone crosses the border.

The threshold and the encounter with the stranger

Bill begins his story by stating that the cottage where he lives has a flagpole. His drawing shows the Swedish flag. Bill was born abroad, but situates himself in Sweden when writing about his future life. A number of Bill's classmates were immigrants, several of whom wrote about living in their birth country in their future life while the others wrote about living in Sweden. Bill does not present his family, but goes directly to the encounter:

> My house is a cottage. I live in a garden. I have a flag pole. One morning I heard something when I was eating breakfast. It was somebody scratching at my door I went and opened the door where I saw a dog it was a Alsashun the dog was a he and he was dirty I brought him inside I washed him then I gave him some dog food. After a few months my terrier got puppies.[2]

In his very condensed style Bill lets us know that he and his dog have a visitor. As noted above, the narrative does not introduce the family members, but the drawing does, portraying Bill with his terrier. Someone is scratching at the door. The stranger is characterised: it is a dog, an 'Alsashun', and the dog's sex is specified: 'the dog was a he'. The dog is dirty and hungry. He is let into the house, cleaned and fed and a few months later 'my terrier got puppies'. The door to the house separates the inside world were Bill lives with his dog and the outside world from whence the stranger has come. By starting the story with himself eating breakfast, Bill indicates that this is an ordinary morning. When Bill opens the door he is confronted with a strange dog that is dirty and hungry. This stranger is brought inside and taken care of, and his entrance changes the life of those living inside. In Bill's short story he manages to establish two worlds: the one outside where the strangers are and the one inside where the family lives. The door, symbolising the dividing line, is opened and the stranger is welcomed in and cared for. Bill uses few details when describing his house; we are told that it is a cottage surrounded by a garden and that he has a flagpole. The main character lives an ordinary life where few major events occur; but then a stranger crosses his threshold and this encounter is an important event. We can see it as marking the creation of a family. The stranger was a 'he' and the life of a single man with a she-dog changes into a family with 'children'. Children need to be cared for and they can cause trouble. Under the title 'Then I got disappointed', a heading the teacher had suggested, Bill writes:

> then I got disappointed. One day I called my Alsashun puppies but they didn't come so I call them again but still they don't come so I went and looked in the whole house but they weren't there then I got disappointed then I went out and there they were.

The puppies have disappeared and he looks for them everywhere in the house. They are supposed to be inside, but he cannot find them and this makes him disappointed. What does this mean? Is Bill anxious that something may have happened to the puppies and that he may lose them, or is he disappointed at their having broken the rule forbidding them to go outside? We do not know, but the narrative can be interpreted as showing worry and then relief when Bill finds them. The drama is situated on the edge. He searches inside and finds them outside. They have crossed the threshold and, in a sense, the borders of the family. The story ends with a passage that supports the interpretation that the puppies are children who were born into the family when the stranger entered the house: 'After a few years my puppies became big dogs and they could look after themselves.'

The end of the story connects to the way the story began. Bill begins the story with himself living alone with a dog. The encounter with the stranger leads to the birth of puppies and the start of family life with its worries about the little ones. The ending closes the story with the 'children' growing up and moving out: having fulfilled his caring mission Bill is again living on his own with his dog.

The transition between order and chaos and night and day

In her narrative Barbara gives a detailed picture of the house where her family lives. It is a big house with lots of space for different activities. This is an affluent family, and it is Barbara who organises life and keeps order in the house.

> My house is in town, I live in a villa. Outside the villa is a big swimming pool with lots of things also I have two children. And three kittens too and a cat mother too.
>
> The littlest one is Alexander and he's five months. And the biggest is Emma and she's two years. And the kids' Dad is Lasse and he's twenty three.
>
> And we have a garage too. And we have our own cars and we have our own workrooms. But we have everything else together. Everything else and the children have their own rooms. And that's all about our family. Goodbye.

In emphasising caring routines Barbara gives herself an important role as the person who organises family life and protects the family members from chaos. The detailed descriptions underscore her role as the head of the family. Her way of writing has much in common with children playing with a doll's house. The important events are feeding, cleaning and bathing the children.

> One morning Alexander woke up he wanted oatmeal. I stood at the sink and made breakfast. We had warm sandwiches and hot chocolate, at

about nine o'clock in the morning. In the morning I took a hot shower and then I gave Emma a shower and then I gave Alexander a hot bath. And then I made the beds and cleaned the whole house. I cleaned the windows and took the vacuum cleaner and got rid of all the dust and then I washed the floors and washed the clothes in the washing-machine in the home. And Lasse cleaned the car and mowed the lawn.

The house is Barbara's domain; the text indicates that she takes pride in this important duty of keeping the house in proper order. In Carolyn Steedman's (1982) analysis of three little working-class girls writing about family life, she interprets it as socialisation to motherhood. The little girls' writing about the struggle to keep the house tidy is understood both as an identification with their mothers and as part of a working-class identity of respectability. We can see the same pattern in Barbara's writings: a little girl's attempt to identify important issues. The house is the central area and the main character spares no effort in creating order. In this house everything must be kept clean and tidy and this is the wife's duty. The husband's (Lasse's) areas of responsibility are the garage and the lawn. Barbara's careful way of minding the house forms a way to create a home and to establish a barrier to a threatening disorder.

Hot baths and showers are also a frequently recurring theme. Is this mainly a way of keeping order or does it have another meaning as well? I see this emphasis on hot baths and showers as a way to mark the border between night and day. Nighttime is a period of dreams, happy or frightening, and waking up is the transition back to reality. Douglas has written about the importance of rituals in protecting the transitions in life (Douglas 1966). When we go from one period in life to another, we become more vulnerable. Rituals have the function of protection and caring during the transition. When Barbara writes about hot showers and hot baths she is, however, not only cleaning the body and marking the border between night and day, but also creating a sensual feeling. Together with serving her family hot chocolate, this can be seen as a ritual to emphasise the border and the need for protection.

The house as a scene where the good life is orchestrated by an important main character is even more developed via the relationship to neighbours. In a sense the family is not enough for the creation of a good life. Relationships with other families are also needed.

When I looked out the window. A new family had moved in a whole new family who lives next door to us now. It's lots of fun having a new neighbour. Cause then Emma has someone to play with. I said that was really great. 'Mummy can I go out and play with her. Of course why shouldn't I let you. But wait up for me.' Emma waits. 'I'm just gonna get Alexander dressed first and put him in the carriage. Then I can get you dressed Emma.'

The new family opens up possibilities for establishing friendships. The daughter may possibly get a new playmate. But Barbara does not comment further on the new neighbours; instead she gets bogged down in the details of putting on clothes and going shopping. Detailed descriptions of daily routines are the main content of her story. Even when more dramatic events and existential episodes occur, such as Barbara's giving birth to twins and the cat's giving birth to kittens and then dying, they are followed by accounts of daily routines.

> And next morning I told Lasse to call the hospital and the ambulance came and picked me up there was no time to lose and I was in the hospital and the twins came a girl and a boy, they bathed them and changed their diapers and then Lasse came with the pram and with a whole suitcase filled with baby clothes to the hospital and then I could go home again and then we were in the car and were so happy that I had twins we were very very happy.

The important transition that occurs when a child is born is Barbara's business alone. In an interview I had with her at the end of the project, she told me that the fictional mother had not told the family in advance about the expected birth, but taken the full responsibility upon herself. The narrative underscores that this is a drama: there is an emergency and an ambulance comes to take her to the hospital. In a place outside the home she gives birth to twins. The movement from the home, which is characterised by order and respectability, to the hospital, which signifies disease and all-powerful doctors, establishes two scenes between which the main character moves back and forth. Not only is the transition her business alone, but it also occurs outside the home. The persons who protect her in these rites of passage are located outside the home. She is the one who gives the order to call the ambulance, and when the twins are born 'they' (that is, the hospital nurses) bathe the infants and dress them in clean clothes. The rituals that Barbara uses to manage the situation occur in a place outside the home that is under the care of others. When she returns home, she resumes the role of the one who creates the routines for re-establishing order.

In the stories by Bill and Barbara we find both dramatic and everyday episodes. Both need to be taken into account to prevent dangerous things from happening. The way the episodes are accounted for shows how the outside world is important as a resource and a potentiality, but also that the secure place of the home must be guarded and cared for.

Time and place: a way to handle transition and belonging

In Barbara's and Bill's narratives, we find a main character who takes care of the family members and in doing so establishes a place of importance. The house needs a person to live in it, someone to create routines for everyday life and to bring in new family members. The border is accounted for both as a marking of the threshold, with its chronotopic value (Bakhtin 1937 (1981)), where the stranger enters the home, and as a ritualistic way of emphasising the border between night and day (Douglas 1966). The family is created in a house that becomes a home through the caring routines carried out by the main character. This can be described as locating a place and becoming attached to it. Issues of identity and belonging are part of this process. Life is not lived in an abstract way, but in relation to a certain place, and we can describe that place as being associated with knowledge. The place provides opportunities for a life, and in describing the place the main character can appear as someone who is capable of taking action. The place is a frame for the narrative and it opens up certain positions for the main character. In Barbara's and Bill's stories, reproduction and caring are the key to homemaking. This can be found in many other narratives as well. Reproduction and caring are accounted for in different ways, but a main point is to distinguish who is and who is not part of the community. In their 'border work' our young narrators engage in an inclusion/exclusion process. The relationship between inside and outside is important, and the inside is partly constituted by contact with the outside world.

In Bill's narrative the border is accounted for when the stranger scratches on the door. In fact, the establishment of a generation chain is strongly connected to a place in other narratives as well, where the main character displays competence and fellowship (Halldén 1998, 1999). The house is a shelter for the main character and her or his family, and as a key site for 'belonging', for creating and maintaining intimate social ties and relationships. The encounter with a stranger plays a crucial part in establishing the border and illustrates how the stranger is taken up as a family member and thus becomes included in the home. Making a home from a house is implemented in contact with the outside world. The same theme can be found when Bill writes about being disappointed. The puppies cannot be found indoors and Bill gets upset, but after a while he finds them outside. This could be interpreted as indicating that dangers lurk outside. The house, which is supposed to be a shelter, is empty and Bill is anxious until he finds the puppies. To have the responsibility of caring for and protecting the rising generation is here associated with a feeling of uneasiness and a request to prevent misfortune. This part of the narrative also shows us that the border is important and that the outside world actually creates some of the qualities of the inside.

Bill describes in his story the new-born puppies as his responsibility, but they will eventually grow up to be big and strong 'and they could look after themselves'. Bill's relation to the puppies is characterised as a caring mission. In Barbara's story a cat gives birth to kittens and then dies. Her story is more threatening, and the idyll is maintained only with great effort on the part of the main character. There is a parallel between her giving birth to twins and the cat giving birth to kittens. The narrative casts a shadow over the act of giving birth and establishes a connection to death. Both the familiar and the alien are explored and the frame for the process of exploration is the family and the home.

The work on order and respectability, which is so prominent in Barbara's narrative, has the purpose of incorporating the family members into the daily routines and excluding the diffuse periods of the night. This is, as in Bill's story, a way to protect the family and to maintain control. Chaos is always kept at a distance, and the arranging of the house is an important part of this process. When the main character transports herself and her children from the sheltered home to the daycare centre or to the shopping centre, she is very keen to present all the details of these excursions.

> And now I was at the shop and now I got out of the car, then I put up the pram. And then I took Jacob and Linda out of the car. And now I was in the shop and bought food, and now I was ready, and now we were outside the shop, and first I put the twins in the middle of the car, and now I shut down the pram, and packed the goods into the car. And now I drove home.

We can read this passage as being a way to emphasise the different locations between which the main character has to move in the process of caring for her family. She arranges the house in an orderly fashion and brings the family out into the daylight, represented by offering them hot showers and hot chocolate. Furthermore, she goes shopping as well, and here she is very careful not to forget anything. Coming home marks the end of the passage and can be interpreted as returning to the sheltered area – the place. In this narrative, as in Bill's, the relationship to the outside world is important for establishing the secure sphere of caring. Christensen *et al.* (2000) have pointed out the importance of material space for belonging and identity. In their research on the construction of 'family time', they show that the family is 'made and remade by children and parents through negotiation and the juxtaposition of time and space' (Christensen *et al.* 2000: 154). This is obvious in the narratives analysed here as well. The family is closely connected to the house that forms a home.

Conclusion

To understand how children identify a place and attach symbolic meaning to it is crucial for disentangling the relationship between time and space in children's narratives about the family and the home. Mary Douglas (1991) writes about how the home is organised around an ongoing co-ordination of people's time and space. A space is needed but not necessarily a fixed space, and time needs to be regulated. 'So a home is not only a space, it has some structure in time; and because it is for people who are living in that time and space, it has aesthetic and moral dimensions' (Douglas 1991: 289). The home is created by the persons who live in it and who participate in this complexity of co-ordination. In my analysis I have looked for the threshold chronotope (Bakhtin 1937 (1981)) to identify how this co-ordination is accounted for in children's narratives. How can we understand how children, when writing about a future family, account for this co-ordination of time and space? And how is the chronotopic value used in creating the border between outside and inside that is the subtext?

In Bill's and Barbara's texts, the threshold chronotope indicates that an underlying issue is the inclusion of persons in a way of life, and what is excluded is an uncontrolled outside world. At the threshold transitions take place: those between night and day, between order and disorder, between single life and family life. The place that is guarded and symbolised by the threshold is the house and the home of the family. The transitions are closely connected to the reproduction of daily routines and to reproduction in terms of childbirth. The narratives are, in that sense, inscribed in both everyday time and lifetime. The life of the family goes on in the narrative, and making time is as important an issue as space.

The issues I have raised are the connection between time and space and the way we can identify important places in children's narratives. The data were collected in connection with an assignment where the children were asked to write about their future family. In doing this they provided the narrative with a venue and established a place of importance where life is lived. In the narratives analysed here, the place is the house. In this house a life is lived that is regulated. Through regulation a home is established that has borders to the outside world and is regulated in relation to time and place/space. In writing about a future life, the young writers distinguished between outside and inside. In Bill's and Barbara's stories, for example, inside is the house or home and outside is the alien world. It is in the contact with the outside world that important events take place, and it is inside that the work of consolidating the family takes place. The important point here is that the narrators explore the inside/outside, 'the well-known/the strange' and the house as a potential area for positioning the main character as a competent person. In this process of narration, place is used to raise the issue of time. With the occurrence of important events a mediation between time and place is established. And following Bakhtin (1937 (1981)), we can talk about a chronotopic value of that part of the narrative – a turning point where the children's narrators draw attention to essential meanings.

The introductory parts of this chapter indicate that there is a connection between children and nature and that this is especially true for the Nordic countries. When Bill draws a picture of the house, he draws a Swedish flag. This is an archetype symbolising nationality, and furthermore it gives an association to nature with blue sky and sunshine. In media contexts the Swedish flag is often used in advertising as a symbol for summer, sunshine and countryside. As has been shown in research on children's drawings, Swedish children often use the nation's flag to introduce an element of the idyllic in their drawings (Aronsson 1997). In their analysis of the image of the Swedish child, Aronsson and Sandin (1996) describe the child as free, unbound and active, just like the little naked boy on Einar Nerman's picture adorning Swedish match boxes. Freedom, nature and sunshine are associated with the flag and in that sense nationality is very much connected to nature. All the children in the younger age group participating in the study lived in blocks of flats, but their pictures were of villas or even more often little cottages set amidst green grass, flowers and trees. These houses were depicted as idyllic places; they are attached to nature and thus, in extension, to the image of a rural idyllic childhood. An important aspect of this idyll in the children's accounts is the reproduction of life, the birth of children and the routines of caring. In the narratives children and animals are interconnected. Bill writes about an encounter with a stranger that becomes part of the family, and this stranger is a dog. In Barbara's story there is an episode where the cat gives birth and then dies, which underscores the risks involved in childbirth. The animals are important members of children's families, but they also have a broader symbolic meaning indicating a relationship to strangers that can change the life course.

In this chapter I have used children's narratives about a future family life in a discussion about the process of creating a place of importance. My point is that a place is colonised through the people who use it and give it meaning. This process is important to discuss from children's perspective. Which places are important to children and what makes them important? How do children attach themselves to a place? Although ethnographic fieldwork perhaps is the most obvious way to obtain material about children's colonising projects, I have shown that children's narratives are another important source for understanding children's relation to place.

Acknowledgements

Many thanks to Pia Christensen and Margaret O'Brien for their comments on earlier drafts of this chapter.

Notes

1 The research reported here was financed by the Swedish Council for Social Research and the Swedish Council for Research in Humanities and Social Sciences.
2 The quotations are translated from Swedish and I have purposely followed the children's grammar as closely as possible.

References

Appadurai, A., 1995, 'The production of locality'. In R. Fardon (ed.), *Counterworks, Managing the Diversity of Knowledge* (London: Routledge).
Aronsson, K., 1997, *Barns världar – barns bilder* [*Children's Worlds – Children's Drawings*] (Stockholm: Natur och Kultur).

Aronsson, K. and Sandin, B., 1996, 'The sun match boy and plant metaphors: a Swedish image of a 20th-century childhood'. In P. Hwang, M. Lamb and I. Siegel (eds), *Images of Childhood* (Mahwah, NJ: Lawrence Erlbaum).

Asplund, J., 1983, *Tid, rum, individ och kollektiv* [*Time, place, individual and collective*] (Stockholm: Liber Förlag).

Bakhtin, M., 1937 (1981), *The Dialogical Imagination: Four Essays by M. M. Bakhtin* (Austin, TX: University of Texas Press).

Christensen, P., James, A. and Jenks, C., 2000, 'Home and movement: children constructing "family time"'. In S. L. Holloway and G. Valentine (eds), *Children's Geographies: Playing, Living, Learning* (London: Routledge).

Cohen, A. P., 1982, 'Belonging, identity and social organisation'. In *British Rural Cultures* (Manchester: Manchester University Press).

De Conick-Smith, N., Sandin, B. and Schrumpf, E. (eds), 1997, *Industrious Children: Work and Childhood in the Nordic Countries 1850–1990* (Odense: Odense University Press).

Douglas, M., 1966, *Purity and Danger: An Analysis of Concepts of Pollution and Taboo* (Harmondsworth: Penguin Books).

Douglas, M., 1991, 'The idea of a home: a kind of space'. *Social Research*, 58, 287–307.

Eckert, G., 2001, *Wasting Time or Having Fun? Cultural Meanings of Children and Childhood* (Linköping Studies in Arts and Science (Dissertation)).

Grewin, A.-M., 2001 (Dissertation), *Unga flickor skriver in sig i sin kultur: möjliga sätt att vara – uttryck i text och bild* [*Young Girls Inscribe Themselves in Their Culture: Possible Ways of Being as Expressed in Texts and Pictures*] (Stockholm: Department of Education Stockholm University).

Gullestad, M., 1997, 'A passion for boundaries: reflections on connections between everyday lives of children and discourses on the nation in contemporary Norway.' *Childhood*, 4, 19–42.

Halldén, G., 1994a, 'Establishing order: small girls write about family life'. *Gender and Education*, 6, 3–17.

Halldén, G., 1994b, 'The family: a refuge from demands or an arena for the exercise of power and control. Children's fiction on their future families'. In B. Mayall (ed.), *Children's Childhoods Observed and Experienced* (London: The Falmer Press).

Halldén, G., 1997, 'Competence and connection: gender and generation in boys' narratives'. *Gender and Education*, 9, 307–16.

Halldén, G., 1998, 'Boyhood and fatherhood: narratives about a future family life'. *Childhood*, 5, 23–39.

Halldén, G., 1999, '"To be or not to be": absurd and humoristic descriptions as a strategy to avoid idyllic life stories – boys write about family life'. *Gender and Education*, 11, 469–79.

Halldén, G., 2001, *Barnet och boet: familjen – drömmar om det goda, det spännande och det farliga* [*The Child and the Nest: The Family – Dreams of the Good, the Exciting and the Dangerous*] (Stockholm: Carlssons Förlag).

Hendrick, H., 1997, *Children, Childhood and English Society 1880–1990* (Cambridge: Cambridge University Press).

Holloway, S. L. and Valentine, G., 2000, 'Children's geographies and the new social studies of childhood'. In Holloway and Valentine (eds), *Children's Geographies: Playing, Living, Learning* (London: Routledge).

Johannesson, K., 2001, *Nostalgia* [*Nostalgia*] (Stockholm: Bonniers Bokförlag).

Jones, O., 1997, 'Little figures, big shadows: country childhood stories'. In P. Cloke and J. Little (eds), *Contested Countryside Cultures: Otherness, Marginalisation and Rurality* (London: Routledge).

Matthews, H., Taylor, M., Percy-Smith, B. and Limb, M., 2000, 'The unacceptable *flaneur*: the shopping mall as a teenage hangout'. *Childhood*, 7, 279–94.

Munger, A.-C., 2000, *Stadens barn på landet: Stockholms sommarlovskolonier och den moderna välfärden* [*City Children in the Countryside Stockholm Summer Camp and Modern Welfare*] (Linköping Studies in Arts and Science (Dissertation)).

Olsson, O., 1999, *Från arbete till hobby: en studie av pedagogisk filantropi i de svenska arbetsstugorna* [*From Work to Hobby: A Study of Pedagogical Philanthropy in the Swedish Arbetsstugor*] (Linköping Studies in Arts and Science (Dissertation)).

Olwig, K. F., 2000, 'Barn i lokalsamfund – barns lokalsamfund' ['Children in the local community – children's local community'], *Barn*, 3–4, 5–22.

Philo, C., 2000, ' "The corner-stones of my world": editorial introduction to special issue on spaces of childhood. *Childhood*, 7 (3), 243–56.

Sandin, B., 1992, *The Century of the Child: On the Changed Meaning of Childhood in the Twentieth Century* (Linköping: Department of Child Studies, Linköping University).

Sandin, B., 1997, 'In the large factory town: child labour legislation, child labour and school compulsion'. In De Coninck-Smith, Sandin and Schrumpf (eds), *Industrious Children: Work and Childhood in the Nordic Countries 1850–1990* (Odense: Odense University Press).

Swedish Official Reports, 2001, *Barns och ungdomars välfärd* [*The Welfare of Children and Youth*] (Stockholm: Graphium/Norsteds AB), 55.

Steedman, C., 1982, *The Tidy House: Little Girls Writing* (London: Virago Press).

Steedman, C., 1990, *Childhood, Culture and Class in Britain; Margaret McMillan 1860–1931* (London: Virago Press).

Söderlind, I., 1999, *Barnhem för flickor: barn, familj och institutionsliv i Stockholm 1870–1920* [*Orphanages for Girls: Children, Families and Institutional Life in Stockholm 1870–1920*] (Stockholm: Stockholmia Förlag (Dissertation)).

Thorne, B., 1993, *Gender Play: Girls and Boys in School* (London: Open University Press).

Weiner, G., 1995, *De räddade barnen: om fattiga barn, mödrar och fäder och deras möte med filantropin i Hagalund 1900–1940* [*The Saved Children: On Poor Children, Mothers and Fathers and Their Encounter with the Philanthropy in Hagalund 1900–1940*] (Uppsala: Hjelms Förlag (Dissertation)).

Welles-Nyström, B., New, R. and Richman, A., 1994, 'The "good mother": a comparative study of Swedish, Italian and American maternal behavior and goals'. *Scandinavian Journal of Caring Sciences*, 8, 81–6.

Woodhead, M., 1990, 'Psychology and the cultural construction of children's needs'. In A. James and A. Prout (eds), *Constructing and Reconstructing Childhood: Contemporary Issues in the Sociological Study of Childhood* (London: The Falmer Press).

4 'Displaced' children?

Risks and opportunities in a Caribbean urban environment

Karen Fog Olwig

During the nineteenth and early twentieth century many children on the Danish West Indian island of St John moved alone to the city of Charlotte Amalie on neighbouring St Thomas in order to stay in the homes of better-off people. For the children, this move to St Thomas constituted a dramatic change in environment. On St John they had lived with their families in scattered rural settlements in an African-Caribbean community of poor small farmers. On St Thomas they stayed with strangers in the fast-moving, multicultural urban environment of the port city of Charlotte Amalie. For the children, life in Charlotte Amalie constituted both a danger of being exploited as inexpensive domestic labour and an opportunity to experience the more cosmopolitan ways of life in the city and take advantage of the resources that it had to offer. On the basis of archival research and interviews with St Johnians who spent all or part of their childhood in Charlotte Amalie, this chapter explores children's move to the city as both risk and opportunity. In exploring this urban experience of St Johnian children the chapter seeks to provide historical depth to and a cross-cultural perspective on contemporary studies of urban childhood.[1]

According to the historian Harry Hendrick, it is difficult to elucidate children's experiences in the past, because children's points of view are rarely documented in the public records and thus they are not recognised as 'historical actors' (Hendrick 2000: 42–3). Hendrick goes on to argue, however, that the purpose of historians

> is not simply to describe, however objectively, past cultures. It is rather to unmask the hidden and apparently *natural* structures of inequalities that existed (and continue to exist) between adults and children, to show how these affected the latter as historical subjects, to examine their influence on the evolution of age relations and to illustrate their significance for the varying concepts of childhood.
>
> (Hendrick 2000: 45–6)

I suggest that a focus on structures of inequality sheds important light on the St Johnian children's position as historical actors on St Thomas. Structures

Figure 4.1 Boy in Charlotte Amalie, 1915 The Royal Library, Copenhagen, Department of Maps, Prints and Photographs

of inequality, however, not only obtain in interpersonal relations between adults and children, but also are inscribed within wider societal structures of social and economic inequality that may present major barriers to general social mobility. I shall here argue that the presence of St Johnian children on St Thomas must be seen in the light of children's particular position as possible agents of social and economic improvement at a moment in history when few avenues of progress were available to their parents. Children did not act alone, however, but within the context of a kinship system based on networks of relations where the exchange of children was common and did not result in loss of family ties. I therefore suggest that, when studying children in the city, it is important to conceptualise the city as a socio-cultural, rather than a physical site. This means seeing it as a place that people create and practise as they develop social and economic relationships and cultural values in relation to particular localities under varying historical, social and personal circumstances (Olwig 1997; Olwig 2000).

Charlotte Amalie – An urban site in a West Indian colony

The Danish West Indies first emerged when the Danes colonised St Thomas in the 1670s.[2] The island's fine natural harbour Charlotte Amalie, which was granted free port status, allowing all nations to trade in the harbour, soon became a major entrepôt in the north-eastern part of the Caribbean. It

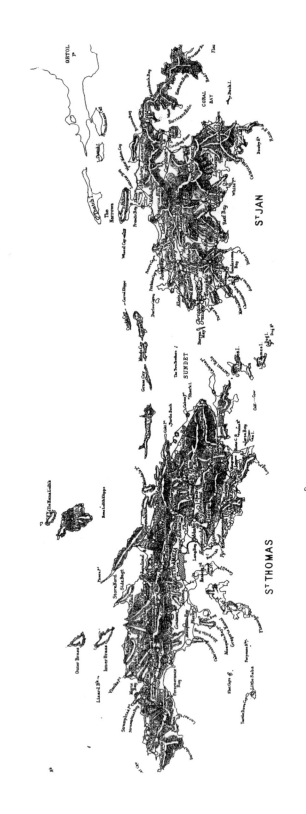

1:120000

Figure 4.2 St Thomas and St John (called St Jan in Danish), part of a map of the Danish West Indies published by the organisation De Danske Atlanterhavsøer (The Danish Atlantic Islands) in 1907. St Johnians travelled by boat directly to Charlotte Amalie (here spelled Charlotte Amalia) on the southern coast of St Thomas. While the sound between the two islands was only a few miles wide, the distance between St John and Charlotte Amalie was considerably longer. Moreover, many of the St Johnian children in Charlotte Amalie came from the Coral Bay area, in the eastern most part of St John

attracted merchants from Europe and North and South America, becoming a central port in the trans-Atlantic slave trade as well as an important regional trans-shipment point. When steamships were introduced in the nineteenth century, it also became a significant coal loading station. Unlike most other Caribbean islands, St Thomas never developed a major plantation economy, and it attracted a large population of *free coloured* from other Caribbean islands. The system of slavery that did emerge on the island was limited and primarily used slaves as domestic servants, artisans, traders or workers loading and unloading ships (Hall 1983).

St John, colonised by the Danes in 1717, and St Croix, purchased from the French in 1734, by contrast developed as plantation societies controlled by a small plantocracy who owned not just most of the land, but also most of the population on the islands. St Croix, with its flat topography and fertile soil, offered the best prospects for sugarcane cultivation, and the most significant plantation interests soon concentrated on that island. Being located 40 miles south of St Thomas, this island developed fairly independently of St Thomas. St John, with its mountainous and rocky soil, was considerably less attractive for sugar production and plantations were only marginally profitable. By 1800, St John nevertheless was a full-fledged plantation society with a slave population of more than 2,500 who lived and worked on the sugar estates that dominated the plantation economy.[3] After emancipation in 1848, sugar production declined rapidly, and during the 1860s the plantations were turned into cattle estates. After the collapse of the sugar plantations St Johnians purchased small plots of land and settled as subsistence farmers in their own villages, developing tightly knit communities based on exchange relations involving food, labour and use rights in land. St Thomas, located a few miles from St John, across a narrow sound, became a major economic centre for St Johnians where they might sell their produce, purchase imported items not available on St John and seek wage employment.

As a large, relatively prosperous urban area, Charlotte Amalie offered opportunities unheard of on St John. At the same time, it constituted a complex social and economic system that St Johnians often experienced difficulty negotiating, and they therefore developed a rather ambiguous relationship toward the city. St Johnian children came to play an important role in this relationship.

St Johnian children during and after slavery

During slavery, children were forced to enter the work force at the sugar plantations as soon as they were capable of performing physical labour. Plantation records from the 1840s show that children 6 to 7 years of age were used to carry water to the field slaves, look after calves and help care for smaller children (Olwig 1985: 17). As they were able to perform more physically demanding labour they were assigned to new tasks until most of them, finally, ended up in the work gangs labouring in the cane fields.

During the last years of slavery, the colonial government instituted mandatory education for children, but only the youngest children were allowed to attend school on a daily basis, the older ones being confined to receiving education on Saturdays. This education, nevertheless, was touted by the colonial government as an important and necessary step in the slaves' preparation for freedom so that they might become responsible citizens in society. Thus the government pointed to the children as those who really would be able to harvest the fruits of freedom, and in 1847 it passed an emancipation act which declared that all children born after the promulgation of the law would be born free. Others would have to wait an additional twelve years before they could become emancipated. The anger caused by this act, which left all but the new-born enslaved, is believed to have prompted the slave uprising on St Croix that led to general emancipation in 1848.

The freedom gained by this declaration of emancipation was seriously curtailed by a Servants Act, which forced all former slaves to enter contracts with their former owners. The Servants Act also included children and stipulated that they were to be paid in food and clothing for their labour (Olwig 1985: 84). Many parents, however, decided to send their children to school on a full-time basis after emancipation, apparently in accordance with the colonial government's wish that the freed should be better prepared for freedom. The planters, however, did not accept this loss of labour power and complained to the colonial authorities that children who were old enough to labour on the estates were being sent to school. Consequently, a school ordinance was passed in 1849 that allowed only children from 5 to 8 years old to attend school on working days from 8 a.m. to 11 a.m. As formerly, older children had to seek education on Saturdays. Four years later, school attendance was extended to include children 6 to 10 years of age (Olwig 1985: 87). This improvement in the children's education was not so much a reflection of the authorities' growing concern for the well-being of children. It was rather a sign of the colonial government losing control over the children, because many parents, realising that all but the youngest children would be forced to work on the plantations, had sent their children to St Thomas, where the Servants Act was not in effect. Thus the revised school ordinance noted that 'during the latter years, a considerable number of children have been removed clandestinely from the estates to St Thomas' (Olwig 1985: 87). Furthermore, the ordinance included a reminder that children as well as adults needed a permit to travel to St Thomas.

The population censuses show that the new school ordinance, and the increased pressure to place children in labour contracts, did not prevent parents from sending their children to St Thomas. The St Thomas censuses document a growing number of St Johnian children living there without their parents, even though the St John origins of these children was mostly likely underreported in order to avoid their being deported to St John.

According to the 1857 census, thirty-four children born on St John were listed as living without their parents on St Thomas. In the 1860 census the

Table 4.1 The household status of St Johnians 0–15 years old living without their parents in St Thomas (% in parentheses)

	Servant	Other	God or foster child or relative	Total
1857	15 (44)	14 (41)	5 (15)	34
1860	24 (55)	15 (34)	5 (11)	44
1870	28 (49)	25 (44)	4 (7)	57
1880	13 (35)	18 (49)	6 (16)	37
1901	20 (57)		15 (43)	35

Source: Population Returns from St Thomas, Folketællingerne, Dansk Vestindien, Det Statistiske Departement [The Population Censuses, Danish West Indies, Statistical Department], 1857, 1860, 1870, 1880, 1901. The figure of 15 for 1901 may refer to more varied household statuses that were included in the 'other' category in previous years.

figure had increased to forty-four children, and in the 1870 census, the last one to be taken before the Servants Act was abolished in 1872, the number had grown to fifty-seven children. In 1880, the number of St Johnian children living without their parents in Charlotte Amalie had declined to thirty-seven, underlining that a primary motive for sending children to St Thomas was to avoid their being subjected to the plantation labour regime. Furthermore, it is important to remember that this may be the first year when the origins of St Johnian children was not underreported, and that the actual decline therefore may have been considerably larger. Although the number of St Johnian children living without their parents in St Thomas decreased considerably by 1880, it is apparent that the custom of sending St Johnian children to St Thomas did not disappear. Thus in 1901[4] thirty-five St Johnian children of 15 years and below were reported living on St Thomas, more than 9 per cent of all children born on St John. This indicates that St Johnians also had other motives for sending their children to St Thomas. I shall analyse this further below by examining the sort of positions the children had in St Thomian households.

'Giving' St Johnian children to St Thomian homes

According to the population censuses, approximately half of the St Johnian children were listed as living in the St Thomian homes as servants. It may therefore seem rather ironic that children were moved from St John to avoid the Servants' Act only to become servants in Charlotte Amalie. Nevertheless, as servants in Charlotte Amalie they were not required to labour in canefields, as they would have been on St John. They were rather doing domestic work, which had been a relatively high-status occupation in the hierarchical structure of the plantation regime. During slavery, it was usually the offspring of white–black unions who were used for domestic labour, and this type of work was generally less physically strenuous than the labour required of the field gangs. Being a servant in a private home in Charlotte Amalie therefore was to be preferred to working under the Servants' Act on St John. It is moreover likely that the category 'servant' covered a wide range of conditions in the household. The conditions of 'servants' may therefore not have been so different from those which prevailed for the children who were listed as living 'with others' (more than a third), or with persons with whom they had a kin or kin-like relationship, such as aunts and uncles, godparents or foster parents (between 5 and 15 per cent).

It is difficult to interpret the status of the children in the home on the basis of census material alone. Fortunately, in the mid-1970s I interviewed a number of St Johnians who had spent part of their childhood in Charlotte Amalie. These interviews were part of a more general historical anthropological study of the development of African Caribbean culture on St John from the eighteenth century to the late twentieth century. This study was based partly on archival research, partly on one year of field work on St John in 1974–75. An important part of the field research was oral history interviews with elderly St Johnians.[5] Many of them were then in their seventies and eighties, and their recollections dated back to the turn of the century. The recollections of those who had spent part of their childhood in St Thomas therefore shed light on what it meant to be sent as a child to St Thomas and how children might have experienced this.

In the following description of the practice of sending children from St John to St Thomas, Amos Fraser[6] provided important insights into the complexity of the custom of sending children to St Thomas:

> I grew up in St Thomas with my aunt. My brothers also grew up with people in St Thomas, except for one or two. Things were very, very hard, and somehow it seems that the St Thomians were a little better off than we were . . . I didn't see any of my brothers and sisters when I lived in St Thomas. Emmanuel lived with the Monsantos who were with the port authority . . . And such people could afford to take care of a child, so you could give your child to them knowing that they wouldn't be starved or going naked. I stayed with my Aunt Alexandrine. She had no children in the house at the time . . . In most cases, the households that accepted these children, or wanted them, had women who had no children of their own living with them. In this way, you would have a little person to send around to do a little shopping and all like that. I was 6 years when I went to St Thomas, I think. I stayed there for nine years. When I left St John, I hardly knew anything about it, but my mother used to come visit me very often. Whatever she could find to bring with her, she would bring for me and the household where I stayed. She brought provisions, ground food. I came home when I became big enough to work, and my mother was glad for that because I could help out. My stepfather died young, when I had come home.

Amos Fraser begins his account by explaining that St Johnian children were sent to homes on St Thomas that were better off because their parents were so poor that they found it difficult to provide for their children. The practice of sending St Johnian children to St Thomas therefore can be portrayed as a rather desperate means whereby poverty-stricken parents sought to ensure that their children received food and clothing, basic subsistence requirements that, apparently, were not a certitude on St John. Furthermore, it seems that the practice involved the scattering of families, because Amos Fraser noted that he and his siblings were sent to different homes and that they did not see each other at all while on St Thomas. In the light of these rather stark circumstances, it is rather surprising that he described the practice as the *giving* of children to others. Indeed, as he continues his account of his own experiences it becomes apparent that he did not perceive of the custom as involving poor people abandoning their children by having them placed in wealthy homes where they might work for their living. He rather thought of it in terms of people with many children and limited economic means giving homes with better economic means, but lacking children, the company and help of these children in return for their upkeep. Even so it is apparent that at least some of the St Johnian parents continued to help with their children's upkeep, because Amos Fraser related that his mother brought root crops that she had cultivated on St John to the home where he lived whenever she travelled to St Thomas. Apparently she came 'very often', so even though he had little recollection of St John, when he finally returned after nine years in St Thomas, he knew his mother well and regarded St John as 'home.'

Amos Fraser's mother was not unusual in making frequent visits to St Thomas. Indeed, most St Johnians travelled periodically to St Thomas in order to sell charcoal, fish and root crops and to purchase imported goods. The practice of sending St Johnian children to St Thomas therefore seems to have been inscribed within a more generalised network of social and economic relations between child givers in the community of subsistence farmers on St John and child receivers in the city of Charlotte Amalie on St Thomas. What might initially be described as well-to-do people's exploitation of poor rural children's labour becomes, in Amos Fraser's account, an aspect of a wider network of personal exchange relations involving rural and urban homes. This network of relations did not just operate between households in St John and St Thomas, but was, to a great extent, an extension of exchange relations that already existed on St John. These exchange relations involved the giving of food, labour and children between homes according to the ability and need of the various homes. There were, generally speaking, no commercial transactions involved in these exchanges. Rather they were based on the idea that what is given will go around and eventually come back when there is a need. In terms of children, it was therefore common to give children to older people or couples with no children of their own on both St Thomas and St John, so that they might have the children's company and help. As Ralph Prince explained: 'I lived with my grandparents from when I was 1 year and 11 months. I was my grandparents' first grandchild so it was only natural that they should want to raise me.' But it was also common that homes with many children gave children to better-off homes that would be able to provide well for the children and could use their help around the house. In some cases, this 'help' might turn into labour exploitation, especially if the children had little support from their families, as happened when their parents were deceased. There is little indication, however, that the children were ever merely exploited as free labour force. Thus, they all seem to have attended school on a regular basis.[7] Child exchange therefore included a wide range of social and economic situations, but it was, basically, regarded as an integral, and fully accepted, part of social relations in the St Johnian community. Indeed, the custom of exchanging children was so prevalent at the turn of the nineteenth century that a third of all children 15 years and below born on St John were listed in the 1901 population census for St Thomas and St John as living in homes without their parents (Olwig 1985: 133). The children who ended up on St Thomas therefore were part of a more general system of child exchange.[8]

The children who had been sent to homes on St Thomas had a central position in the network of relations that extended between St John and St Thomas. This is particularly apparent in Julia Peterson's account of her childhood on St Thomas:

> My father promised me away to my godmother. When my mother was making me, he told her that if the child turned out to be a girl he would give the child to this woman ... My godmother [who was a baker] had one of the big brick ovens with the chimney, and my father would bring wood and charcoal for this oven, so that she could do her baking. And my father would stay with us until he was ready to go back ...
>
> My father would come every month and bring the charcoal and wood and provisions such as potatoes and peas ... He would sell ground food from the boat and he would always bring some for me and my godmother.

Julia Peterson explained that her mother had been quite unhappy about her going to St Thomas as a young child, because she was her mother's only child, her only sibling, a brother, having died as an infant. Apparently, the next four children to follow Julia Petersen, all boys, also died and only the last two children, both girls, survived. This was therefore not a case of a poor household sending a child to a relatively well-to-do household in St Thomas, because it was unable to rear a great number of children. Julia Peterson's father rather seems to have given his only child to a home on St Thomas as a means of strengthening ties that he had developed with this woman by virtue of her being a good customer for his wood and charcoal because of her bakery business. By giving his child to the home, Julia Peterson's father not only established a firm trading relationship with the baker; he also created a home base on St Thomas where he might stay whenever he was in Charlotte Amalie.

When I interviewed Julia Peterson, she explained that she had been like a daughter of the home, and it was apparent that she had been treated better than other children who had stayed there:

> My godmother never married, she had no children, so she was an old maid. But she had liked children, and so people used to see to it that she had children around . . . It wasn't hard to grow up with my godmother, because they used to call me the black daughter. My godmother raised me from when I was a baby, and I was the only one at first, so my godmother became especially attached to me. Some of the other god-children were children of people who were hired to her, so they were different.

This description of Julia Peterson's status makes apparent that members of the household were distinguished according to various factors, such as their length of stay in the household, their colour and their parents' relationship with the household. Thus because she had lived, as the only child, in the home since she was a baby, Julia Peterson had become like a daughter. This kin-like status was probably reinforced by her father's frequent visits to the home, where he did not just come briefly to sell his wood, but sometimes stayed for several days in the house. It is important that her father came as a business partner and friend, and not as a hired hand, because this placed Julia Peterson on a level above that of the children of the domestic servant who lived in the home. This special position is reflected in the fact that Julia Peterson, unlike most other St Johnian children living in private homes on St Thomas, visited her family on St John quite often as a child and stayed there for extended periods of time. She therefore knew her relatives on St John quite well. She never returned to live on St John, however, but remained with her godmother on St Thomas, took care of her when she became ill and eventually inherited her house. Julia Peterson noted that she was called her godmother's 'black daughter', indicating that she was a good deal darker than her godmother who, she later explained, was of mixed descent, her father being Danish. In the colour-conscious urban environment of Charlotte Amalie, Julia Peterson therefore would have had a relatively low status compared to that of her lighter-skinned godmother.

Not all St Johnian children were placed in homes that had a kin, or kin-like, relation to the children's parents. Indeed, it was quite common to ask persons from St John living on St Thomas to help them find a St Johnian child that they could have in the home. This was how Reuben Jackson happened to spend six years on St Thomas as a child:

I lived with some Jacksons in St Thomas, but they were no relatives of mine. My aunt was living in St Thomas, and she sent for me to live with these people . . . I was 8 years when they first took me to St Thomas, and I just went home for Christmas once while I was in St Thomas. Otherwise I never came home while I stayed in St Thomas as a child . . . [My parents never went to the Jackson family's home, and they] never gave anything to the people I lived with. I helped the people I lived with, especially with the painting. They had property there, so they weren't poorly off. I left before Mr Jackson died, and the lady sent for me, but I wasn't able to get to St Thomas before she had left. I think that I would have gotten something for all that I had done for them . . . The lady had a son in the States, but I don't know where she was from.

In this case, Reuben Jackson's aunt arranged for him to be placed in a home on St Thomas, and there was no personal relationship between this home and his parents on St John. This was probably the main reason why Reuben Jackson's family never came to see him at the home where he stayed on St Thomas. A contributing reason why the Reuben Jackson's family did not develop a personal relationship with the family on St Thomas may have been that this family was not local. Furthermore, it was described as propertied, and therefore as fairly well off, though hardly wealthy since Mr Jackson was a house painter. Nevertheless, the family was not in need of any provisions from St John. There was therefore no reason for Reuben Jackson's family to go to the house.

His case was not unusual. Most of the St Johnians who had lived in the homes of strangers explained that their parents had never visited them in the home where they stayed. Thus when Emmanuelita Matthias told me about her childhood in Charlotte Amalie, she noted, 'I was with the Hartmanns the whole time, and from I was 7 to 18 years old, I never came home once. I wanted to come back.' When I asked her whether she had missed her family she denied this, because she had seen her family in St Thomas. I suggest that what she, and some of the other St Johnian children who lived with strangers on St Thomas, might have been missing in St Thomas was a sense of a home that offered a place of belonging. Thus the children who were placed in the homes of strangers with whom their parents had little direct contact tended to be treated as servants and not as 'children' of the home. For them, the St Thomian home was a place of work. This work, however, involved spending some time in the streets, and I shall argue that the streets offered an important context in which the children were able to maintain a life of their own and a link with their family and friends on St John. The city streets of Charlotte Amalie also presented the St Johnian children with an urban arena that was completely different from the rural communities of St John. The children who learned to master this environment therefore acquired skills that proved useful later in their life after they had returned to St John.

Children in the street

Julia Peterson and Reuben Jackson described performing various kinds of work in the home. Julia Peterson had to wash dishes and sweep up the yard every day, and Reuben Jackson had helped with the painting. However, it was apparent that one of their most important tasks was that of running errands. In the case of Julia Peterson, whose godmother was a baker, this involved carrying bread to customers throughout the city. Indeed, Julia Peterson seemed to remember the city of her childhood by the various customers to whom she delivered bread:

> A lady they called Dana had a store with bread and cake where the Chase Manhattan Bank is now, and as a child I would carry bread there. In Back Street were Bomas and Miss Zoom, and I would carry bread there to them. My godmother supplied bread to different places.

The St Johnians who had grown up in St Thomian homes believed that an important reason why they were wanted was that the homes were inhabited by single or elderly women who had no children of their own who could run errands for them. This was the case as far as Julia Peterson's godmother was concerned, because Julia Peterson described her as 'an old maid' who had no children of her own. Since she had a bakery business, where bread had to be delivered every day, children were a rather vital source of help to her. Even in ordinary homes, however, children were regarded as indispensable. As Amos Fraser noted, by having a child in the home 'you would have a little person to send around to do a little shopping and all like that'.

The desire to have a child in the home reflected a general idea, also prevalent on St John, that the running of errands was children's work and therefore not something that adults should do. Furthermore, in the colonial environment of Charlotte Amalie, women who desired a social standing in the better circles sought to avoid spending much time in the streets. This desire was related to the prevailing notion of respectability, introduced by European missionaries and educators, which held that women belonged in the home if they were of a certain status in society. Respectability has been described as an important aspect of social status throughout the English-speaking Caribbean and it has been contrasted with ideas of reputation, associated with lower-class male street life that includes drinking, playing around, joking and storytelling, often with sexual overtones (Abrahams 1983; Eriksen 1990; Miller 1994; Olwig 1993; Wilson 1969, 1973). According to the tenets of respectability, children belong in the family home, under the moral guardianship of their mother, and well-to-do homes usually had adult servants perform tasks outside the home, such as shopping in the market. Children's position in the sexual division of the city's space seems to have been somewhat ambiguous, however, because as sexually immature persons they were not yet fully gendered. There are, for example, pictures of white children of upper-class colonial families accompanying a black servant to the market on St Thomas, a place where respectable woman did not venture to go. These children would not go out in the city on their own, however. Children of lower-class families, especially children from St John who had not learned the 'bad' ways of the street, were expected to go out on the street alone in order to run errands for the adults in the home where they stayed, and all the St Johnians described the running of errands as a major task. Maggiana Matthias explained:

> When I lived in these different houses, I had to help, of course. I was sent out on errands . . . They had me up and down like that . . .
>
> At that time, they had no servants like they have now,[9] everybody now has servants to cook and to wash and to do everything, but at that time it didn't use to be so. You would ask for a child to live with you who would run errands and you would send the child when you needed something.

This indicates that the homes that received St Johnian children were of lower middle-class background, but socially ambitious. A St Johnian child allowed them to keep the outward appearance of respectability, without having to pay for the expense of hiring a domestic servant.

By sending the children out to the street, the respectable St Thomian homes, paradoxically, enabled the St Johnian children to maintain relations with their home on St John from which they had become displaced, because they often met relatives from St John on the street. Reuben Jackson explained:

> I used to see my parents sometimes when I went into the street, because they would come to St Thomas now and again sailing with the boats, and then I got a chance to see them and talk to them. The family might give you 5 to 10 cents when they saw you, to buy some peppermint.

Similarly, Emmanuelita Matthias had seen her family in the street: 'I used to see my family, because my mother and father would come down selling things.' It seems that at least some of the children preferred the street to the home, where they were closely supervised, and this may have caused some tension in relations between the St Thomian family and the St Johnian child.[10] It is apparent in Emmanuelita Matthias's statements below that she was watched closely and prevented from spending more time on the errands than absolutely necessary. Unnecessary time spent in the streets would not just take her away from work that needed to be done in the home, but it might also involve her in activities that would not have been acceptable in homes seeking respectability in society: 'When they sent me to the street to buy something, they would spit on the pavement, and I would have to be back before the spit was dry!'

The spitting on the pavement indicates that some of these homes may not have been of quite as high social status, and respectability, as they would have liked to think. Emmanuelita Matthias regretted that she was not able to participate in the fun that took place in the street: 'I loved to watch the masquerade pass by, but I didn't go to the masquerade – I never used to go nowhere. They didn't let me go to anything . . . They were very strict with me.'

Other children shared Emmanuelita Matthias's feeling of being trapped in the home. It could become a serious problem in those cases where the children had lost contact with their St John family, because it was in such situations, that children might not always be treated well. This had happened to Chrystalia Stevens, who had only bitter memories of her childhood on St Thomas:

> My grandmother was in St Thomas, and she sent for me to live with a family . . . My mother didn't mind sending me off to live in another house because she had a lot of children of her own. A mother wouldn't mind if they treated her child well. But I wasn't treated well. I did not get enough clothes to wear, so I got cold and took sick. My mother took me back when she found out about this. She used to send things for me through my grandmother. But my grandmother never came. She sent the things with her sister, who stayed with her, so she never knew. She never came, so that I could tell her that they had taken away some of my clothes and that I wasn't well.

The St Johnians who remembered feeling abandoned and left to the whim of the persons who had taken them into their homes had little good to say about their childhood experiences in St Thomas. Indeed, a few St Johnian women expressed strong feelings against the whole custom of sending children to live in other homes, whether on St John or St Thomas, and they emphasised that they had taken care of all their children themselves. Most of the elderly St Johnians I interviewed, however, did not express such negative feelings towards their childhood experiences on St Thomas. Indeed, it is remarkable that many St Johnians described their having grown up on St Thomas in a very matter-of-fact way, as if their circumstances had been quite ordinary. This was, to a great extent, the case.

As noted, in 1901 about a third of all St Johnian children were living in homes without their parents. In the St Johnian scheme of things, probably few children spent their entire childhood with one or both parents. Many lived for shorter or longer periods of time with grandparents, aunts and uncles or godparents and some were placed in the homes of strangers. For the children it does not seem to have been crucial exactly where they were living, but rather that they continued to have close ties with their parents and other close relatives, who kept an eye on them and made sure that they were treated well. For those who were living outside St John, maintaining a close relationship to their parents was also a question of their continuing to be part of the St Johnian community. This community consisted of networks of social and economic relations that often extended beyond St John to places of opportunity, most notably St Thomas. It was therefore quite possible for children to grow up as staunch St Johnians, even when they spent most of their childhood years in St Thomas, as long as they were integrated into the network of social and economic exchanges that comprised the St Johnian community. Indeed, their being sent to St Thomas was an integral aspect of the dynamics of this network of exchange relations, where the placement of children in relatively well-to-do homes might be an important strategy of improvement. This strategy could benefit both the parents, who might gain useful contacts on St Thomas, and the children, who learned new skills and were potential beneficiaries of some of the St Thomian family's resources. This was highlighted when I interviewed Henry Samuel, who, I thought, had lived his entire life on St John. It turned out, however, that when he was 12 years old he had been sent to live with an aunt in New York. When I asked him why he had been sent so far away, he explained that she was doing well and had no children of her own. The implication was that since she was doing well in New York she offered important social and economic opportunities that the family ought to take advantage of by sending a child to live with her. At the same time, the family was doing her a favour because she needed the company of a child. When the aunt became ill within a couple of years, however, both of them returned to St John, and he did not benefit much from his brief New York sojourn.

Learning the ways of the city

Most of the St Johnians who had spent a number of years in St Thomas emphasised that they had benefited from their exposure to urban life. They had watched how sellers in the street and the market negotiated the best price for a product. Such trade relations did not exist on St John, where subsistence farming predominated and there was no public market. This St Thomas experience provided vital knowledge for Amos Fraser when, later in life, he earned a living as a boat captain sailing between St John and St Thomas, selling St John produce and buying imported goods in St Thomas for his customers on St John. Many children also learned skills in the homes where they grew up. They cherished this even when they did not use these skills later on. Julia Peterson learned about the bakery business from her godmother and stayed on helping her until she died. She eventually inherited her godmother's house and lived all of her life there with her family.[11] Reuben Jackson emphasised that St Thomas offered children important opportunities unknown in St John. Indeed, he denied that there were any economic reasons for sending a child to St Thomas – it was strictly a matter of the parents wanting their children to 'experience different things, see different places and learn something':

Parents liked to send their children to St Thomas, because they could learn different trades there. On St John you only learned how to cut bush and burn charcoal, but here were more opportunities on St Thomas. Mr. Jackson was a painter and so I used to do a lot of painting with him, learning the trade so to speak.

Emmanuelita Matthias expressed pride that on St Thomas she had learned fine housekeeping of a kind that belonged in the best homes in the highest layers of society: 'I lived with some white[12] people, and they trained me, they couldn't have trained me better. I know how to clean brass, silver, I know how to lay the table and everything. I could go to the government house tomorrow and do it!'

Because of their upbringing on St Thomas, these elderly St Johnians generally speaking regarded themselves as more experienced and exposed to the world than their fellow islanders who had never left St John. Several of them related their experiences with Danish colonial officials in the city and demonstrated their knowledge of Danish, which was taught in the schools on St Thomas, but never introduced in the St Johnian schools. Reuben Jackson, for example, entertained me with a Danish children's song 'Bæ, bæ, lille lam' ('Baa, baa, little lamb') that I had all but forgotten. Its lyrics, about how the lamb has enough wool to make a winter coat for father, a winter dress for mother and a pair of stockings for little brother, seemed absurd, to say the least, in the tropical Caribbean. For Reuben Jackson, however, the song provided a means of showing that he was a man of wider horizons than the local community of small farmers on St John.

Children in the city

This study of St John children on St Thomas sheds light on the current debate on children in the city. From a child welfarist point of view, the removal of children from their family homes on rural St John to the homes of strangers in urban Charlotte Amalie might be interpreted as a highly questionable practice. None of the children seems to have been asked whether or not they wanted to go to St Thomas. Rather they appear to have been moved around by their parents, whether or not they wanted to leave their homes. Indeed, many of them were so young that they probably barely realised what was happening to them before they had been installed in another home. Amos Fraser, for example, stated, 'When I left St John, I hardly knew anything about it.' The custom of sending children to St Thomas thus contains all the elements usually identified with the mistreatment of children, such as displacing of children from their homes without their informed consent and preventing them from visiting their home on St John; using the children as cheap labour in domestic work; forcing the children to perform various tasks in the city streets; prohibiting the children from participating in what little fun they might have enjoyed. There is no doubt that adults and children were not equal partners in the system of child exchange that brought St Johnian children to St Thomas, but neither were the adults. Thus, the structure of inequality obtained not just between adults and children, but also between adults in rural St John and in urban St Thomas. Given St John's historic social and economic dependency on St Thomas, one might instead suggest that poverty-stricken parents felt obliged to let their children grow up under better circumstances on St Thomas. This interpretation is also born out by Amos Fraser, who added to the sentence above: 'but my mother used to come visit me very often', which indicates that she went to a great deal of effort to maintain a close tie with her child.

Both of these interpretations, however, are too one-sided, and I have here suggested that the custom of sending children to St Thomas is better interpreted as related to a complex system of exchange that was closely interwoven with St John's particular social, economic and cultural relation to St Thomas. These factors are apparent in the relationship between adults and children in the receiving homes on St Thomas, which was characterised by local systems of kin, or kin-like, relations as well as by colonial structures of gender and class relations. These multifaceted structures suggest that the St Johnian children experienced life in St Thomas from many different viewpoints, depending on their position in these networks of relations. This, in turn, means that the city came to mean many different things to the St Johnian children, and to the St Johnian adults who remembered their childhoods in Charlotte Amalie. The city was not only a physical site with certain characteristics of its own, but rather a place that attained particular significance as the St Johnian community developed through time. In this exploration of the city as a socio-cultural site in the St Johnian community the oral history interviews proved to be an important research tool, illuminating aspects of urban life in St Thomas that were of little concern to the colonial records. I do not thereby mean that my oral history interviews with elderly St Johnians during the 1970s described life in Charlotte Amalie in the late nineteenth and early twentieth centuries, as experienced then by the children. This was clearly not the case, because the St Johnians related their childhood experiences from the hindsight of older persons reminiscing about their childhoods. This means that they probably highlighted both the most negative and the most positive aspects about growing up on St Thomas, which made their childhoods distinct in relation to those of their fellow St Johnians, and forgot about the more mundane everyday matters where St Thomian and St Johnian children's lives were similar. The negative aspects included being treated as servants who had to work for their living, and risking mistreatment if the parents were not able to keep a close eye on their children. The positive aspects meant living in better-off homes, acquiring special skills, getting well acquainted with the Charlotte Amalie, the economic, social and political centre of the Danish West Indies. The oral history interviews therefore provide important insights on the significance of Charlotte Amalie in the St Johnian community, and how children, because of their particular position in the intergenerational network of kin relations, were able to help the family establish a foothold in this urban centre that the family was dependent on for its living. This, in turn, means that the oral history interviews helped generate a social and cultural framework within which to interpret the custom of sending St Johnian children to St Thomas.

From a contemporary European or North American view, children are regarded as individuals belonging to particular family homes located in specific physical sites. From a historical St Johnian perspective, however, children were rather part of a socio-cultural field of relations that could be extended and restructured according to the particular situations in which the children and their families found themselves. Children therefore were not out of place in Charlotte Amalie, even though the city had many of the physical characteristics of modern urban environments, as long as they remained part of the St Johnian community of relations. They were out of place, and in a vulnerable position, when they lost contact with this community and became incorporated as isolated dependents into a city of strangers. This study therefore points to the importance of examining children in the city in relation to the ways in which the city is constructed as place, and as a social and cultural site, in the lives of children. This perspective should be equally valid whether the researcher is concerned with children 'confined' to urban institutions in Europe or North America, or children 'exposed' to street life in the developing world. This chapter therefore calls for detailed studies of children's place in the generational, and the wider socio-cultural, order that may allow for more in-depth and culturally sensitive analysis of what life in the city means to children.

Notes

1 Among recent studies can be mentioned: Aptekar and Abebe (1997); Blanc (1996); Glauser (1997); Matthews *et al.* (2000); O'Brien *et al.* (2000). For overviews of the literature see: Holloway and Valentine (2000); James *et al.* (1998: 47–52); Philo (2000).
2 For further documentation of the historical development of the Danish West Indies see: Bro-Jørgensen (1967); Hall (1992); Hornby (1980); Nørregaard (1967); Skrubbeltrang (1967); Vibæk (1967).
3 The discussion of St John's historical development draws on Olwig (1985).
4 Unfortunately, the enumerators' lists from the 1890 census on St John were missing in the Danish West Indian Archives.
5 I did oral history interview with approximately fifty St Johnians. At least seven had spent several years in St Thomian homes. I wish to express my gratitude toward Amos Fraser and the other St Johnians who helped me with my research in 1974–75.
6 I am here using the real names of the persons that I interviewed in 1974–75.
7 Literacy was very high in the Danish West Indies, and the colonial authorities fined parents, or wards of children, if they did not send their children to school (Olwig 1985: 119). Most of the parents who were fined for not sending their children in school had a great number of children and were keeping the older children at home in order that they might take care of the younger ones. Since

St Johnian children were staying in more well-to-do homes on St Thomas with few young children it is likely that they attended school on a regular basis.

8 The exchange of children is also known from other Caribbean societies: see, for example: Goosen (1972); Sanford (1975, 1976); Soto (1987). For a discussion of child exchange among Black Americans, see Powdermaker (1968 (1939)).

9 She is referring to the fact that a large number of migrants from the former British West Indies have been working as domestic servants for native American Virgin Islanders since the 1960s.

10 In their recent study of contemporary British children aged between 9 and 16, Matthews *et al.* (2000: 66) have shown that the street is an important place for children because it allows them to retain some autonomy and escape the 'adult gaze'.

11 She did not mention having carried on the bakery business after the godmother's death, but explained that she had lived in the house with her husband and children.

12 It is quite likely that they were not entirely 'white', but rather very light-coloured persons of mixed Danish and African descent.

References

Abrahams, R., 1983, *The Man-of-words in the West Indies* (Baltimore: The Johns Hopkins University Press).

Aptekar, L. and Abebe, B., 1997, 'Conflict in the neighbourhood: street and working children in the public space'. *Childhood*, 4 (4), 477–90.

Blanc, C. S., 1996, 'Life paths of urban children and youth in comparative perspective'. *Childhood*, 3 (3), 375–402.

Bro-Jørgensen, J. O., 1967, 'Dansk Vestindien indtil 1755' [The Danish West Indies until 1755], vol. 1. In J. Brøndsted (ed.), *Vore gamle tropekolonier* [*Our Old Colonies in the Tropics*] (Copenhagen: Fremad).

Eriksen, T. H., 1990, 'Liming in Trinidad: the art of doing nothing'. *Folk*, 32, 23–43.

Folketællingerne, Dansk Vestindien, Det Statistiske Departement [The Population Censuses, Danish West Indies, Statistical Department], *Folketællingslisterne for St Jan* [*Population Census Returns for John*] *1901* (Rigsarkivet [National Archives], Copenhagen) (unpublished).

Folketællingerne, Dansk Vestindien, Det Statistiske Departement [The Population Censuses, Danish West Indies, Statistical Department], *Folketællingslisterne for St Thomas* [*Population Census Returns for Thomas*] *1857, 1860, 1870, 1880, 1901* (Rigsarkivet [National Archives], Copenhagen) (unpublished).

Glauser, B., 1997, 'Street children: deconstructing a construct'. In A. James and A. Prout (eds), *Constructing and Reconstructing Childhood*, 2nd ed. (London: Falmer Press), 145–64.

Goossen, J., 1972, 'Child sharing and foster parenthood in the French West Indies'. Paper presented at the American Anthropological Association, New York.

Hall, N., 1983, 'Slavery in Three West Indian towns: Christiansed, Fredericksted and Charlotte Amalie in the late eighteenth century and early nineteenth century'. In B. W. Higman (ed.), *Trade, Government and Society in Caribbean History, 1700–1920* (Kingston: Heinemann Educational Books Caribbean), 21–38.

Hall, N., 1992, *Slave Society in the Danish West Indies* (Mona: The University of the West Indies Press).

Hendrick, H., 2000, 'The child as social actor in historical sources: problems of identification and interpretation'. In P. Christensen and A. James (eds), *Research with Children: Perspectives and Practices* (London: Falmer Press), 36–61.

Holloway, S. L. and Valentine, G. (eds), 2000, *Children's Geographies: Playing, Living and Learning* (London: Routledge).

Hornby, O., 1980, *Kolonierne i Vestindien* [*The Colonies in the West Indies*] (Copenhagen: Politikens Forlag).

James, A., Jenks, C. and Prout, A., 1998, *Theorizing Childhood* (Cambridge: Polity Press).

Matthews, H., Limb, M. and Taylor, M., 2000, 'The Street as Thirdspace'. In S. L. Holloway and G. Valentine (eds), *Children's Geographies: Playing, Living and Learning* (London: Routledge), 63–79.

Miller, D., 1994, *Modernity, an Ethnographic Approach* (Oxford: Berg).

Nørregaard, G., 1967, 'Dansk Vestindien 1880–1917' [The Danish West Indies 1880–1917], vol. 4. In J. Brøndsted (ed.), *Vore gamle tropekolonier* [*Our Old Colonies in the Tropics*] (Copenhagen: Fremad).

O'Brien, M., Jones, D., Sloan, D. and Rustin, M., 2000, 'Children's independent spatial mobility in the urban public realm'. *Childhood*, 7 (3), 257–77.

Olwig, K. F., 1985, *Cultural Adaptation & Resistance on St John: Three Centuries of Afro-Caribbean Life* (Gainesville: University of Florida Press).

Olwig, K. F., 1993, *Global Culture, Island Identity: Continuity and Change in the Afro-Caribbean Community of Nevis* (Reading: Harwood Academic Publishers).

Olwig, K. F., 1997, 'Cultural sites: sustaining a home in a deterritorialized world'. In Olwig and K. Hastrup (eds), *Siting Culture: The Shifting Anthropological Object* (London: Routledge), 18–38.

Olwig, K. R., 2000, '(Be)tydningen af barndommens "sted"'. [The meaning of the 'place' of childhood]. *Barn*, 18 (3/4), 33–55.

Philo, C., 2000, 'The corner-stones of my world.' Editorial introduction to special issue on spaces of childhood. *Childhood*, 7 (3), 243–56.

Powdermaker, H., 1968 (1939), *After Freedom: A Cultural Study in the Deep South* (New York: Russell & Russell).

Sanford, M., 1975, 'To be treated as a child of the home: black Carib child lending in a British West Indian society'. In T. R. Williams (ed.), *Socialization and Communication in Primary Groups* (The Hague: Mouton Publishers), 159–81.

Sanford, M., 1976, 'Child lending in Belize'. *Belizean Studies*, 4 (2), 26–36.

Skrubbeltrang, F., 1967, 'Dansk Vestindien 1848–1880' [The Danish West Indies 1848–1880], vol. 4. In J. Brøndsted (ed.), *Vore gamle tropekolonier* [*Our Old Colonies in the tropics*] (Copenhagen: Fremad).

Soto, I. M., 1987, 'West Indian child fostering: its role in migrant exchanges'. In C. R. Sutton and E. M. Chaney (eds), *Caribbean Life in New York City: Sociocultural Dimensions* (New York: Center for Migration Studies), 131–49.

Vibæk, J., 1967, 'Dansk Vestindien 1755–1848' [The Danish West Indies 1755–1848], vol. 2. In J. Brøndsted (ed.), *Vore gamle tropekolonier* [*Our Old Colonies in the Tropics*] (Copenhagen: Fremad).

Wilson, P., 1969, 'Reputation and respectability: a suggestion for Caribbean ethnology'. *Man*, 4 (1), 70–84.

Wilson, P., 1973, *Crab Antics* (New Haven: Yale University Press).

5 Shaping daily life in urban environments

Helga Zeiher

Insularisation, domestication, and shaping daily life

In our cities, children play ball games in sports clubs rather than on the streets, and climb playground apparatus rather than trees. Where urban areas are formed by functional differentiation, particular opportunities for and constraints on the actions of individuals are spatially fixed in specialised centres. Some are also temporally fixed by time-scheduled activity programmes. Places geared toward children's needs, often toward the needs of children of a particular age, are scattered like islands on the map of the city at greater or lesser distances from one another. Other places are specialised for the purposes of adults' use, and are often inaccessible, dangerous or simply not of interest to children. Thus, the societal differentiation of childhood is reflected in the urban landscape as segregation of places for children and for adults.

How do children live in and move around such landscapes of islands? This question shifts the focus from urban space to children's daily lives and addresses the interplay between the spatial and temporal organisation of children's urban environments and children's ways of living their daily lives in the course of time within these environments. In the research project from which I would like to report in this chapter, Hartmut J. Zeiher and the author conceptualised this interconnection between spatial and temporal aspects of childhood structure and children's agency, developed related case study methods, and studied 10-year-olds in Berlin (Zeiher and Zeiher 1994; H. J. Zeiher 2001a).

Day after day, over the course of the day, a child engages in one activity after another, often at different locations. The places that a child uses in the course of time can be seen as strung together by the individual life path. This sequence of places constitutes his or her *individual temporalised life space*. During the daily and weekly repetitions of everyday life, the frequented places form a pattern that is characteristic of the individual life space. In functionally differentiated urban landscapes, the patterns of the children's movements reflect the fact of spatial fragmentation as well as of centralisation. Children spend much of their time within the confines of islands such as houses, day-care and recreation centre buildings, sports fields, and playgrounds, and they have to go on their own or to be escorted and ferried by adults between these urban islands. Thus, children's individual life spaces can be seen as characterised by *insularisation*. When most of the children who live in the same neighbourhood spend much time in child-specific institutions, there is not much time left for playing in the streets near the home. Even if the spatial conditions of a neighbourhood allow for playing outdoors, and a child living there would prefer doing so, this child will not find playmates there and therefore has to adjust to the use of specialised facilities, too. Of course, there may be very different shapes of insularised individual life spaces for different children varying with the increasing age of a child, between children living in different parts of a town, between children of different family background, or between individuals with different interests (H. J. Zeiher 2001b).

Urban landscapes can also be seen as 'landscapes of power' (Matthews *et al.* 2000). In a functional differentiated urban space, social control over children is less than in former times (Behnken *et al.* 1989) exerted personally by adults, rather than anonymously by set arrangements at fixed locations with prede-termined purposes and programmes and organisational structures. Children spend much of their time within walls, fences and hedges. Following Norbert Elias (1969), Zinnecker (1990) described this as 'domestication of childhood' relating to children being confined as well as controlled within houses or other sheltered places. Whereas the concept of insularisation results from an overarching view on all places, whether in urban space or in a person's temporalised life space, the concept of domestication relates to single places. Both concepts complement one another in order to reveal certain aspects of control on children's action possibilities imposed by structural features of the urban landscape.

Within some of the sheltered places specialised for children's purposes, control is exerted through formal organisational regulations. No less import-ant is control that operates not through force but through enticement. Rec-reation facilities as for example playground equipment leave it up to the child to decide whether or not to make use of them. Yet, the more specialised a place is for a particular activity, the more favourable the conditions are for that activity, the more likely it is that the child will be attracted to do the activity and not an other. Children's action opportunities are also influenced by the distances between islands. As long as young children are not able or are not allowed to overcome the distances by themselves they are dependent on their parents to explore activity options and on being transported between the islands; to playgrounds, kindergartens, the homes of their playmates and other places scattered throughout an area which may extend rather far. Under conditions of insularisation, and in order to enrich their daily life activities, children therefore are forced to think about their personal interests, to find opportunities within a wide area, to organise their daily time including adapt-ing to the time schedules of activity programmes and of other persons, and to find ways to overcome the spatial distances involved. To shape daily life and to navigate the life path through the spatial world becomes a task of its own to be handled by children themselves or, in early childhood, with the help of their parents.

Thus by the functional differentiation of urban space, children have experienced conditions that increase external control imposed by the structural characteristics of places and of institutionalised activity programmes as well as greater opportunities than before to determine their daily actions by themselves. This raises questions about children's agency such as: How do individual children in their particular everyday worlds meet these contradictory constraints and possibilities? How do children who live in certain urban environments develop their agency? The activity questioned here is *shaping daily life*. It is an activity superordinate to all the particular activities which are performed in the course of the day as playing or watching television. Shaping daily life is choosing, defining, arranging, and organising what is to be done, where, when, and with whom. Environmental factors influencing disposition and sequence formation of activities play an important role. These factors, generally considered characteristic of modern societies (see for example Elias 1969; Berger *et al.* 1973), include spatial ones resulting from specialisation and centralisation as well as temporal ones such as institutional prestructuring of activity programmes and the high degree of temporal interconnectedness of contemporary social life. Hence, by questioning how it comes about that children shape their daily lives within particular environments in a particular way our research focuses on the interconnection between children's shaping their daily lives and structural phenomena of childhood in our contemporary society. Such a focus enables us to reveal features of children's everyday lives as imbedded in major societal processes (Qvortrup 2000).

We conceptualised the activity of shaping daily life as follows (H. J. Zeiher 2001; Zeiher and Zeiher 1994). Just as the course of the day consists of a sequence of activities, the process by which it is shaped consists of a sequence of consciously or unconsciously made *decisions*, each of them determining which new activity shall follow when an activity has come to an end. Such decisions may be prepared long before the change of activity occurs. They may be embedded in intentions which extend into the past or future, sometimes spanning considerable time periods, and produce more than one activity (i.e. habits or projects which the person is working on). The decision-making process takes place in an environment produced by a flow of events that extends throughout the course of the individual's life. The flow consists of a mixture of single and recurring events, with regularities in terms of times, locations, arrangements, and other social agents. Through the temporalised environment, societal processes and structures become relevant in a person's decisions. In the very moment of a decision the person's temporalised environment influences the decision through the possibilities and constraints given in the part of the world which he or she can reach from the present location in space and time, as well as through individual competencies and intentions which have been developed earlier when the person made decisions and performed activities in former situations. On the other hand, by taking the initiative to do one thing or another the person selects environmental elements to become relevant in his or her life now and in future time, and by performing activities the individual changes, develops, and produces elements of the environment that may be of influence in his or her future activity decisions. In the course of time, by again and again negotiating between his or her own intentions and the prevailing environmental factors, each person develops his or her own habitual means of deciding what to do next over the course of the day.

This approach forms the basis of the research design. The investigation which is reported in this chapter[1] covered the course of seven days in the lives of a small number of 10-year-old children who resided in two districts of West Berlin, both urban areas with four- or five-storey apartment houses built before the First World War, one of them a traditional working-class area, the other an area traditionally with a greater proportion of the educated middle-class in the population. After choosing neighbourhoods within these areas we selected a child who lived in each, and then the three children of the same age who were his or her closest neighbours. The children reported on their days themselves.[2] Each child carried a notebook in which he or she was asked to keep a short record of each activity from waking up in the morning until going to sleep in the night (activity, time, place, persons involved). The next day, an interview was conducted following the sequence of activities recorded in the interview. The child related how each activity came about, and described the social and environmental circumstances and background of the activity, as well as its origin and history in his or her life. This one-day record, next-day interview procedure was carried out seven times over a two-week period, thus providing a record of roughly 150 activities per child on chronological sequence, along with the time, place, and social circumstances in which each activity occurred. Further information was gathered by interviewing the children's parents about the child's biography and about the family's life management, by observations during the visits to the families, and during inspections of the neighbourhoods made in children's company. Inquiries into recreational facilities for children were made in interviews with adults working in those facilities.

Data analyses proceeded on three levels. Firstly, for each activity the child's decision-making process was reconstructed in its situation-specific and bio-graphical context. Secondly, features recurring over the seven-day period were explored, involving the identification of typical characteristics of the child's individual environment, of the child's intentions, and of the child's way of decision-making. This step resulted in case studies of each child's shaping his or her daily life within his or her temporalised environment and biographical background. Thirdly, between all children similarities and differ-ences with respect to these characteristics were studied. This was done firstly within each neighbourhood, and finally across neighbourhoods.

In this chapter, I present a comparison of two boys' ways of shaping their social life among peers in the afternoons. In Germany, school ends at midday. The proportion of children in after-school day-care is low. Many mothers work half days, and younger schoolchildren whose parents cannot be at home at midday are often cared for by grandparents, or arrangements of care for some midday hours are made with other families. However, most 10-year-olds are supposed to be able to look after themselves when no adult is at home. Besides doing a little homework (often less than an hour), they spend about five hours between the midday meal and the evening meal doing things they want to do, whether alone or with friends, in institutional settings, at home, or outdoors. Most German parents allow their children from the age of 10 to leave the house for walks or bicycle rides in the neighbourhood and to play outdoors with friends without being accompanied by an adult.[3] The afternoon is therefore the part of the day when children have to decide on their activities more or less by themselves; when they may meet friends and make use of playgrounds or institutional facilities such as sport or culture-related courses. Here, they shape their daily life by negotiating their interests and intentions not only with their parents but also with peers, institutional provided options, and features of the urban landscape. Children who are used to playing together in their free afternoon time will often produce a collective way of shaping these common activities, and when a child decides to play with friends on a particular day, he or she has to consider the collective social rules and habits governing such meetings. In the research study, by exploring the sequences of decisions in the lives of several children living nearby in a neighbourhood, it was possible to identify both the social rules and the type of self-determination that are possible and customary among children in this particular environment.

Both of the two 10-year-old boys, Daniel and Thomas, discussed in this chapter, enjoyed moving around and playing outdoors with friends, and both of them were able to do this. This public life took place within their different spatial and physical environments and different social class milieux. The comparison focuses on the interplay between the children's ways of shaping their social life and these features of urban environment.

Two ways of using time

Ten-year-old Daniel lives in a working-class area near the centre of Berlin. When this area of apartment houses was built about a hundred years ago, no place was left for play areas. Later in the 1970s, gaps made by the bombings during the Second World War were used to provide specialised places for children. As a result of this, in the direct vicinity of Daniel's home several facilities for children are located close together, forming an unusual large children's island: two large playgrounds with a variety of apparatus, two football 'cages' surrounded by high wire meshing, and a youth recreation centre. This consists of group rooms and workshops, another small football pitch, and a supervised building playground where children can borrow tools to work with old timber. This area, which is so well equipped with places for children to play, attracts children from the surroundings in large numbers. Daniel grew up in this part of the city. He spends almost all of his afternoons playing outside with other children. His circle of friends consists of a group of at least thirteen boys aged between 8 and 13.

Let us take a closer look at the sequence of decisions determining Daniel's actions over the course of a particular afternoon.

> On the way home from school at lunchtime, Daniel meets Jens in the playground opposite his home. Jens has been waiting for Daniel in the hope that they can play table tennis together, but Daniel first has to return home for lunch. He promises to come back immediately afterwards. This he does, and the two boys are soon joined by two more friends.
>
> After two hours of table tennis, the others leave the playground. Daniel remains behind, still with a good deal of spare time before he is expected home in the evening. He can choose between two possibilities in the immediate vicinity: the recreation centre football pitch or the building playground, also located at the recreation centre. As Daniel is a keen football player, he decides to go to the football pitch.
>
> There is nobody else there, however, and even after waiting and looking around for people to play with, he is unable to find either team-mates or opponents. He then notices some of his friends, who are making huts out of old timber on the adjacent building playground. They are preparing for a children's festival which is to be held in nine days' time and is to culminate with the children camping out in the huts they have constructed themselves. Daniel has already participated in the preparations over the past few days, so it would seem a reasonable idea to go and join in again.
>
> He does so for about an hour, at which point he sees a group of boys on the football pitch. This immediately revives his interest in playing football, and he runs over to join them.
>
> However, it emerges that one of the players is someone Daniel had an argument with on the previous day, which means that he cannot join in the game. He returns to building huts, and stays there until the playground closes at 7 p.m.

At the beginning of the afternoon, Daniel had no detailed plans for the rest of the day, with the exception of the arrangement made at short notice to play table tennis with Jens. Daniel only ever decides on a new activity when the previous activity has been concluded, at the end of the table tennis game, for example, or when something more appealing 'catches his eye', such as the possibility of playing football after all. Daniel looks around the spatial locality, detects a possible activity, and seizes the opportunity immediately. His way of making decisions is tied to the moment at which the change of activity occurs, and determined by what is happening around him in the location at the present time. The temporal structure of his afternoon is correspondingly simple: the idea of embarking upon a new activity coincides with the beginning of that activity.

Thomas lives in a middle-class district of Berlin that is characterised by apartment houses as old and high as in Daniel's quarter but with small front gardens, and by a population not rich but many of them affluent and educated. The few playgrounds within about ten minutes' walk of his home are small and geared to younger children; they are scattered throughout the area and hold little attraction for 10-year-olds. The places that are of interest to Thomas, a sports field, a swimming pool, the city park, and the banks of the canal, are situated further away. Thomas and the other children use the streets of their residential area almost exclusively as a means of getting from one place to another, either on foot or by bicycle.

I would like to present Thomas's sequence of decisions for an afternoon he has decided to spend at the canal. He enjoys going to the canal, which is about half an hour's walk away from his home, to roam around and observe wildlife. Thomas needs the company of a friend in order to embark on such a trek, as he thinks it is no fun for him to go there alone, and furthermore his parents do not like him going such distances by himself. It is the general practice for the children in Thomas's class at school, both boys and girls, to arrange each morning at school to meet one of their friends that afternoon. Back home for lunch, each child checks with his or her family to see if the meeting can go ahead as planned, and the children then telephone to confirm the arrangement. As a rule, these children only ever spend their afternoons in pairs. The entire afternoon is 'booked' for a single partner, and no other children are allowed to join in. From one day to the next, Thomas meets up with various friends, in various different locations. He enjoys going to the canal with one friend, going to another friend's home to play with his train set, and going on cycling or swimming trips with various different classmates.

This morning, Thomas had arranged to meet up with Markus. After lunch at home, the telephone rings. Contrary to expectations, however, it is not Markus calling, but another friend, Stefan, asking if Thomas has time to play that afternoon. Because he already has a 'booking' with Markus, Thomas declines Stefan's offer and continues to wait for Markus to call.

While he is waiting, he lies down on his bed and reads a book as he often does during such waiting time.

Markus rings to confirm their arrangement. This not only means that the trip to the canal can go ahead, but also implies that Thomas will not be able to watch an interesting television programme being broadcast that afternoon. Because the video recorder cannot be programmed, he asks his mother to record the programme for him. He then sets off on the half-hour walk to meet Markus, who lives near the canal.

When he arrives, however, Markus is nowhere to be seen. This calls for a decision. Going to the canal on his own is no alternative, because he has never done so before, it would be no fun, and he would not feel safe there on his own. Trying to find another friend to spend the afternoon with is pointless – not only because all of his friends live some distance away, but because the rules governing the children's afternoon arrangements state that Thomas can no longer contact the other children today. Thomas first hopes that he will run into Markus after all, and stays there looking for him.

After twenty minutes Thomas decides to return home since the only options that would be available to him here and now without Markus – playing alone in the city park playground or wandering aimlessly through the streets, for example – are not part of his repertoire of activities and are unlikely to be in keeping with his disappointed mood.

When he arrives back home, he is alone in the apartment. He remembers the television programme his mother has recorded for him and uses this unexpected free time to watch it.

What is then the significance of time use in Thomas's decision-making process? Almost everything that Thomas does on the afternoon under consideration was planned some time in advance. He decided to spend the afternoon at the canal, and made a plan to this effect. He arranged to meet Markus and waited for him to call, turning down Stefan's alternative offer in the meantime. A few hours before an interesting television programme was due to be broadcast, he organised for this to be recorded.

Unlike Daniel, Thomas cannot simply rely on the local environment providing him with the opportunity to engage in activities he enjoys whenever he is ready and willing. Every morning, Thomas has to contemplate which of his interests he would like to pursue that afternoon. He has to anticipate what he will feel like doing, and which opportunities will be available to him. He has to identify the conditions that need to be satisfied in advance, and to draw up plans for his daily life at a temporal distance and make the appropriate arrangements. This process can become very complex, as it may be necessary to co-ordinate a planned activity with other future activities, and to make separate arrangements for the latter. For example, the planned trip to the canal has implications for Thomas's television viewing, and he has to make special arrangements to ensure that the latter can also be fitted into his schedule. New opportunities and constraints may emerge after the plan has been forged, but before it is carried out. This is the case, for example, when Stefan calls to suggest an alternative plan for the afternoon. Events sometimes even go contrary to plan, when Markus does not keep to the arrangement, for example. In such cases, new goals have to be set, and options reviewed. In contrast to Daniel, Thomas also has to manage his time in a second respect: he has to keep track of time to make sure that he is punctual for his various arrangements and appointments.

Two ways of relating to one another

These contrasting ways of children's determining the temporal structure of the afternoon are connected with the particular ways that the children relate to one another and shape their relationships.

Daniel and his friends have been meeting up at the recreation centre and in the surrounding playgrounds for years now. This shared past means that each individual child can rely on being able to join in with the others at any time, without having to ask permission. Furthermore, because there are so many of them, it is almost certain that a group of friends will meet up somewhere by chance each afternoon. Aside from these certainties, each child has a great deal of individual freedom, not only in physical space, but also in social space. Daniel can join in with the activities of an existing group, and can leave a group before the other children. This will not result in conflict of interests, as the other children can simply carry on without him. The members of an existing group are interchangeable. A group of playmates is not dependent on the presence of a single child for its survival, and neither is the group of friends as a whole. Each child is primarily concerned with the local 'venues' and the activities occurring there, and only within this framework do they relate to the other children present at any given moment. As such, the social relations among the children do not need to be particularly intense or personal. It suffices to know the other children and to accept them as playmates.

Being accepted, that is, having social access to the other children, is the prerequisite for Daniel being able to spend his afternoons playing outside with the rest of the group. It is important that he does not undermine this by allowing conflicts to escalate and falling out with the other children. Daniel is dependent on these children, who have been his playfellows for years now. He has got along with them, and thus constantly has to work on resolving any conflicts that may arise. There is no viable alternative. As such, the security of the fixed spatial structure goes hand in hand with the obligation to conform to the conventions and norms of the group.

Thomas's and his friends' afternoon meetings, however, have no fixed location. The only fixtures are temporal ones; these are not placed in the 'outer world', rather in the life times of the children involved. In consequence, the quality of interpersonal relations is of great importance here. When two children spend the entire afternoon together, they are much more closely involved with each other than children playing in larger groups. Moreover, successful arrangements are dependent, among other things, on the current quality of the relationship. Thomas and his friends have taken steps to ensure that they nevertheless always maintain a certain measure of independence from one another. The rule stipulating that partners are to be changed on a daily basis means that friends do not begin to take it for granted that they can meet up every day. In principle, when a number of different friendships are cultivated at the same time, every child is free to choose a new partner every day. The close personal relationships the children enjoy during their shared afternoons stand in contrast to a certain distance the rest of the time. Every arrangement implies approaching a new potential partner, and whether or not this approach will be successful is an open question. When Thomas approaches a friend in the morning to suggest a joint activity for the afternoon, it is uncertain whether this friend will have the time or the inclination to accept his offer, or whether he will chose to spend the afternoon with someone else. Thomas needs to cultivate his social relations carefully to ensure that he will be able to attract partners in the future. In other words, Thomas's need to plan and make arrangements ahead of time applies not only to his activities, but also to his social relationships.

This means that not only activities but also relationships are objects of reflection. The children view one another with a critical and evaluative eye. Whom do I like having as a friend? What can I do to make sure that other children like me? Individual children perceive themselves as being more or less in competition with their peers, and try to find ways of making themselves appear attractive. The children are separated by reflective distance. For each individual child, this represents a dangerous balancing act, with hazards to both sides. On the one hand, the children do not want to give up either their independence or their temporal and social freedom; on the other hand, there is always a risk of ending up alone. Conflicts among Thomas's friends usually result in the friendship being broken off entirely. It is easier to end a friendship in the context of the one-on-one relations maintained by these children than among Daniel's friends, where it would result in a split with the whole group. In Thomas's circle of friends, children who fall out with one another simply no longer arrange to meet. The remaining friendships are not adversely affected, and the children involved have the option of looking for new friends. However, Thomas is also limited in his ability to substitute new friends for old, as his only source of new friendships is his class at school.

The interplay between urban and family environments

Why do these children shape their social life in the different ways? To find answers, the first step is to look at the possibilities and constraints that their particular neighbourhoods offer to them now, and offered to them in the early years of their lives.

Each urban environment under investigation has been shaped, though in contrasting ways, by the same societal process of spatial differentiation described at the beginning of this chapter, namely the tendency to specialise places and centralise activity opportunities, leading to spatially fixed activity structures. Besides the fixation in space it is the fixation in time which may constrain activity possibilities. Some facilities are not only spatially limited, but also subject to temporal access restrictions, with opening hours, course times, and registration requirements. Others are temporally open, children can come and go as they please, and determine the temporal structure of their activities themselves. It is quite an interesting outcome of the comparison between Daniel and Thomas that neither accepts institutional time-structured options as part of their individual life space. This will be discussed later.

Daniel and his friends not only live near to child-specific places, as they have access to an agglomeration of several attractive islands: a large, multi-purpose children's area. These places are open to all children, at any time of the afternoon they choose. There are no temporal restrictions on any of the activities on offer. Being able to play table tennis or football, however, is dependent on several children being present at the same time, and on them also wanting to play. On the same lines, Daniel does not enjoy working on the wooden huts on his own. Because many of his friends go there fre-quently, however, this does not pose a problem for Daniel. It is sufficient to go and join in, wait until a friend arrives, or call on a friend. Individual children are not in a position to predict, or indeed have much bearing on, when and where a new opportunity will arise, who will join in, or how long the group will stay together. Because of the spatial proximity of the facilities in this area, the children can soon establish what is going on in each of their play areas at any particular moment. They may come and go between these places, alone or in small groups. Individual schedules or arrangements with other children would be futile.

The residential area where Thomas lives is a rather different section of the urban landscape. In the vicinity of their homes, Thomas and his friends do not find enough children's places which they like to use. Their playgrounds are as islands scattered across in a larger area of the city and do not constitute a cohesive spatial segment of the urban world. If social events cannot be initiated and nurtured simply by going to a specific place, temporal activity is called for. It takes time to get from one place to the next, and long distances make one dependent on transport and timetables. And because none of the children likes going long stretches 'on the off-chance', arrangements are made in advance. As the opportunities available to Thomas are not physically apparent in the spatial environment, he has to anticipate his options mentally. The spatial distances mean that he has to establish his own goals, and make conscious choices and decisions in advance.

Yet, it is not only daily spatial conditions that influence the children's different ways of shaping daily life. Individual ways of shaping daily life develop across the life span, in a lifelong sequence of negotiations with the existing spatial, temporal, material, and social realities. And these realities are also influenced or produced by the individuals' activities and ways of shap-ing their lives, as mentioned at the beginning of this chapter. Here, I can only give a very short report on Daniel's and Thomas's former temporalised environments.

Up to this point in their lives, Daniel and his friends have not experi-enced any other way of organising their social life. Most of the parents in this district have never been particularly interested in how their children find friends to play with, considering this to be a concern for the children themselves. Some parents are rather anxious and do not allow their children to play outside. Others, such as Daniel's mother, have allowed their children to go out alone from an early age. This was possible because the children's outside activities are taken care of by other adults. The youth welfare department and playground designers have equipped the residential area with a wealth of sheltered places for children, and in the youth recreation centre the children are supervised by professionals. A particular effort to provide children with special places was made here because of the widespread lack of parents' engagement in their children's after-school lives.

Thomas and his friends have learnt to organise their own social lives across the spatial distances with the involvement of their mothers. The middle-class parents living in this local district saw it as their duty to provide their children with good developmental and learning opportunities, including the chance to engage in social learning by playing with peers. When Thomas was younger, his mother ferried him from one island to the next, often by car, to playgrounds, an organised playgroup, the swimming pool, his friends' homes. His friends' mothers did the same. The mothers built up networks to ensure that their children had friends to play with, and made arrangements for them to meet. Since then, Thomas is used to moving on the road only as a passenger between home and the scattered islands where he meets friends to play with, rather than playing outdoors in the vicinity of the house.

I have already mentioned that both children's environments mirror the spatial segregation of the generations, each in another form. The two environments also share another factor that is specific to modern society, in that certain conditions have been created to make possible social life among children, each by other agents and in other forms. For Daniel and his friends, these conditions take the form of finished products in the spatial environment. Playground designers and social education workers have worked to create an attractive environment for all children who want to come here, and have succeeded in establishing a large, well-equipped children's area. In contrast, Thomas and his friends are responsible for recreating the conditions for their social life on a daily basis. Here, it is a matter not of conditions that are fixed in space, but of temporal conditions that are in constant need of renegotiation. In Thomas's environment, organisation occurs in the temporal rather than the spatial medium: it is not a matter of equipping the urban environment, but of planning one's time in the anticipated future. Here, too, adults have made efforts to ensure that children have the opportunity to play with their peers. In past years, this was the parents' task, and by doing so they gave their children the chance to learn how to shape their daily lives in that way.

Children's agency and temporal freedom

Children are actors not only by living their social lives among peers but also by shaping it. By shaping life they permanently negotiate, modify, and produce the opportunities and constraints which they meet outdoors and at home. Our research showed that knowing the particular opportunities and constraints relevant in individual children's lives is a prerequisite in order to reveal this aspect of the children's agency as well as the child's preferences and interests. Concerning afternoon outdoor life, the parents are negotiation partners in that they tend to restrict the time and the distances for their children to move from home whereas children try to extend these. This is the case for Thomas (see more about Thomas's relationship to his parents: Zeiher 2001a: 43–5). Out of home, children may get into conflict about the use of space with passengers in the streets, householders, or police. But this is not the case for Daniel and Thomas, who keep within the confines of children's islands or move through the streets like adults as passengers. Is there any resistance to being determined in their way of playing with friends outside school and what are their ways of self-determination?

In Daniel's environment, the recreation centre and the surrounding playgrounds are pivotal points for the development of social events. The children have tied their social life to these spatial locations. Because the opportunities provided there are so attractive, however, the children also limit their range of activities to whatever is on offer there. Daniel and his friends do the same things day after day, mainly playing table tennis or football and building huts, and occasionally joining in with activities organised by the social education workers at the recreation centre, such as trips to the swimming pool or art and craft sessions in the workshop. The life of these children differs from life in more traditional neighbourhood groups of playmates in that it was previously adults who planned what children could do. Here, the adults' influence is indirect: the fact that places and objects have been specialised for certain activities makes it tempting to do just that. The children see no necessity to overcome these restrictions by exploring new activities or going elsewhere to pursue them.

The fact that these children accept the spatial and material restrictions on the range of activities available to them is connected to the fact that they are not constrained by fixed temporal structures. Each child is free to decide what to do with his or her own time. The conditions governing the social life allow the children to meet up with one another spontaneously at any time. This temporal freedom is shown to be of central importance to Daniel and his friends, as they refuse to comply with temporal restrictions whenever they emerge in their afternoon environments. In the past, the educators responsible for the recreation centre have tried to set up football training with regular dates and times. Despite being keen on playing football, Daniel and his friends did not keep to the times and the experiment had to be abandoned. When they provided courses, other institutions in this district of Berlin had similar experiences with children either arriving far too early or coming late, failing to attend regularly, and eventually not turning up at all. As a result, the institutions have had to adopt their temporal structures to suit the children's ways of using time, and no longer offer courses with fixed dates and times. In other words, the children have seen to it that the institutions in their local environment correspond to their preferences for open temporal arrangements.

The spatial structure of Thomas's environment is not characterised by appealing locations, but rather by the lack of such attractions. This means that Thomas, in contrast to Daniel, is not restricted to the material realities of a confined area. Thomas can look for opportunities to pursue his interests over a more extensive area, and select the children he wishes to spend time with. Because he is not tied to the close vicinity of his home, he has a broader range of options. And because he is not restricted to opportunities that are immediately available to him, he has more scope than Daniel to pursue his own inclinations, goals, and interests. The restrictions and freedoms of Thomas's daily life are of a completely different nature than those experienced by Daniel. Here, it is the need to plan that curbs the temporal spontaneity of Thomas and his friends. Organising opportunities for the future, for example, by arranging to meet classmates, means that Thomas and his friends have to commit themselves to particular undertakings and exclude any other possibilities that might crop up unexpectedly. On the afternoon described above, negative aspects of this need for commitment become apparent. Because Thomas has arranged to meet Markus, he is unable to take up Stefan's alternative offer. And when Markus fails to keep to their arrangement, Thomas has no contingency plan to fall back on, as it is then too late in the day to contact Stefan.

Thomas and his friends show a need for unrestricted and flexible time and self-determination, too. In order to be as free as possible despite the need to plan, they have established a particular kind of social rule for making arrangements with one another, meaning that they start each day free to decide on how to spend their time. They do not commit themselves to particular friends in the long term, and they accept the downside of this arrangement: that they will, occasionally, have no choice but to spend the afternoon alone. And, like Daniel and his friends, Thomas and his friends avoid time-scheduled institutional arrangements. They have been used to attending some afternoon activities and courses in earlier years orchestrated by parents. However, since the age of about 9, Thomas, and also some others, began to refuse continuing these activities. Thomas, who is committed to playing football like Daniel, explicitly refuses to join a football club for the reason of it being overly organised. These children defend their temporal freedom against institutional attempts to restrict it through a common aspiration to temporal self-determination. The prerequisite for this is that the time available to them is left as open as possible. Both of them go to much effort to achieve this goal, as can be seen from the ways in which they deal with the specific temporal opportunities and constraints they encounter.

The overall tendency toward the functional specialisation of urban spaces in contemporary society can occur in different children's local environments, and in interplay with a child's family and other conditions they may impact on the daily lives of individual children in very different ways. From our studies a larger spectrum of childhoods than could be displayed in this chapter was revealed, including girls shaping their social life in similar ways to Thomas and, to a lesser degree, to Daniel, girls and boys who were attached only to formal organised afternoon activities, and also some children who mostly stayed at home without having a chance at all to play with peers. In this chapter, I chose Daniel and Thomas as examples of children who, living in two very different urban and social class environments, succeed in shaping a social life among peers, and produce ways of doing so that are appropriate to features of their environments. In each of these contexts, these boys succeed in finding ways to realise their aspirations and achieve self-determined agency. The world around these children provides them with certain opportunities, and indeed imposes certain constraints, but the children themselves deal with these conditions, sometimes taking, sometimes rejecting, and sometimes adapting them.

Acknowledgement

Translated from German by Susannah Goss.

Notes

1 More investigations with the same method were made in other districts of Berlin, some of them in East Berlin after the fall of the wall (Kirchhöfer 1996), and in a West German village (Schick 1992). With these data, also other problems were analysed (H. Zeiher 2001a).
2 All of the children performed the task with great commitment, appreciating being asked to co-operate in the research project as experts on children's ways of living (and being paid for the work).
3 This is different in England, either because parents seem to be more afraid of traffic and stranger danger or because this danger is actually greater (see the comparison between England and Germany by Hillman *et al.* 1990).

References

Behnken, I., Du Bois-Reymond, M. and Zinnecker, J., 1989, *Stadtgeschichte als Kindheitsgeschichte: Lebensräume von Grosstadtkindern in Deutschland und Holland um 1900* [*Urban History as Childhood History: Lifespaces of Children in German and Dutch Towns*] (Opladen: Leske & Budrich).

Berger, P. L., Berger, B. and Kellner, H., 1973, *The Homeless Mind: Modernization and Consciousness* (New York: Random House).

Elias, N., 1969, *Über den Prozess der Zivilisation: Soziogenetische und psychogenetische Untersuchungen* [*The Civilising Process: Sociogenetic and Psychogenetic Investigations*] (Bern: Francke).

Hillman, M., Adams, J. and Whitelegg, J., 1990, *One False Move: A Study of Children's Independent Mobility* (London: Policy Studies Institute).

Matthews, H., Taylor, M., Percy-Smith, B. and Limb, M., 2000, 'The unacceptable *flaneur*: the shopping mall as a teenage hangout'. *Childhood*, 7 (3), 279–94.

Kirchhöfer, D., 1989, *Aufwachsen in Ostdeutschland: Langzeitstudie über Tagesläufe 10- bis 14jähriger Kinder* [*Growing Up in East Germany: An Extended Study of the Day Courses of 10–14-year-old Children*] (Weinheim and Munich: Juventa).

Qvortrup, J., 2000, 'Macroanalysis of childhood'. In P. Christensen and A. James (eds) *Research with Children: Perspectives and Practices* (London and New York: Falmer Press).

Schick, M., 1992, *Kindheit in einem Dorf: Fallstudien zur Alltagsorganisation zehnjähriger Kinder* [*Childhood in a Village: Case Studies on the Organisation of Ten-year-olds' Daily Lives*] (Berlin: Max-Planck-Institut für Bildungsforschung).

Zeiher, H., 2001a, 'Dependent, independent and interdependent relations: children as members of the family household'. In L. Alanen and B. Mayall (eds), *Conceptualising Child–Adult Relations* (London and New York: Routledge Falmer).

Zeiher, H., 2001b, 'Children's islands in space and time: the impact of spatial differentiation on children's ways of shaping social life'. In M. Du Bois-Reymond, H. Sünker and H. H. Krüger (eds), *Childhood in Europe: Approaches – Trends – Findings* (New York: Peter Lang).

Zeiher, H. J., 2001, 'Alltägliche Lebensführung: ein Ansatz bei Handlungsentscheidungen' [Shaping daily life: a decision-making approach]. In G. G. Voss and M. Weihrich (eds), *tagaus – tagein: Neue Beiträge zur Soziologie alltäglicher Lebensführung* [*Day after Day: New Contributions to the Sociology of Shaping Daily Lives*] (Munich and Mering: Rainer Hampp).

Zeiher, H. J. and Zeiher, H., 1994, *Orte und Zeiten der Kinder: Soziales Leben im Alltag von Grossstadtkindern* [*Spaces and Times of Children: Urban Children's Social Life*] (Weinheim and Munich: Juventa).

Zinnecker, J., 1990, 'Vom Strassenkind zum verhäuslichten Kind: Kindheitsgeschichte im Prozess der Zivilisation' [From the street child to the domesticated child: childhood history in the process of civilisation]. In I. Behnken (ed.), *Stadtgeschichte im Prozess der Zivilisation* [*Urban History in the Process of Civilisation*] (Opladen: Leske & Budrich), 142–62.

6 Children in the neighbourhood

The neighbourhood in the children

Kim Rasmussen and Søren Smidt

As part of an empirical research project about how children experience and perceive modern institutionalised childhood,[1] eighty-eight Danish children between 5 and 12 years old have been telling us about the many arenas of their everyday life including their neighbourhoods. The children lived in thirteen different parts of Denmark from cities and provincial towns to small villages and islands, reflecting the varied locations in which Danish children live their childhoods. In the course of one week, the children photographed the places they frequented, collecting images about what they were doing, who they were with and what was important and meaningful to them. Subsequently, we carried out interviews with the children, where they told us about the details of the photographs and elaborated on the significance of the places and spaces in their everyday lives. The material presented in this chapter consists of photographic documentation and oral narratives, as photographed and told by the children themselves.

Profound changes in the nature of childhood have occurred over the course of the past hundred years through the process of institutionalisation, whereby more and more of children's activities are taking place in formal and organised settings. This development has been particularly pronounced in Denmark and the other Scandinavian welfare societies where children's play has moved from the street and into specially designed areas and physically confined spaces (Myhre 1994). In our project we have been trying to understand Danish children's everyday life in contemporary societal contexts and have been inspired by a range of theoretical orientations; in particular the socio-constructive approach of childhood sociology in which children are regarded as competent social actors, and the approach of body phenomenology which stresses the physicality and bodily nature of children's interactions with their environment (Merleau-Ponty 2000). Within a general critical theory stance (Habermas 1981; Horkheimer 1968) we have turned to the emerging childhood sociology (Brannan and O'Brien 1995; Corsaro 1997; Honig 1999; James *et al.* 1998; James and Prout 1997; Negt 1984; Qvortrup 1994; Ziehe 1989), in particular its geographical research on children's neighbourhoods (Blades and Spencer

1986; Halseth and Doddridge 2000; Holloway and Valentine 2000; Matthews and Limb 1999). Cultural studies have provided a key background paradigm to our understanding of children's everyday life and culture and their meaning. We have been influenced by Willis (1990). We have used all these ideas throughout, in so far as they allow the primary aim of a critical analysis to be preserved.

In contrast to other neighbourhood studies, we have not focused on any one specific theme, for instance whether children perceive the neighbourhood as safe or dangerous, good or bad (Buss 1995; O'Brien 2000; Woolley *et al.* 1999; and others) but have been open-ended in our approach. Our prime interest has been to let the participating children tell and show us, in as autonomous a manner as possible, the issues they were most keen to discuss and photograph. The interesting part then was whether this approach would contribute to shedding light on the general trend of institutionalisation including the institutionalisation of the neighbourhood, which we believe is an essential characteristic of childhood in the modern world of today (cf. Buckingham 2000; Zeiher 2001; Zinnecker 1990).

Introducing a child's neighbourhood photo-narrative

After we had asked children to photograph significant places, items and persons we received a large number of photographs featuring a wide range of topics. Many of the topics were connected to the children's neighbourhoods as illustrated in Figure 6.1, a photograph taken by a 9-year-old boy living in a

Figure 6.1 The 'den'

suburban district to Copenhagen. When we asked the child what was in his photograph, an interesting story suddenly unravelled that gave us an insight into the life of the child and also the neighbourhood in which he lived. Using the photograph as a starting point, we gained insight into the child's perception of the neighbourhood environment which he and his friend helped to create themselves. The conversation about the picture (Figure 6.1) began like this:

Researcher: Please tell me a little about the photograph.
Child: It's an old den that Troels and I built when we were in first grade, and it has been vandalised in a big way.
Researcher: By whom?
Child: We think it was some drunk bastards, because that's what one of the educational workers told us. At weekends there are often drunk idiots wandering around in the playground and throwing bottles and all sorts.
Researcher: Do you often play in the den?
Child: No, not any more. Because there are a lot of nails sticking out and there are cobwebs all over the place. So it's not a very nice place to be.
Researcher: Why did you photograph the den?
Child: Because we thought it was a shame that it should just sit there, without being photographed, since it's one of the things we have spent the most time on making over here.
Researcher: How long did it take you to make it?
Child: Well, I don't really know. I think it took about a month before we'd finished it and we would sweep it out every day and do all sorts of things. But then it was wrecked.

What does this story tell us about the children and their views of their neighbourhood? It reveals several things to us that were similarly revealed in many of the photographs and narratives of the other children.

First of all, the photograph and the narrative reveal that *children contribute to, create and direct their own lives* and environment. In the narrative referred to here, the important part is that the boys have created something important in their neighbourhood, that is a den that they have been working on for almost a month. The building of the den accounts for a large part of the physical as well as mental energies of the boys, and we suggest that they had attached a lot of symbolic creative force to the building of the den. The result is not just a den to play in. It is also the creation of an important place, the meaning of which was designed by the children. Not only do children often redefine what the adults have made for them; they also frequently build exactly that which is right for them provided they are not being prevented in so doing.

Secondly, the narrative reveals that *children may often be in conflict with the adults in arenas that are commonly used by both parties*. In this narrative the sad conclusion is that drunken adults vandalised the boys' den. Consequently the boys abandon it. This particular turn of events has additional interest, since usually we hear mostly about children and juveniles vandalising the property and belongings of adults. However, in this instance, the tables are turned: the adults destroy the property of the children, and the adults are the destructive ones.

Thirdly, the photograph and the narrative may indicate that *children perceive their neighbourhood in a particular and concrete manner*. Children's knowledge of their neighbourhood is imparted through their experiences of places, items and persons that symbolise the neighbourhood and a sense of belonging, proximity and familiarity (see Christensen, Chapter 2, above). Children hold many detailed observations as well as knowledge about their neighbourhood, and their perception is active through their use of sensors and their own bodies. Their perception of the neighbourhood is of a less general nature than that of the adults.

One important detail to be noted, we will argue, is that the children's perception is rooted in their day-care institution. This is not surprising since, during the last third of the twentieth century, childhood, including the neighbourhood of the children, has been strongly institutionalised (Halseth and Doddrige 2000); an increasing number of day-care institutions and facilities have emerged in this period. Children spend ever more time in institutions, and more areas are being fenced in and watched over by educational workers. However, this does not prevent children from creating and organising parts of their own everyday lives partly on their own and partly in interaction with professional adults (Rasmussen and Smidt 2001).

Method and reflections on the methodology

As mentioned above, eighty-eight children from 5 to 18 years of age participated in this project. In the planning stages consent was firstly sought from the children in their school and neighbourhood contexts and then parents give their written permission. We met with the children, and gave each of them a disposable camera and some simple instructions. These were:

- remember to take the camera with you everywhere you go during the week
- take one or two photographs of each place and of the things you are involved with
- get as close to your image as possible so it will be easier to make out in the photograph afterwards
- remember to stand with the sun or the light behind you, otherwise the photographs will be too dark

Following this first encounter, the children went off to take photographs on their own for a week. The films were developed and we met with the children again. Together we opened the envelopes with the photographs, and the children saw again the images they had captured. At the time of the reunion we interviewed the children, primarily in order to let them tell us about the things they had photographed. It was on this occasion that, together with photographs of their families, friends, schools, institutions, media and leisure-time activities, we were introduced to a series of photographs of the neighbourhoods that the children lived in.

In this chapter we shall present our reflections about the methodology, the children's photographs and our understanding of the child as a social actor. Using this as a foundation we shall then return to the actual subject of this chapter: the neighbourhood arena as perceived by children.

Our method is founded on a view of *children being actors*; that is, actively creating their own lives. This is not to say that they do so independently of the adults, or that we believe that the many rules, structures and conditions imposed on the children by the adults, and which have a profound impact on the lives of the children, may be disregarded. Nevertheless, in the children's everyday lives they perform acts of varying importance every day, which prove that they are human beings who act and who have intentions, interests and desires. Hence, children and the lives of children may, in accordance with this view, be studied in manners that are not basically different from the manners in which adult lives are studied. We therefore find it important to employ empirical methods that support the active role of children. Thus, when children are informants in empirical studies we consider it important that it is done in a way that supports and contributes to this understanding.

It is in this context that the active photographing by the children followed by their vivid narratives about parts of their lives become instructive. Traditional interviews of children generally display a certain degree of asymmetry between the children and the adults (the child is being interviewed and the adult is doing the interviewing). The method of using photographs to some extent departs from this asymmetry.

First of all, it involves the actual process of photographing, where the children are active in taking the photographs. They are active in the same way as when they are taking part in a game, physical activities, communication or negotiation with other children and adults.

Secondly, the camera contributes to increasing the child's power. Through the camera, the child can capture and freeze scenes from his or her everyday life that she would not otherwise be able to control in the same way. Although the power that the child obtains through the camera is fleeting and temporary, it supports the child's experience of being an actor. In principle, the child can photograph whatever he or she wants to. In reality, however, children photograph only segments of life. Cultural taboos are reproduced in the children's photographs. Children do not take embarrassing photographs. But once in possession of the power from the camera, they know full well how to use it against, for instance, an older sister who is chased under the table, or they can photograph a den which has been vandalised by 'drunk bastards'.

The comments about the photograph of the den – that it was a shame that it should just sit there without being photographed when it was one of the things they have spent the most time on making – illustrates that in this instance the camera may be viewed as an important object of power for the boys in their exasperation over the vandalised den. The camera supports the active doings of children and motivates them for further activities.

In the third place, the subsequent interviews differ from more traditional interviews. As researchers and adults we needed to be extra attentive and open-minded about what the children showed and told us in order to grasp the meaning and cohesion. In principle, one should always be so when interviewing children, but thematic delimitation and interview guides traditionally add a strong element of control. When, on the other hand, children's photographs are used as a starting point, is was our experience that the materialised life of the child (the photograph) forced us to look very closely from the child's perspective (Rasmussen 1999, 2000). The point about a photograph, as noted by Becker, is that it generates meaning through its context (Becker 1998: 88).

As mentioned in the introduction, our approach is determined on the one hand by the understanding of the actor role pertaining to childhood sociology. On the other hand, though, we have also been inspired by phenomenology, which facilitates an understanding between subject and object (actor and environment), in which it is attempted to neutralise the dualistic separation. It is not within the scope of this chapter to give a detailed account of the relationship between the socio-constructive approach of childhood sociology and the approach of phenomenology, but we will, nevertheless, point out the main theoretical differences between the two approaches.

'Phenomenology concerns itself with *phenomena in the way they are perceived by our senses*' (Merleau-Ponty 2000, our emphasis). The reason for us turning to phenomenology for inspiration is partly that 'a phenomenological perspective could enable us to gain insight into an existential and generative sense of sociality that emerges from within the consciousness of the child' (Jenks 1996: 49), and partly because the phenomenological perspective contributes to focusing on the body and body perceptions. It is, after all, through the child's body that the neighbourhood is perceived. This is an area of attention that is also inherent in the new childhood sociology (Prout 2000).

French phenomenology challenges the tradition founded by Descartes (that is, the traditional perception of subject/object). Thus, in line with Merleau-Ponty it could be argued on the subject of the understanding of children's relationship to their neighbourhood that 'paradoxically, . . . *for us* [is] an *in-itself*' (Merleau-Ponty 2000: 71). In other words, *within* the subject there is an 'in-itself', a sensual perception of the object, such as the physical cultural environment. The physical cultural environment already exists as a sensed reality. It exists before any form of analysis is possible, Merleau-Ponty argues. At the same time the human body works as a kind of community of the senses. Or in the words of O'Neill: 'Because the human body is a "community of the senses" and not a bundle of contingently related impressions, it functions as the universal setting or schema for all possible styles or structures of the world' (O'Neill 1989: 50).

Using this framework it makes sense to claim that the *children are in the neighbourhood, and that the neighbourhood is in the children*. That the children are in the neighbourhood seems obvious to anyone: this can be observed by a chance external observer as well as by the children themselves. That the children are present in their neighbourhood is evident from their narratives about what they do, what they perceive and what they feel. However, that the neighbourhood is also inside the child's body may seem more difficult to grasp. The phenomenological approach helps us to acknowledge the neighbourhood as a sensed, perceived and experienced reality; it is stored within the child's body as tactile knowledge and a 'community of the senses'. The body and its movements are vital building blocks in making meaning of the environment. The creation of meaning is basically a physical manifestation (Skantze 1990). Knowledge about the neighbourhood is therefore not always expressed in verbal language, but is rather expressed through a physical 'know-how', for instance about how to scale a tall fence, or the specific manner of climbing a certain tree, or a sense of which shortcut to choose between two locations when in a hurry. We suggest that part of the physical knowledge about the neighbourhood that children have may be expressed through a photograph. The visual language of a photograph can show us the way the child through their body is related to certain things, persons and places or spaces. Often, but not always, a child's photograph of the neighbourhood was supplemented by their own words. However, the segment of the neighbourhood shown on the children's photographs has to be perceived as something in itself. It may not always be expressed in words, or it may contain something other and more than mere words. Children's photographs of these things, places and persons in their neighbourhood that they physically turn towards to photograph, and which they know, sense and feel, will often give us an indication of what they think is important. Or at least what they are fascinated by. It is to such understanding that the phenomenological approach can contribute an important aspect (see Tuan 1977).

To some degree a neighbourhood is an abstract concept defined by adults, but it is also a very concrete socio-physical concept that, as we will go on to show, is primary to children's perception of neighbourhood. The manner in which an adult defines, perceives and not least talks about a neighbourhood is very different from the more straightforward and concrete manner of the children. Where adults talk in a general and outlining manner about the neighbourhood, the children have a greater concrete and tactile knowledge of it. This is not least because the children who move around in the neighbourhood breathe it in, have physical experiences of it, as do adults. The understanding of children's neighbourhoods which we seek to explore in this chapter is thus based on a phenomenological approach in that the photographs are used as a way to achieve greater understanding of how the children perceive their neighbourhood.[2]

Children perceive their neighbourhood as something concrete and visible, with a physical appearance, and therefore it may be represented in a photograph. However, children also experience their neighbourhood through their bodies. As we inhabit the world through our body (Merleau-Ponty 2000), the child's body will know something about the neighbourhood that will be unknown territory to most adults. The child also perceives the neighbourhood through anecdotes and narratives (about the road accident, the runaway cat, the garden with the dog that always barks, the poisonous tree, the child molester, and so on). As a result, at least three approaches for gaining knowledge about children's neighbourhoods may be employed: the visual perspective, the physical perspective and the narrative perspective.

The first perspective is supported by the photograph and that which may be shown in a photograph.[3] The second perspective is supported by the body and bodily knowledge which children can illustrate by using body language, such as the best way to climb a certain tree or the safe way to tackle a certain fence. The third perspective is supported by the children's anecdotes and narratives about their place and their local environment.

In our study of children's photographs of their everyday lives, we saw many photographs that we as adults immediately defined as depicting the neighbourhood. However, when the children themselves described these photographs they never used the word *neighbourhood*. Children's initial replies to the question 'Where was this taken?' would never be, 'This is from my neighbourhood'. The children's answers were far more concrete: 'This is our backyard', 'This is from our garden', 'This is from the parking lot', 'This is the fence in the backyard', 'This is my mate and our bicycles', 'This is my next-door neighbour'. It is therefore justifiable, we would argue, that the concept of neighbourhood does not belong to the immediate pattern of concepts of children and is not an active part of their vocabulary, at least not the vocabulary of the 5–10-year-olds in this study (but see Baraldi, Christensen, Morrow, Chawla and Malone, in this volume). We suggest that the neighbourhood of younger children is revealed through a number of neighbourhood markers. These may be physical and pertaining to space (e.g. houses, blocks of flats, pavements, bicycle paths, playgrounds and dens) or they may be of a social nature (e.g. my mates, my neighbour, my dog and my pet rabbit).

In the following, we will to give some examples of the children's neighbourhood as represented through neighbourhood markers and also as it was represented to us through the children's narratives about the neighbourhood.

The neighbourhood: a multitude of places, items and persons

At first glance the neighbourhood depicted in the children's photographs came across as a chaotic multitude of places, items and persons. It was a source of constant surprise to us just how many different images the children

Places to be used by children in the neighbourhood
Photographs of playgrounds or nature playgrounds, slides, earth mounds for the children to dig in, hills for sleighing in the winter, Wendy houses, cabins, shacks, dens, handball goals, playing fields, old rowing boats, campfire sites, swings in trees. In the vast majority of cases adults have created and organised those things for the children. However, there are examples where the children had made their own playing fields.

Means of transportation used in the neighbourhood
Photographs show: roller-skates, bicycles, home-made go-carts, sleighs, but also the school bus and the parents' car were photographed. Means of transportation such as bicycles symbolise the children's opportunities for independently going more or less where they please within the neighourhood.

Nature spots and objects from nature
These have been manifested through the following images: trees, felled tree trunks, shrubs, stone walls, flowers, flower beds, front gardens, herb gardens, fallow fields, the beach and sand dunes, field of dandelions, open space, pruning of trees and wood chips. The children's accompanying narratives are often tainted by them having a consumer-type relationship with nature. They pick the flowers, they climb the trees, they play in the dandelion field, they closely watch the pruning of the trees etc. At the same time, nature spots and objects from nature are neighbourhood markers – landmarks with which they feel familiar, and which serve to identify the neighbourhood.

Public buildings and places of cultural interest
This category comprises photographs of: water towers, water tanks, building sites, corner shops, shopping centres, sports centres, parking lots etc. Those are places where children go for different purposes and where they stay for varying lengths of time sometimes on their own and sometimes together with the adults.

Private buildings, places and areas
This category includes photographs of: single family houses and their gardens, the next-door neighbour's garden, holiday cottages and holiday areas (which give the children a dual sense of belonging), residential streets, their patio, their herb garden, the front of their house, the common green belonging to a street of terraced houses, the backyard belonging to a block of flats, the block of flats, a system of footpaths, fences, railings, bicycle paths and pavements.

Figure 6.2 Thematic categories

Special persons with a connection to the neighbourhood
The children have photographed some of the residents from the neighbourhood. It could be said that the neighbourhood is perceived through
certain people who belong there. Those are persons that the children
know and are able to tell stories about, as opposed to children and
persons who are known only marginally or not at all. In this sense, the
neighbourhood should be perceived as relating to space and sociability,
where the space aspect is not entirely separate from the social aspect.

Animals
The last category comes into being through the large number of animal
photographs taken by the children. The children's photographs reveal
that there is in fact a multitude of animals in the neighbourhood, which
many people may not notice nor imagine. The children have photographed small birds, ducks, chickens, cats, dogs, rabbits, guinea pigs,
mice, horses, sheep and cattle.

Figure 6.2 (continued)

have managed to capture through their photographs. Many of the narratives
and photographs that the children have come up with stemmed from areas
that geographers have called 'the fourth environment', that is the places
beyond school, home and playground (Matthews *et al.* 1998).

We have chosen to sort the photographic images into seven general categories determined by what we interpreted as being the most important
element in the photograph. The categories are shown and summarised in
Figure 6.2. In the following section we will present some photographs together with the narratives and comments of the children as examples of these
themes.

Places to be used by children

One of the children's views of the neighbourhood is what may be termed
places to be used by children. It is hardly surprising that a large number of
the children's photographs are of very traditional childhood places such as
established playgrounds with playground equipment including swings, see-
saws, slides, sand pits, Wendy houses and so on. More unconventional places
were also chosen, as seen in the photograph taken by 6-year-old Kristine
(Figure 6.3).

Child: It is from the mounds. In the after-school centre we have some
              mounds.
Researcher: Do you often play there?

Figure 6.3 Photograph by 6-year-old Kristine

Child: Yes.
Researcher: What do you play on the mounds?
Child: Oh, you can play all sorts of things . . . (pointing) . . . this is some-
                one called 'Morten'. He is just about to fall down and then he
                grabbed hold of something. It's a sort of place where you can
                slide.
Researcher: Why is it so good to play there?
Child: Because it is very slippery, and then you can skid, and you never
                know when you're going to start skidding.
Researcher: Is that exciting?
Child: Yes.

From the child's comments it becomes evident that it is the *excitement factor*
and the *imaginative factor* of the place that are important. These two factors are
difficult to attain in many neighbourhoods in part because they often challenge and provoke the sense of order, neatness, control and safety of many
adults, and also because the potential for excitement and imagination at
accessible playgrounds differs a great deal from one neighbourhood to the
next. A series of tests reveals that the layout of playgrounds have a large
influence on the games and activities of the children (Susa and Benedict
1994; Titman 1994; Grahn *et al.* 1997). At the same time, a number of
empirical examinations confirm the generalised findings of German sociologist Oskar Negt:

If children are to objectify their specific form of sensuousness and recognise themselves within its framework, they need areas in which to experiment, spaces, an open field for activities where things have not once and for all been determined, defined, provided with definite names and had rules laid down for them by the means of directions and prohibitions.

(Negt 1984: 5)

Numerous empirical investigations confirm this thesis (see Holm 1998: 29e–62e). When playgrounds are empty, the explanation is probably not only that children today spend most of their time at school or in a day-care institution. It could also be because a large number of traditional playgrounds are anything but exciting, they are lacking imagination and they do not appeal to the sensuousness of children. The empty playgrounds to be encountered in many places may, therefore, be interpreted as a criticism from the children. Who wants to spend time in a boring place? It is against this backdrop that it becomes interesting to watch and listen to what the children show and tell us about the places they find important in their neighbourhoods. As expressed in the example above, a giant earth mound ('the mounds') may turn out to be an exciting place to play, among other things because one runs the risk of skidding, and it is likewise fascinating that one can never quite know when one does. This story tells us, then, that it is not so much the place or neighbourhood in itself that is interesting. It is the place as a setting for performing certain activities that is crucial to the experience of the child.

There is no doubt that the children have a physical knowledge of the places and of the significance of the places for playing certain games. Yet, this knowledge does not always find linguistic expression, as indicated in the next case (see Figure 6.4).

Child: This is at Teis's place, . . . in his yard. We're playing football. It's Mikkel kicking the ball.

Researcher: Is he the goalkeeper, and are you using the shed as the goal?

Child: Yes, but we can also play outside the shed. Further down there are some wooden thingamajigs, and there we can play football using a big goal.

This boy knows where they can play football in the neighbourhood, but he is having difficulties expressing it in words (by the 'wooden thingamajigs'). He is able to show where it is by pointing at the photograph, and he knows exactly where it is, when he is there. You can choose between playing in front of the large or the small goals. The fact that the goals are of those sizes, and that you can choose between them, contributes to the identity of the place. This is an identity that the boys give to the place, whereas none or only a few of the adults even know about this identity. Similarly, girls may not know so much about this particular aspect. The great majority of Danish

Figure 6.4 Teis's place

boys play football, some more than others. In most neighbourhoods there is not just one football pitch, but many places to play: some have been designed for the purpose (adults have erected goals and planted shrubs or trees in order to cater for this function), whilst others have been created by the boys themselves, as in the photograph, where the pillars of a pavilion are being used as the goalposts. The boys, in particular, are quick to spot and occupy the most suitable places for playing football in the neighbourhood.

The neighbourhood becomes the story about what they do in the neighbourhood 'the mounds where we skid' or 'where we play football using the large and the small goals'. The neighbourhood comes into being and goes through changes by means of the children's narratives. And since the activities, experiences and narratives within the neighbourhood are in some ways rather different from those of adults, the children's perception and narratives about the neighbourhood will not be identical to those of the adults. Children are quick to spot the areas that they see as being 'for them', and children tend to frequent different places from the adults. Such places in the neighbourhood are created by adults for the children (e.g. the mounds). Other places have been made by the adults for adults. This is done with a certain function in mind: however, they may then be redefined and taken over by the children (e.g. a covered pavilion with a bench and table that is changed into a perfect small football goal). Still other places appear to be potential areas for the constructions and the taking over by the children. This pattern is especially valid in connection with the transitional areas between that which

is planned and organised (playgrounds, parking lots, etc.) and the prop
or overgrown areas in the neighbourhood: the transitional area betw
categories 'places for children' and 'nature spots and objects from nat

The children's own spaces and dens are fine examples of how childr
adults guide themselves differently in the neighbourhood. In addition, different types of neighbourhoods afford different opportunities for children to
discover their 'own' places. As stated by Titman (1994), the children's 'secret'
places may not be prefabricated. Furthermore, there is an inherent latent
conflict between, on the one hand, that which has been planned and organised by adults and, on the other hand, the children's recreation of public
spaces and locations into their own territories. Only rarely are children allowed
to take possession of essential parts of public places. It is for this reason that
dens and secret places are found on the extremities of the recreational areas,
in the country or in the transitional space between the landscaped areas and
the overgrown areas.

Animals

There is a multitude of animals in the children's photographs, and animals
also play a part in the narratives about their neighbourhoods (Titman 1994;
Nordström 1990). Children experience and view their neighbourhood through
animals, and to some extent animals become symbols of the neighbourhood
(just as they are symbols of other aspects such as compassion and intimacy).
Animals are markers for the children, and they appear to form a link between
the children and their neighbourhood.

Obviously, children relate differently to animals, depending on whether
they live in the town or on a farm where animals are an integral part of the
production. Yet, children in the country also photograph animals and tell
stories about them in a way that does not reduce the animals to being mere
units of production. Watching the photographs and listening to the children's
narratives, one becomes aware of the number of animals living in modern
residential neighbourhoods even in the cities. The joint impression is that the
animals are an important part of the children's perception of their neighbourhood, regardless of where they live.

For example one 10-year-old girl describes her neighbourhood not far
from the city centre of Copenhagen by referring to various animals. At home
she has a parrot, rabbits and some mice. She tells us about the mice: 'I bought
four mice: two males and two females. They are forever having young, and
then my dad takes them, wraps them up in a napkin and flushes them out in
the toilet. This way we make sure that we don't end up with so many mice,
that it gets crowded.' Her aunt lives close by, and she has a dog that chases
the mice when they are visiting. In her after-school centre they also have a
lot of animals: rabbits, horses, ducks and chickens. On the subjects of the
ducks she says, 'I'm so fond of the ducks; I think it is fascinating that they are
so pretty.' When the girl is playing herself, the animals also take precedence:

'I mostly play animal games. We love to pretend to be animals. I don't want to do anything else but making animals and drawing animals and people. I can draw the animals' hair and their eyes and mouths, but I can't draw their heads.'

Animals help to add existence and life to the neighbourhoods. The animals in the example above (at home, in the after-school centre, her aunt's dog) form a sense of continuity between the various arenas. The animals contribute to the children creating narratives about the neighbourhood, and they become elements in their games and other creative activities. Secondly, the presence of the animals and their need for care and protection result in certain duties in connection with feeding and caring for the animals, which afford children a certain responsibility which many take on willingly. Their relationship to animals becomes a significant fulcrum for important activities in the residential neighbourhoods. In the third place, the children's relationship to animals gives the neighbourhood a more colourful, interesting and significant meaning. The animals, and the children's relationships to them, afford the children a stronger sense of belonging to the neighbourhood. Those places in the neighbourhood where the children know someone (whether people or animals) become alive for the children, whereas houses and places where the children do not know anyone often remain places that the children are unacquainted with.

Animals can be the reason for children to be moving around in the neighbourhood. It is not uncommon for the destination of a bicycle ride or a walk to be the pond with ducks or some other place where there are animals to look at or feed. With an animal there is an element of coincidence and unpredictability. The German cultural philosopher Walter Benjamin poetically describes this in his famous memoirs *Childhood in Berlin around the Year 1900*. He remembers when he used to chase butterflies as a child: 'that so often had lured me away from the well-tended garden paths and into a wilderness where I was at the mercy of the conspiracy of wind and scents, leaves and sun that also presumably guided the flight of the butterflies' (Benjamin 1992: 21).

When the animals pursue their own course the children will tag along. In this manner they will be taken away from the established roads and paths and into new and unknown places. It appears that animals could be a sixth element to add to Lynch's (1960) five core cityscape elements of path, edge, district, node and landmark. Animals play a mysterious dual role. They can be a kind of landmark (the angry dog in a certain garden), or they can be a kind of alluring 'siren' that seduces the children away from the well-known paths.

Conclusion

The experiences from the project reported on in this chapter have shown that the method of letting children be active participants in research on children and their neighbourhoods is not only possible but also advantageous. It is our experience that once children had agreed to take part, they were fully capable of photographing significant segments of their everyday lives. Photography is a physical act, and as such it enabled, we suggest, the children's physical knowledge and attention towards concrete persons, items and places in their neighbourhood to be expressed. The children enjoyed participating and they were proud of their photographs. At the same time, we, as researchers, gained a valuable insight into the present world of childhood, particularly with our open-ended methodological framework. These experiences link up well with other studies which are also based on child informants who take photographs and narrate (Buss 1995; Schrantz and Steiner-Löffler 1998; Hubbard 1991; Ewald 2000; Woolley *et al.* 1999). This present project has confirmed to us that children do not direct their attention and approach only towards a large unified whole, but also towards many details and concrete singular aspects (Philo 2000). A large part of their knowledge of the neighbourhood is physical and is thus embedded in their bodies.

With regard to the institutionalisation of childhood, the children's accounts suggest that the institutionalisation trend varies and has not yet taken on a standardised character. Even though most children in Denmark live their lives within an institutionalised 'triangle' of home, school, and day-care (against the neighbourhood as a backdrop), there is great *variation* in the form of institutionalisation.

Through the photographs and narratives of the children, this project has also given important insight into how children not only reproduce the neighbourhood, its layout and functions, but also actively emboss and mark it. Although the children did not use the word 'neighbourhood' about the area where they lived, they still had a detailed and extensive knowledge about the persons, animals, places, items, events and stories from the neighbourhood. The neighbourhood is perceived by the children through a number of concrete parts, where social, cultural and physical elements are inseparable and interwoven (see too Buss 1995; Tuan 1977). The children are present *in* the neighbourhood, and they have the neighbourhood 'under their skin'.

Notes

1 This chapter is a part of the project programme Childhood and Welfare Society and supported by a grant from The Danish Research Agency under the programme Children's Living Conditions and Welfare.
2 For general information about photography see Barthes (1983), Berger (1972), Sontag (1977), Price and Wells (1997). For information about a phenomenological approach to photography see Damisch (1980). For information about photography in ethnographic research see Collier and Collier (1986), Banks and Morphy (1997), Banks (2001).
3 Similar studies on children and life in the cities that have also been based on children's photographs are Buss (1995), Orellana (1999), Rasmusson (1998) and Rogers (2000).

References

Banks, M., 2001, *Visual Methods in Social Research* (London, Thousand Oaks and New Delhi: Sage Publications).

Banks, M. and Morphy, H., 1997, *Rethinking Visual Anthropology* (New Haven and London: Yale University Press).

Barthes, R., 1983, *Det lyse kammer.* Camera Lucida [*The Light Chamber*] (Copenhagen: Rævens sorte bibliotek, Politisk Revys Forlag).

Becker, H., 1998, 'Visual sociology, documentary, photography and photojournalism: it's (almost) all a matter of context'. In J. Prosser (ed.) *Image-based Research.* (London: Falmer Press), 84–96.

Benjamin, W., 1992, *Barndom i Berlin omkring år 1900* [*Childhood in Berlin around the Year 1900*] (Copenhagen: Rævens bibliotek, Politisk Revys Forlag).

Berger, J., 1972, *Ways of Seeing* (London: Penguin Books).

Blades, M. and Spencer, C. 1986, 'Map use by young children'. *Geography*, 71, 47–52.

Brannen, J. and O'Brien, M., 1995, 'Review essay childhood and sociological gaze: paradigms and paradoxes'. *Sociology*, 29, 4, 729–37.

Buckingham, D., 2000, *After the Death of Childhood* (Cambridge: Polity Press).

Buss, S., 1995, 'Urban Los Angeles from young people's angle of vision'. *Children's Environments*, 12, 3, 340–51.

Collier, J. and Collier, M., 1986, *Visual Anthropology – Photography as a Research Method* (Albaquerque: University of New Mexico Press).

Corsaro, W. A., 1997, *The Sociology of Childhood* (Thousand Oaks, CA: Pine Forge Press).

Damisch, H., 1980, 'Notes for a phenomenology of the photographic image'. In A. Trachtenberg (ed.), *Classic Essays on Photography* (New Haven: Leete's Island Books).

Ewald, W., 2000, *Secret Games* (New York City: Scalo).

Grahn, P., Mårtensson, F., Lindblad, B., Nilsson, P. and Ekman, A., 1997, 'Ute på dagis. Hur anvender barn daghemsgården? Utformningen av daghemsgården och dess betydelse för lek, motorik och koncenttrationsförmåga' [Away from home during the day. How do children use the day-care institution? The organisation of the day-care institution and its importance for play, motor skills and ability to concentrate]. *Stad och Land*, 145 (MOVIUM och Institutionen för Landskapsplanering Alnarp ved Sveriges Lantbruksuniversitet).

Habermas, J., 1978, *Knowledge and Human Interests* (London: Heinemann).

Habermas, J., 1981, *Theorien des Kommunikativen Handelns* (Frankfurt am Main: Suhrkamp).

Halseth, G. and Doddridge, J., 2000, 'Children's cognitive mapping: a potential tool for neighbourhood planning'. *Environment and Planning B: Planning and Design*, 27, 565–82.

Holloway, S. L. and Valentine, G., 2000, 'Children's geographies and the new social studies of childhood'. In Holloway and Valentine (eds), *Children's Geographies: Playing, Living and Learning* (London: Routledge).

Holm, S., 1998, 'Anvendelse og betydning af parker og grønne områder [Use and importance of parks and recreational areas] (Copenhagen: Den kongelige Veterinær- og Landbohøjskole. Institut for Økonomi, Skov og Landskab. Sektion for Landskab).

Honig, M. S., 1999, *Entwurf einer Theorie der Kindheit* (Frankfurt am Main: Suhrkamp).

Horkheimer, M., 1968, *Traditionelle und kritische Theorie* (Kritische Theorie II. Frankfurt am Main: Fischer Verlag).

Hubbard, J., 1991, *Shooting Back – a Photographic View of Life by Homeless Children* (San Francisco: Chronicle Books).

James, A. and Prout, A. (eds), 1997, *Constructing and Reconstructing Childhood: Contemporary Issues in the Sociological Study of Childhood*, 2nd ed. (London: Falmer).

James, A., Jenks, C. and Prout, A., 1998, *Theorizing Childhood* (Cambridge: Polity Press).

Jenks, C., 1996, *Childhood* (London and New York: Routledge).

Lynch, K., 1960, *The Image of the City* (Cambridge: The MIT Press, Massachusetts Institute of Technology).

McKendrick, J., 2000, 'The geography of children: an annotated bibliography'. *Childhood*, 7, 3, 359–87.

Matthews, H. and Limb, M., 1999, 'Defining an agenda for the geography of children: review and prospect'. *Progress in Human Geography*, 23, 1, 61–90.

Matthews, H., Limb, M. and Percy-Smith, B., 1998, 'Changing worlds: the microgeographies of young teenagers'. *Tijdschrift voor Economishe en Sociale Geografie*, 89, 2 193–202.

Merleau-Ponty, M., 2000, *Phenomenology of Perception* (10th ed.) (London and New York: Routledge).

Myhre, J. E., 1994, *Barndom i storbyen Opvekst i velfærdstatens epoke* [*Childhood in the City Growing Up in the Era of the Welfare State*] (Oslo: Universitets forlaget).

Negt, O., 1984, 'Barndom og børneoffentlighed' [Childhood and the public life of children]. *Kontekst*, 47, 5–17.

Nordström, M., 1990, *Barns boendeforeställingar i et utvecklingspsykologikst perspektiv* [*Children's Perception of Their Neighbourhood Seen from a Psycho-developmental Perspective*] (Gävle: Statens Institut for Byggnadsforskning).

O'Brien, M., 2000, *Reviving Children's Neighbourhoods: What Do Children Want?* Paper to Final Children 5–16 Programme Final Conference (London, 20–1 October 2000).

O'Neill, J., 1989, *The Communicative Body* (Evanston: North Western University Press).

Orellana, M. F., 1999, 'Space and place in an urban landscape: learning from children's views of their social worlds'. *Visual Sociology*, 14, 73–89.

Østerberg, D., 1984, *Sociologiens nøkkelbegreber* [*The Key Concepts of Sociology*] (Trondheim: J. W. Cappelens Forlag).

Philo, C., 2000, 'The corner-stones of my world'. Editorial introduction to special issue on spaces of childhood. *Childhood*, 7, 3, 243–56.

Price, D. and Wells, L., 1997. 'Thinking about photography'. In L. Wells, (ed.), *Photography: A Critical Introduction* (Routledge. London and New York), 11–54.

Prosser, J. (ed.), 1998, *Image-based Research: A Sourcebook for Qualitative Researchers* (London: Falmer Press).

Prout, A., 2000, 'Childhood bodies: construction, agency and hybridity'. In Prout (ed.), *The Body, Childhood and Society* (Basingstoke: Macmillan).

Qvortrup, J., Bardy, M., Sgritta, G. and Wintersberger, H. (eds) 1994, *Childhood Matters: Social Theory, Practice and Politics* (Aldershot: Avebury).

Rasmussen, K., 1999, 'Om fotografering og fotografi som forskningsstrategi i barndomsforskning' [About photography and photographs as a research strategy in research into childhood]. *Sociologi*, 10, 1, 62–78.

Rasmussen, K., 2000, 'Det fotografiske (ind)blik i børns liv' [The photographic insight into the lives of children]. *Barn*, 3–4 (Trondheim: NOSEB), 159–72.

Rasmussen, K. and Smidt, S., 2000, 'Statens børn' [Children of the state]. In C. Clausen and H. Lærum (eds), *Velfærdstatens krise* (Copenhagen: Tiderne Skifter), 117–41.

Rasmussen, K. and Smidt, S., 2001, *Spor af børns institutionsliv* [*Traces of the Institutional Life of Children*] (Copenhagen: Hans Reitzels Forlag).

Rasmusson, B., 1998, *Stadsbarndom: om barns vardag i en modern förort* [*Childhood in the Town: About the Everyday Lives of Children in Modern Suburbia*] (Lund: Meddeladen från Socialhoejskolan).

Rogers, B., 2000, 'Romlig koreografi av barndom i et norsk boligområde' [Space choreography in a Norwegian residential area]. *Barn* (Trondheim: NOSEB), 3–4, 115–32.

Schrantz, M. and Steiner-Löffler, U., 1998, 'Pupils using photographs in school self-evaluation'. In Prosser (ed.), *Image-based Research* (London: Falmer Press), 235–51.

Sigsgaard, E., Rasmussen, K. and Smidt, S., 1998, *Andre måder* [*Other Ways*] (Copenhagen: Hans Reitzels Forlag).

Skantze, A., 1990, 'Hvordan oplever barnet sin skole?' [How does the child perceive its school?]. *S-arkitektur*, 10, 22–5.

Sontag, S., 1979, *On Photography* (Harmondsworth: Penguin).

Susa, A. and Benedict, J., 1994, 'The effects of playground design on pretend play and divergent thinking'. *Journal of Environment and Behaviour*, 26, 4, 264–72.

Titman, W., 1994, *Special Places; Special People, The Hidden Curriculum of School Grounds* (WWF UK: Learning through Landscapes).

Tuan, Y., 1977, *Space and Place: The Perspective of Experience* (London: Edward Arnold).

Wartofsky, M., 1983, 'The child's construction of the world and the world's construction of the child'. In F. Ziegal (ed.), *The Child and Other Cultural Inventions* (New York: Praeger), 188–223.

Willis, P., 1990, *Common Culture: Symbolic Work at Play in the Everyday Cultures of the Young* (Milton Keynes: Open University Press).

Woolley, H., Dunn, J., Spencer, C., Short, T. and Rowley, G., 1999, 'Children describe their experiences of the city centre: a qualitative study of the fears and concerns which may limit their full participation'. *Landscape Research*, 24, 3, 287–301.

Zeiher, H., 2001, 'Children's islands in space and time'. In M. du Bois-Reymond, H. Sünker and H. H. Krüger (eds), *Childhood in Europe: Approaches – Trends – Findings* (New York: Peter Lang Publishers).

Ziehe, T., 1989, *Kulturanalyser* [*Cultural analyses*] (Lund: Symposion).

Zinnecker, J., 1990, 'Vom Strassenkind zum verhäuslichten Kind: Kindheitsgeschichte im Prozess der Zivilisation' [From the street child to the domesticated child: childhood history in the process of civilisation] In I. Behnken (ed.), *Stadtgeschichte im Prozess der Zivilisation* [*Urban History in the Process of Civilisation*] (Opladen: Leske & Budrich), 142–62.

7 The street as a liminal space
The barbed spaces of childhood

Hugh Matthews

In this chapter, I suggest how the street[1], a metaphor for all outdoor spaces within the public domain, acts as a liminal setting or a site of passage, a place which both makes possible and signifies a means of transition through which some young people move away from the restrictions of their childhood roots towards the independence of adulthood. I consider how the street is infused with cultural identity and how, in their attempts to claim socially autonomous space within the public domain, young people frequently collide with adults and with other groups of young people. Confrontations of this sort are the rituals of transition within the socially *barbed spaces* of the street. In order to disentangle these street stories, I pay particular attention to the ways in which age and gender cut across place use. In developing these ideas I draw upon the theoretical notions of *habitus* (Bourdieu 1977, 1992; Cahill 2000) and the *rites of passage* (van Gennep 1909 (1960); Winchester *et al.* 1999), as well as the new literature on the cultural politics of difference and diversity (Bhabha 1994; Matthews *et al.* 2000a; Prout 2000). To pull these ideas together, I critically discuss the social construction of *binaries* (Skelton 2000), in this case those common cultural practices, interpretations and assumptions that unequivocally relegate children to *adult becomings* or persons *not of the adult world*. All of these thoughts are developed with reference to an empirical study that considers how a group of young people aged 9 to 16 years in an East Midlands town within the UK make use of their local neighbourhoods. Children's own words are used extensively in the text.

Locating 'the street'

According to Bourdieu (1992: 134), *habitus* refers to 'a durable, transposable system of definitions' that are gained by 'conscious and unconscious practices' as children move through different social institutions from home, to school and on to the worlds of adulthood. Habitus is both structured and structuring (Brooker 1999: 98). It suggests that whilst children's understanding is the product of embodied histories, 'internalised as second nature and so forgotten as history' (Bourdieu 1990: 56), it is 'open to creative variation as the individual meshes with a relatively stable common habitus and conducts this forward'

(Brooker 1999: 98). Cahill (2000: 268) extends these ideas by considering teenagers behaviour out and about within Lower East Side, Manhattan. She describes how the 'rules of the neighbourhood', that is, what is and what is not acceptable, were bound by an invisible hand of mediation. Actions in the public realm were 'constricted and regulated by social practices and state surveillance (the police)'. Accordingly, young people knew their place and, yet, in the spirit of habitus, different groups of young people responded in different ways to these strictures of acceptability. Keeping teenagers 'invisible' and their presence only within the background was seen to be part of the status quo. Others, too (Matthews *et al.* 2000a, 2000b; Sibley 1995; Valentine 1999), have suggested that within urban society streets are an extension of the private domain of adults and that children on the street are seen as out-of-place, a destabilising presence to the social order. Furthermore, as streets are owned by white, middle-class, heterosexual males, women (girls), people of colour (young Blacks), the poor (working-class youths) and young gays and lesbians are especially conspicuous and vulnerable. What the concept of habitus adds to these observations, however, is an understanding of how young people come to accept their place(s) within urban society and how, given the social structures that surround them, they continue to carve out their own diverse cultural spaces. The habitus is thus a generative rather than a static system, 'a basis from which endless improvisation can derive' (Brooker 1999: 98). For as Bourdieu (1990) suggests, once the rules have been 'mastered' and players have a 'feel for the game', in the case of the street, where or where not to hang out and what can be done and what not, individuals and groups can respond to the circumstances of the moment. In the course of this chapter, I shall discuss how children identify, interpret and respond to the habitus of the street and demonstrate the saliency of their agency within this embodied space.

Van Gennep (1909 (1960)) introduced the concept of rite of passage to describe those rituals and practices that define the various stages through which individuals' pass as they journey from childhood to adulthood. Three processes mark it: separation, transition and incorporation. Each process can be played out in different spatial settings. Winchester *et al.* (1999), for example, describe how during 'Schoolies Week' the Gold Coast in Australia acts as a liminal zone between youth and adulthood, the beach becomes a place where people are in transition from one culturally defined stage in the life cycle to another. Sexual gratification, drink and partying are likened to 'rituals of resistance' whereby teenagers throw away the mantles of childhood. For the purpose of this discussion, the street is presented as a liminal space, a place of separation and a domain of transition. Occupancy of the street, particularly with the exodus of adults after dark, enables young people to take on the fluid identity of the hybrid, persons who are not quite adult but no longer child. In this sense, the street represents a place on the margin (Shields 1991), a location in which young people can establish their independence, display their ambivalence and set out their public identity. For as Turner (1969: 26) has suggested, 'liminal phases and states . . . are . . . about the doffing of masks, the stripping of statuses, the renunciation of roles, the demolishing of structures'.

These ideas lead on to a third set of constructs on which this discussion will draw – hybridity (Bhabba 1994; Prout 2000) and syncretism (Back 1996) – both taken from the new cultural politics of identity that has emerged within postcolonial theory. A hybrid combines unlike parts, which may give rise to mixed or contradictory identities. For Bhabba (1994: 219) 'Hybridity is a fraught, anxious and ambivalent condition. It is about how you survive, how you try to produce a sense of agency or identity in situations in which you are continually having to deal with the symbols of power and identity.' Usually used in relation to race and ethnicity and the contradictions that emerge with the colonisation of one people by another, the phase and state of liminality that young people acquire when on the street, associated with the conjunction between a status that they are attempting to shed (childhood) and an emergent public identity (adulthood), can be likened to the process and condition of hybridisation. When hanging around on the street, young people are symbolic of the oppressed hybrid, a group in-between, 'neither One [*adult*] nor the Other [*child*], but something else besides' (Bhabba 1994: 1). Here, too, notions of syncretism abound. Syncretism is 'the combination of different supposedly opposite things' that arises through cross-cultural exchange (Brooker 1999: 243). Just as different juxtaposed ethnic groups may acquire a shared style of behaviour and speech, so through the agency of young people on the street new syncretic cultural behaviours arise that have something of the superordinancy of adults but which are still riddled with the subordinancy of children. For example, the ways in which young people present themselves when out and about may signify their desire to be recognised as socially autonomous, but at the same time their occupancy of marginalised space is redolent of those opportunities presented to the oppressed. From these perspectives the street becomes a *thirdspace*, a dynamic zone of tension and discontinuity where the newness of [syncretic] hybrid identities can be articulated (Matthews *et al.* 2000b: 282).

When drawing upon these notions of liminality, it is important to recognise that there are multiple transitions into adulthood, such that young people will be at various stages, along different paths, with the possibility of each path splitting into a myriad of directions (Matthews and Limb 1999). In effect, difference and diversity are essential ingredients of any childhood. I emphasise the need to recognise the importance of multiple childhoods and the sterility of the concept of the universal child (Aitken 1994; Aitken and Herman 1997). There is a danger, however, in emphasising the diversity of children's everyday lives that the commonality of generationally based exclusion and of their encountered experiences are underplayed. With this in mind, although the street provides a setting for disparate activities, it also is a space that is deeply invested with cultural values that forms part of the spatiality of *growing up*. In the rest of this chapter, through a detailed case study, I consider how the street acts as a site of identity, a gendered space, and a place of contest and how, when taken together, these ideas contribute to an understanding of the street as a cultural borderland.

The case study

The study area comprises a large public housing estate in an East Midlands town. The estate forms a distinct unit, mostly separated from surrounding lower middle-class housing. Since the closure of the local steel mills the area has been blighted by high unemployment. Above-average levels of crime and a large number of single-parent families living in poor and often unsatisfactory conditions contribute to a sense of collective despair. A Young Person's Support Index,[2] a composite measure used to identify children and families in need by the Northamptonshire County Council, places the estate within the highest category of social deprivation within the county. The area is almost exclusively white, with many families comprising first- and second-generation migrants from Scotland.

The data were derived by means of a doorstep questionnaire survey (n = 140), semi-structured interviews with groups of young people on the street and in-depth discussions held over a series of sessions with mixed-sex and single-sex groups aged 10 to 11 years, 13 to 14 years and 15 to 16 years. The nature of the project was fully explained to all prospective participants, letters of consent from parents or guardians confirmed their willingness to get involved and there was no coercion to take part. Each member of the research team was registered as an outreach youth worker. Wherever possible, in order to get as close as possible to their life worlds, the voices of these young people are incorporated into the text.[3]

The street as a site of identity: cultural crevices and social fissures

The ways in which young people used the street varied by age. For those aged 11 and under, the street was a setting for games, play and adventure. By the age of 13, however, the street was a social haven, a place for meeting with friends, hanging out and 'where things happened' (Table 7.1). For older teenagers, in particular, the street offered opportunities 'to get away from it', sites that offered the freedom and excitement of separation away from the 'humdrum' of daily life.

Despite a lack of formal provision of outdoor spaces in which young people could congregate, for a significant proportion street life was a daily routine. During the summer months, particularly when not at school, nearly half (49 per cent) of the sample used local streets on a daily basis to meet up with friends and even during winter, after school, about a quarter (27 per cent) of all young people regularly met up with each other (Table 7.2). There was some variation with age, with streets becoming more important as stamping grounds during the teenage years. For many young people the street was the

Table 7.1 Most popular activities carried out on the street by age group, % (frequency)

	9–10 years	11–12 years	13–14 years	15–16 years
Informal sport (football, cricket)	31 (8)	29 (8)	27 (12)	21 (9)
Just play	23 (6)	21 (6)	7 (3)	1 (1)
Meet/hang about with friends	19 (5)	25 (7)	30 (13)	38 (16)
'Get away from it'	–	7 (2)	11 (5)	24 (10)
Do nothing	8 (2)	7 (2)	18 (8)	12 (4)
Other activities	19 (5)	11 (3)	7 (3)	4 (2)

Table 7.2 Making use of the street as a place to meet friends, % (frequency)

	9–10 years	11–12 years	13–14 years	15–16 years
Meet friends daily on the street in summer	42 (11)	43 (12)	52 (23)	52 (22)
Meet friends regularly on the street after school in winter (two or more days a week)	15 (4)	18 (5)	32 (14)	36 (15)
Never use the street as a place to meet friends	35 (9)	29 (8)	32 (14)	29 (12)
Never or rarely have friends visit at home	46 (12)	39 (11)	53 (23)	55 (23)

only place where they were able to meet with their peers, with two-fifths of those aged 13 and under and about a half of those aged 16 and under reporting that they never or rarely have friends visit them at home.

The amount of time spent on the streets formed an important part of the day for many young people (Table 7.2). For example, of those regularly using the street in the summer to meet friends, more than two-thirds (68 per cent) spent more than six hours of each day outside of their homes. During the winter as well, four-fifths (80 per cent) of those aged 13 to 16 years who were regular street users commonly spent four or more hours of each day after school with friends out and about. When asked whether they regarded themselves as an indoor or outdoor person more than 70 per cent of 9-year-olds claimed the former. From the age of 13 onwards more than four-fifths of all young people suggested that they were outdoor types.

These observations highlight how streets are places of affordance for young people, in that they offer settings where they can be together, seemingly away from the adult gaze. Unlike their elders who have many social opportunities available to them to mix and meet with friends, for example through their clubs, pubs and places of residence, young people have fewer opportunities, access or obvious rights to such settings. Indeed, for many young people the street is the only place where they can meet informally. As such, streets are places where adultist conventions and moralities about what it is to be a child – that is, less-than-adult – can be put aside. They are spaces that are temporarily outside of adult society, particularly with the withdrawal of adults at particular times of the day (Sibley 1995), fluid domains or a thirdspace set between childhood and adulthood, where the process of separation can be played out (Matthews *et al.* 2000c). Within these interstitial spaces young people can express feelings of belonging and of being apart and celebrate a developing sense of selfhood. In essence, therefore, streets can be grouped among those places where the newness of hybrid identities, no longer a child not yet adult, may be articulated (Rose 1995).

Yet here is a cultural dilemma, for whilst streets appear to offer freedom away from adult mores, occupancy of the public domain is rarely uncontested, particularly when young people come into contact with vigilant adults who are not prepared to relinquish their overarching control. In order to remain on the street, therefore, young people carve out their own *cultural crevices*, and create their own *social fissures*. Often these are places where adults are not commonly found: in this study children regularly congregated in back alleys, on derelict land, around lock-up garages, at the rear of shopping parades, in pockets of green space within neighbouring scrub woodland, in essence, within the forgotten and redundant spaces of the adult world.

The street as a gendered space: boys and girls come out to play

There is a growing recognition that streets are no longer just the leisure domains of boys (Matthews *et al.* 2000c; Skelton 2000). Indeed, recent studies have suggested that with the advent of computer and video games, the home is (re)becoming a significant male leisure site (McNamee 1998). Like the teenage girls of the Rhondda, south Wales (Skelton 2000), where the streets and local parks were the only public spaces where they could spend their spare time, many of the girls participating in this survey similarly reported how they regularly congregated together in outdoor places. Nearly two-thirds of all girls (64 per cent) described themselves as outdoor people. With little money to spend and in the absence of affordable local entertainment, these girls (like many young boys) commonly sought out nooks and crannies within the neighbourhood where they could meet and chat without fear of interruption. 'We're out here from about half six to about half nine, ten' (Girl, aged 13). 'And during the day as well when we're off school. At the end of the day maybe we go in for our dinner, but sometimes we just stay out all day' (Girl, aged 14).

When out alone, however, girls were much more fearful than boys. Nearly two-thirds of all girls suggested they were fearful when out alone, compared to fewer than one-third of boys (Table 7.3). There was also a variation by age (Table 7.4). Younger girls, in particular, were especially fearful and even by the age of 16 girls continued to express considerable anxiety. The reasons for

Table 7.3 Experience of fear when out alone, all boys and girls aged 9–16, % (frequency)

	Yes	No
Male	28 (20)	72 (52)
Female	63 (43)	37 (25)

Table 7.4 Experience of fear when out alone, by sex and age group, % (frequency)

	9–10 years	11–12 years	13–14 years	15–16 years
Male	38 (5)	29 (4)	27 (6)	24 (5)
Female	85 (11)	71 (10)	59 (13)	43 (9)

these fears also differed. Whereas boys were most likely to suggest environmental reasons – for example, 'fear of traffic' was mentioned by more than three-quarters of all male respondents compared to less than two-fifths of girls – girls were more inclined to mention social fears such as 'fear of strangers' (30 per cent), 'fear of being attacked' (18 per cent) and 'fear of bullies and gangs' (13 per cent). Although assaults on young women within the estate were rare events (the last reported incident having occurred more than two years prior to the study), the established habitus equipped these girls with sets of values that guided their outdoor behaviours. In response, a typical coping strategy was to go out with others wherever possible. When with friends fewer than one-third of girls (29 per cent) and fewer than one-fifth of boys (17 per cent) suggested that they felt afraid. 'There's a group of us that goes round together . . . we're just a posse really. Just loads of friends. We always stick together . . . Just wander about' (Girl, aged 14).

The places occupied by boys and girls were often different, particularly when in the company with others of their own sex. Younger boys, for example, congregated together where they could take part in strenuous activities such as football, basketball, skateboarding, rollerblading and cycling. Plots of open land, spaces with brick walls, derelict sites, school fields during the early evening, all provided opportunities for the rough and tumble of boisterous play. Younger girls, on the other hand, sought sanctuary in places where they could just talk, walk about and enjoy each other's company: seemingly, the public domain of girls was more fluid and changeable than that of boys.

In seeking places to hang out, some girls suggested that their access to public space was constrained by the presence of boys, a finding also noted by Tucker and Matthews (2001) in their study of rural children. For example, particular parts of the estate were strongly identified as boys' places. Here groups of male teenagers would meet to drink, smoke and chat. When these boys were around, girls regarded these sites as unsafe and undesirable. 'There's this group of lads right . . . who just act smart . . . drinking, smoking . . . mucking around . . . we don't go near them' (Girl, aged 13).

In contrast, no sites were identified as girls' places. Instead, where boys held social control, many girls felt compelled to stay on the outside. Rather than contesting their right of presence, these girls chose to spend their time on the move or sought opportunities where they could go beyond the estate, for example window shopping with friends. As Matthews *et al.* (2000c: 74) have noted, the dynamic and transient nature of girls' neighbourhood space is perhaps 'one reason why girls were once taken as invisible in discourses about youth subcultures'. 'We walk around, me, Tania, Joely and Ann Louise, checking things out . . . round by the shops is good . . . but then we walk a little bit further and there's a whole lot going on' (Girl, aged 11).

The street as a place of contest: knowing your place

Cahill (2000) introduces the concept of *street literacy* to suggest ways in which young people *read* and make sense of the implicit rules of the neighbourhood. *Knowing your place*, that is, where and where not to go, what to do and when, is indelibly, yet invisibly, inscribed into the environment. Understanding the semiotics of the street is an important part of growing up, and for the youngest children many of these messages are inevitably acquired through the primary habitus of the family and taken on. Heightening children's awareness to possible danger in order to prepare them for forays beyond the home is a formative aspect of socialisation. Within different families and their neighbourhoods, different stories will be told about the dangers that lurk beyond the front door. The harsher and the more blighted an environment, the wilder these stories may be. So, for example, within the narratives of these 9- and 10-year-old children urban myths abound. Some recounted how fearsome strangers would be waiting to pounce should they stray down dark alleys; others how, if playing too far away from home, they would be kidnapped by child-snatchers; whilst in woods and derelict land big black cats prowled waiting for some tasty morsel.

> [So, if you are out and about, playing, where you normally play? What do you think is the biggest danger that you face? What's the thing that frightens you most?]
>
> Being kidnapped . . . my cousin, yeah . . . she was staying and my friends came round . . . Joanna and Stephanie, Christopher and Sophie . . . my cousin . . . goes I'll come round to the garages and . . . we went down there like eight o'clock and we were still there at half nine and these black men were looking at us and I got all worried and that . . . and I remember my mum saying that there's these people who'll take you away . . . we were really frightened and came home.
>
> (Girl, aged 10)

There was these two ladies, riding round the block in their cars when me and my brother and my mates were playing out and I was round my mate's house and . . . my mate's mum said we'd better come in soon because you don't know whether they are kidnappers or not . . . and five minutes after they said that one of the ladies what was in the car . . . grabbed my brother but he punched her in the stomach and he got away. So I don't like playing out very much because this man in a white car keeps going round the block.

(Girl, aged 10)

My auntie lives three doors away from the park and me and my cousin went to go there, right? And when we went on the roundabout there was this great big black thing and I said 'what's that?' He said it was probably just a man walking across . . . the field and I said 'no it's not, it's walking really, really slowly and looking at us' and it was the panther, the black panther . . . And my auntie, yeah . . . She was talking to her friend outside of her house, she came and she looked out and she actually saw the panther, it was outside of her house and . . . she turned round to talk to her friend and . . . her friend had ran into her house and locked herself in.

(Girl, aged 11)

Through such stories and the production of fear young children acquire a sense of which places are in or out-of-bounds. Amongst the youngest children, safe places were commonly regarded as parks, places where they could be seen by observant adults, small patches of open ground in cul-de-sacs and, at night, well-lit places where they could gather and chat.

Pen Green Park is safe . . . it's safe there in the mornings cause there's people there . . . one of them's called Kate . . . she looks after the nursery where my brother is . . . that building's there too . . . and they're often out in the park . . . and we can play near them then.

(Girl, aged 9)

For older teenagers, however, different sets of rules come into play. These are acquired through repeated transactions with place and their own developing routines, aptitudes and assumptions. Lieberg (1995), for example, distinguishes two kinds of social realm currently available to young people: places of retreat and places of social interaction. Each type of place is imbued with social meaning. Places of retreat are backstage places, areas away from the adult gaze, where teenagers can pull back and withdraw from the adult world to be with one's own peers, that is 'the backyards, stairwells, basements, parking lots, or other isolated places' (Lieberg 1995: 722). 'It's quiet down there at night [*local park*] . . . no one's hassling you . . . we just sit around . . . chilling out' (Boy, aged 15).

Places of interaction, on the other hand, are on stage, where young people are on display and out and about to see and to be seen by others. For this group of young people, the local shopping precinct, despite its austerity, acted as a convenient social theatre providing an important venue for young people to gather and show off their new clothes, hairstyles and affiliations with popular culture. Body language and gestures, too, across an entire range of behaviours marked these young people out. Conspicuous occupancy of this kind may be interpreted, drawing upon the work of Bourdieu (1992), as part of a deliberate ploy, a state that arises through confidence with the rules (and a feel for the game). These young people know the limits of their acceptability within the public domain and are prepared to test its boundaries. For, as Brooker (1999: 98) suggests, habitus is also 'embodied', articulated in this case by the syncretic styles, actions and comportment of these young people, that is, choosing not to be labelled as child, yet at the same time standing apart from onlooking adults.

> It's where everybody comes . . . to meet . . . It's where everybody hangs out, sits on walls, smokes cigarettes, chats. It's a place where you're likely to meet with lots of other people . . . Where you meet your mates . . . try to figure out what our next move is going to be.
>
> (Boy, aged 16)

There is a temporal dimension, too, in how young people use places. For example, others (Matthews *et al.* 1998; Sibley 1995) have noted how parks after dark, with the retreat of younger children and their guardians, become important meeting places for teenagers. In this study, for example, the narratives of those aged over 13 repeatedly refer to a place known locally as West Glebe [Park], which offered a sanctuary of retreat during the evening. Other valued places at night included the backyard of a launderette near the outlet pipes, where young people could gather and warm themselves, and amidst the waste skips located at the back of a local pub that was being refurbished, from which cushions and parts of chairs could be extracted for informal seating. 'Kwik Wash or something . . . It's really warm round the back by the pipes . . . we meet there most nights when it's cold . . . we can have a laugh there . . . and keep warm' (Girl, aged 14).

Vying for control (Cahill 2000: 263) is an implicit part of the occupancy of most neighbourhood spaces. McLaughlin (1993) develops the concept of *embedded identities* to describe how young people use place(s) as a means to develop their own identities. What she suggests is that locality matters and, to some extent, shapes how young people grow up. These ideas resonate with the earlier work of James (1986) that focuses on the different forms of cultural expression that distinguish different group identities. She suggests that group identity is maintained by using markers such as style to define boundaries to the self and others. James (1986: 167) states that cultural style amongst adolescents is primarily body-based, such that boundaries to the body represent the boundaries of the self. James goes on to argue that it is not just a matter of how to look, but also how to act stylishly through performance that defines cultural identity. The exercise of power, for example, through displays of machismo by adolescent boys, is one way in which boundaries between self and other are explored, tested and negotiated. When these performances are extended into various place settings, such as the home, school and neighbourhood, what arises is a complex turf politics of inter-personal and inter-group relationships, an expression of differences in power and identity between groups. As a result, different groups will have different spatial and temporal calls upon and ties with the physical landscape. Within the estate, for example, access to particular sites depended upon an explicit pecking order. As a rule of thumb, older groups had priority over younger groups, and certain gangs had ascendancy over others. There was a keen awareness of these rules of the road. For example, the 'Stephenson Way Crew', a mixed-aged, mixed-sex gang of older teenagers, enjoyed notoriety throughout the locality. Others generally kept away from places where this Crew hung out.

> At the corner of Stephenson Road, down that end, the furthest bit . . . we doesn't go there no more. We were riding round the corner and they said 'Oi you can't go on that bit of pavement because that's ours.' So I carried on riding round and they knocked me off my bike . . . on another part of Stephenson Road we were walking round the corner to come and see Paul and these big teenagers . . . they were about eighteen to nineteen and some of them were even twenty-one, and they had big sticks and were circling around and, and once Daniel was on his own and he was coming round to my house and they knocked Daniel over and Daniel had an asthma attack and they gave him a karate kick and when he had enough energy . . . he ran away . . . that's a no go area for us.
>
> (Boy, aged 13)

> you get like different areas, like the Westies . . . you have a Westies Crew and a Pleasure Crew at Pleasure Park and a North Park Crew . . . The Pleasure Park Crew, they normally meet on a Friday night . . . we just have a laugh there . . . there's a lot like us
> [So the different crew from different places don't mix with each other?]
> Sometimes, it depends whether they have a fall-out.
> [What sort of age group is this?]
> They go from about twelve to eighteen and some people who's like losers come down until about twenty-one.
> [Is this mixed groups?]
> Yeah.
>
> (Girl, aged 13)

Younger children, too, demonstrated a heightened understanding of the limits of their place acceptability with their elders. Misreading of these implicit rules led to possible intra-generational conflict.

> I'm not exactly scared but these teenagers are always hanging round our street and threatening us with knives. But I'm not exactly scared, I just ride away . . . I haven't seen it but one of my friends said that the teenagers have drugs and that's why I stay in my garden cause I'm scared.
>
> (Boy, aged 10)

> In the local basketball court . . . [in the park] . . . it is mostly overrun by teenagers and it doesn't give me or anybody else a chance to play basketball or football in the courts and it's just not fair because they've overrun it . . . I just don't think it's fair . . . if we try to get in and say it's our turn they chase us away.
>
> (Boy, aged 12)

Also strongly marked out were the boundary lines drawn by vigilant adults. Spatial and temporal bands, which determined where or where not young people would be tolerated, criss-crossed the environment. Transgressions, often frequently trivial, inevitably led to clashes. Valentine (1997) notes how media reports of child gangs and unruly and troublesome youths mobilise fears that all groups of young people hanging around together are potentially up to no good. Within urban neighbourhoods, given their containment by private property and the limited nature of public open space, many of the places where children like to meet are often highly visible and exposed, such as around local shops or in a bus shelter. From their responses there was a clear sense that many young people felt unwelcome and under scrutiny when out and about. Children of all ages reported how adults frequently intervened in their social activities in order to (re)impose control and order.

> There's this small green bit of land down the road from us . . . I like to go there with me mates to play football . . . it's the only place nearby because of the traffic . . . there's this woman . . . and even if we're standing there she tells us to go away . . . we can't play there . . . 'No ball games allowed', she says.
>
> (Boy, aged 12)

> Me and my friends and my brother were sitting on the wall down by the shops . . . and this man comes flying out of one the shops and says what do we think we're doing there . . . we say, nothing just chatting and that . . . he goes mad and says go away we're trouble . . . we weren't doing nothing.
>
> (Boy, aged 14)

> Say you were standing round, hanging round there, people report you to the police, and say, 'Oh they're breaking into houses' and you get blamed for things you didn't do.
>
> (Girl, aged 13)

Jones's (2000: 37) suggestion that spaces commonly comprise several types is useful when considering adult responses to the visibility of children in the public domain. First there are *monomorphic* spaces, sites frequently dominated by a particular use that exclude the possibility of *other* uses. Then there are *polymorphic* spaces, 'which are in use within adult structures but which can also accommodate subordinate "other" uses' (Jones 2000: 38). Lastly, there are *disordered spaces*, places that can be in some way be *otherable*, 'in that children can use and reconstruct them without incurring the outright hostility and opposition of adults' (Jones 2000: 37). For example, a shopping mall is a monomorphic space, a temple of consumption, where the visible presence of young people who are neither shopping nor spending money means that their behaviour is beyond the pale (Matthews *et al.* 2000b). On the estate, for example, young people who gathered in a warm cranny at the rear of a public house, a bastion of male adulthood, were deemed as highly undesirable and regularly chased away. Similarly, when they were too near a local parade of shops, a convenient and well-lit meeting point, shopkeepers frequently moved these teenagers on. However, when the same group reassembled on nearby derelict land, a place largely abandoned by adults, although they were still visible and doing nothing different, their presence was tolerated. In a different vein, with nightfall poorly lit alleyways that provided adults with well-used short cuts during the day, but which were avoided with the onset of darkness, were spaces that young people could colonise without threat of intervention.

Conclusion

Skelton (2000: 81) and others (James *et al.* 1998; Sibley 1995) draw attention to how cultural meanings and interpretations often rely on the construction of binaries. One side of a binary is usually regarded as the obverse of the other and is invariably of a lesser order. Binaries frequently incorporate assumptions that shape actions and determine opportunities. Of core significance to the way in which young people are regarded within many western societies[4] is the notion of an adult/child binary. Implicit within this construction is that children are less-than-adult or adults-in-the-making, a script firmly written into legislation and played out across a broad range of social institutions and through social practices. Binaries, however, frequently obscure the import-ance of social agency, especially on the part of the oppressed, and obfuscate the importance of transition. Indeed, binaries imply sudden change, such that with the onset of an age-given threshold children will move effortlessly into adulthood.

Binaries, however, frequently lead to ambiguities, especially within par-ticular spatial or temporal settings where the boundaries of social acceptability may be transgressed. From this study and other recent studies (see reviews in Holloway and Valentine 2000; Skelton and Valentine 1998) the street emerges as one such *fuzzy zone*, a place that offers children the space and opportunity to pull away from the constraints of childhood, but in which their presence is seen as uncomfortable and discrepant by many adults. Through their disordering of adult space, as a result of their crossing of spatial or temporal boundaries (Jones 2000), children enter into a liminal world of hybridity and in-betweeness. For the majority of young people, however, their occupancy of the street was not a deliberate attempt to provoke the mores and sensibilities of vigilant adults. Indeed, from the surveys there was a sense that the street was neither a symbolic site for cultural resistance nor a place where adult values – such as those that comprise the prevailing habitus, which requires the invisibility of children in the public domain – were challenged as a matter of course. There was little, too, that could be described as spectacular or carnavalesque. For as Corrigan (1979) has noted, rule-breaking acts are not the normality of hanging out. Instead, young people were simply out and about on the street as there was nowhere else to go and nothing else to do.

Other socially constructed binaries, too, are frequently contested within the confines of the street. For example, notions that outdoor places are masculine spaces, where only older boys choose to congregate is not supported by this or other recent studies (for example, Matthews *et al.* 2000a, 2000b, 2000c; Skelton 2000). On this estate, children of both sexes, from a young age, used the street as an important social haunt. The recent work of James (1995) provides a useful context for understanding children's occupancy of and behaviour in these public domains. Researching the acquisition of language, she sees children as active agents capable of developing their own social argot, often at odds with adult formulations. In essence, adults provide the limits and rules of language but children will develop their own vocabulary and particular patterns of use. Through their own discourse children carve out their own identities, and 'patterns of belonging are laid down' (James 1995: 59). James suggests that there is a temporal culture which children move into and out of during the process of their socialisation. Each step along this social transition is associated with patterns of language and behaviour that defines membership. Likewise, in their physical worlds children are active cultural producers. Adults produce their own patterns of land use and consumption, and children learn to operate within this framework, in this case carving out their own cultural locations. Street corners, local shopping parades and public parks are *cultural gateways* that afford sites of passage where young people can meet, share and create their own syncretic identities (a volatile cocktail of their own cultures and those of their elders) that will in due course lead to their admission to the world of adults.

Lastly, I suggest that streets are sites of latent contradiction for many young people, marginal places that are simultaneously dangerous and yet empowering. For as Bhabba (1994) contends, the very act of colonisation, in this case young people's occupancy of the street, shifts certainties and sureties. By crossing the borders of identity, literally by hanging out in these adult spaces, young people challenge both its and their definition. We have observed too, as Bhabba (1994) has shown elsewhere, the pain that results through displacement and the triumph of psychological survival. Turner's (1969, 1974) earlier ideas are particularly salient to my concluding observations. Some thirty years ago, Turner turned his attention to van Gennep's notion of the rites of passage. He went on to propose that 'man' [*sic*] is both a 'structural' and an 'anti-structural' entity. Structure, Turner suggested, is all that holds people apart, defines their difference and constrains their actions. Anti-structure, on the other hand, is any condition or state that exists outside or on the boundaries or edges of everyday life. Times and places of transition, where anti-structure comes into being, are always liminal, 'temporally, spatially and socially ambiguous, unsettled and unsettling' (Turner 1974: 274). Accordingly, in these terms streets are domains of anti-structure, one of the places where young people push up against the limits, establish their hybridity and set out on a transition towards incorporation into the adult world.

Acknowledgements

I am very grateful to my colleagues Mark Taylor and Melanie Limb who assisted with the data collection and to all of the young people who gave up their time to take part in this project. Grants from the ESRC Children 5–16: Growing into the 21st Century research programme (Award No. L129251031) and the Nuffield Foundation made much of this research possible.

Notes

1 The term *the street* is used as a metaphor for all public outdoor places in which children are found, such as roads, cul-de-sacs, alleyways, walkways, shopping areas, car parks, vacant plots and derelict sites (see Matthews *et al.* 2000a and b).
2 The index was based on a set of indicators associated with the risk of children being taken into care.
3 For reasons of confidentiality, the voices of the young people are anonymised. At the outset of every interview and discussion group assurance was given that the views to be recorded would not be attributable to any individual or to any specific location – this guarantee was provided so that the young people would be secure in knowing that they could talk freely and openly about matters close to their daily experiences without fear of recourse or comeback.
4 The notion of western societies is used to refer to shared sets of values that transcend geographical milieux.

References

Aitken, S., 1994, *Putting Children in their Place* (Washington, DC: Association of American Geographers).
Aitken, S. and Herman, T., 1997, 'Gender, power and crib geography: transitional spaces and potential places'. *Gender, Place and Culture*, 4 (1), 63–88.
Back, L., 1996, *New Ethnicities and Urban Culture* (London: University College London Press).
Bhabba, H., 1994, *The Location of Culture* (New York: Routledge).

Bourdieu, P., 1977, *Outline of a Theory of Practice* (Cambridge: Cambridge University Press).

Bourdieu, P., 1990, *The Logic of Practice* (Cambridge: Polity Press).

Bourdieu, P. with Wacquant, L., 1992, *An Invitation to Reflexive Sociology* (Cambridge, Polity Press).

Brooker, P., 1999, *A Concise Glossary of Cultural Theory* (London: Arnold).

Cahill, C., 2000, 'Street literacy: urban teenagers' strategies for negotiating their neighbourhood'. *Journal of Youth Studies*, 3 (3), 251–78.

Corrigan, P., 1979, *Schooling the Smash Street Kids* (Basingstoke: Macmillan).

Holloway, S. L. and Valentine, G. (eds), 2000, *Children's Geographies: Playing, Living, Learning* (London: Routledge).

James, A., 1986, 'Learning to belong: the boundaries of adolescence'. In A. P. Cohen (ed.), *Symbolising Boundaries* (Manchester: Manchester University Press).

James, A., 1995, 'Talking of children and youth: language, socialisation and culture'. In V. Amit-Talai and H. Wulff (eds), *Youth Cultures: A Cross-Cultural Perspective* (London: Routledge).

James, A., Jenks, C. and Prout, A., 1998, *Theorizing Childhood* (Cambridge: Polity Press).

Jones, O., 2000, 'Melting geography: purity, disorder, childhood and space'. In S. L. Holloway and G. Valentine (eds), *Children's Geographies: Playing, Living, Learning* (London: Routledge).

Lieberg, M., 1995, 'Teenagers and public space'. *Communication Research*, 22 (3), 720–44.

McLaughlin, M., 1993, 'Embedded identities'. In S. Heath and M. McLaughlin (eds), *Identity and Inner City Youth: Beyond Ethnicity and Gender* (New York: Teachers College Press).

McNamee, S., 1998, 'Youth, gender and video games: power and control in the home'. In Skelton and Valentine (eds), *Cool Places: Geographies of Youth Cultures* (London: Routledge).

Matthews, H. and Limb, M., 1999, 'Defining an agenda for the geography of children: review and prospect'. *Progress in Human Geography*, 23 (1), 61–90.

Matthews, H., Limb, M. and Percy-Smith, B., 1998, 'Changing worlds: the microgeographies of young teenagers'. *Tijdschrift voor Economische en Sociale Geografie*, 89 (2), 193–202.

Matthews, H., Limb, M. and Taylor, M., 2000a, 'Reclaiming the street: the discourse of curfew'. *Environment and Planning A*, 31 (10), 1713–30.

Matthews, H., Taylor, M., Percy-Smith, B. and Limb, M., 2000b, 'The unacceptable *flaneur*: the shopping mall as a teenage hangout'. *Childhood*, 7 (3), 279–94.

Matthews, H., Limb, M. and Taylor, M., 2000c, 'The street as thirdspace'. In S. L. Holloway and G. Valentine (eds), *Children's Geographies: Playing, Living, Learning* (London: Routledge).

Prout, A., 2000, 'Childhood bodies: construction, agency and hybridity'. In Prout (ed.), *The Body, Childhood and Society* (Basingstoke: Macmillan).

Rose, G., 1995, 'The interstitial perspective: a review essay on Homi Bhabha's "The Location of Culture"'. *Environment and Planning D: Society and Space*, 13, 365–73.

Shields, R., 1991, 'Ritual pleasures of a seaside resort: liminality, carnivalesque and dirty weekends'. In Shields (ed.), *Places on the Margin: Alternative Geographies of Modernity* (London: Routledge).

Sibley, D., 1995, *Geographies of Exclusion* (London: Routledge).

Skelton, T., 2000, ' "Nothing to do, nowhere to go?" Teenage girls and "public" space in Rhondda Valleys, south Wales'. In Holloway and Valentine (eds), *Children's Geographies: Playing, Living, Learning* (London: Routledge).

Skelton, T. and Valentine, G., 1998, *Cool Places: Geographies of Youth Cultures* (London: Routledge).

Tucker, F. and Matthews, H., 2001, ' "They don't like girls hanging around there": conflicts over recreational space in rural Northamptonshire'. *Area*, 31 (2), 161–80.

Turner, V., 1969, *The Ritual Process: Structure and Anti-Structure* (London: Routledge and Kegan Paul).

Turner, V., 1974, *Dramas, Fields, and Metaphors: Symbolic Action in Human Society* (Ithaca: Cornell University Press).

Valentine, G., 1997, ' "Oh yes I can". "Oh no you can't": children and parents' understanding of kids competence to negotiate public space safely'. *Antipode*, 29, 65–89.

Valentine, G., 1999, ' "Oh please, Mum. Oh please, dad", negotiating children's spatial boundaries'. In M. McKie, S. Bowlby and S. Gregory (eds), *Gender, Power and the Household* (Basingstoke: Macmillan).

Van Gennep, A., 1909 (1960), *The Rites of Passage* (London: Routledge and Kegan Paul).

Winchester, H., McGuirk, P. and Everett, K., 1999, ' "Schoolies Week" as a rite of passage'. In E. Teather (ed.), *Embodied Geographies: Spaces, Bodies and Rites of Passage* (London: Routledge).

Neighbourhood quality
in children's eyes

Louise Chawla and Karen Malone

'To depict the child is to depict the city'

So stated Victor Hugo in *Les Misérables* (cited in Aitken and Ginsberg 1988: 69). Broad as this claim is, there are a number of ways in which it can be argued to be true. Cities are the cultural and political centres of their societies, and how they treat their children and other vulnerable inhabitants is a basic measure of whether they are negligent and cruel or generous and humane. Therefore a city's political and moral dimensions can be judged by the condition of its children, in terms of their health, opportunities for development and sense of well-being. When it comes to the future, the child of today is the city-maker of tomorrow. To predict the probable future outline of a city, it is necessary to look, again, at the condition of its children.

Historically, the child was also considered an expert on the panorama of the city's streets and yards, who slipped most mobilely through its public spaces, a shrewd observer of its seasons and all levels of its society (Ward 1978). It is in this sense that Hugo chose the child, 'the outspoken sparrow', to study 'this eagle', the city. Through the eyes of the child, he as a novelist could best depict the city in all its complex and conflicting expressions of negligence, cruelty, generosity and humanity.

This chapter examines cities through these different dimensions. It emphasises understanding how cities appear to children themselves, and compares their priorities in using and evaluating their cities to adult-defined indicators of urban quality for children.[1] In doing so, it draws primarily on material from Growing Up in Cities (GUIC), an international effort to understand young people's own perspectives on the urban environment and their own proposals for change. The chapter also describes possibilities for enlisting children in studying and shaping their cities, to help prepare them to be city-makers of the most informed and confident kind. Therefore it will close by featuring two innovative Australian locations of GUIC that illustrate different ways of moving from research with young people to engaging their ideas, energy and creativity in processes of urban change.

Growing Up in Cities uses participatory action research to involve young people in low- and mixed-income districts in evaluating their urban environments and collaborating with adults to plan and implement improvements. The project was initiated in the 1970s by Kevin Lynch (1977), an urban designer and advocacy planner, who co-ordinated project locations in four countries under the sponsorship of UNESCO. In 1995, the project was revived and implemented in eight countries with the support of the MOST (Management of Social Transformations) Programme of UNESCO, Childwatch International, the Norwegian Centre for Child Research and other sponsoring organisations. This phase of the project, which mainly involved 10–15-year-olds, has been described in Chawla (2002) and Driskell (2002). Since this time, the project has continued to spread to new locations.[2]

Growing Up in Cities has gathered a wealth of material about how children use and evaluate their cities. Typically, participants engage in a variety of activities, including interviews, drawings of their area, small-group discussions, child-led walks and child-taken photographs and commentaries. Participants are male and female, and at different project sites their numbers have ranged from around twenty to more than a hundred. Project facilitators also document each location's history, geography, economy and demographics; observe the roles that young people play in local public life; and talk with parents, community leaders and urban officials about their views of how the city functions for its children. Wherever possible, this information is then used as the basis for the design of programmes and places for young people and more child-sensitive urban policies. This chapter will begin by summarising how the young people at GUIC sites in the 1970s and 1990s evaluated their city environments: the urban qualities that, in their view, alienate them from their societies and surroundings or create a good place in which to grow up.

Young people's urban values across place and time

Growing Up in Cities seeks to work in representative urban areas or areas undergoing rapid change, where a better understanding of children's experience can influence policy-making and the practice of urban planning and design. Since the project was first conceived in the 1970s, its goals have gained new relevance, given the principle of children's right to participation in decisions that affect their lives according to the Convention on the Rights of the Child, and the extension of this right to decisions that affect their environments, according to the United Nations Conference on Environment and Development (United Nations 1992), the Second United Nations Conference on Human Settlements (UNCHS 1997), and Local Agenda 21 processes (Chawla 2001).

With these goals, the project has worked in a wide range of environments: in self-built settlements in Mexico City, Caracas, Bangalore and Johannesburg; in communities with high rates of immigrant families in Trondheim (Norway) and Oakland (California, USA); in an indigenous community in Port Moresby (Papua New Guinea); in old working-class neighbourhoods in Trondheim, Warsaw, Buenos Aires and Northampton; in peripheral postwar developments in Toluca (Mexico), Salta (Argentina), Melbourne, Warsaw and Cracow; and in the historic city centres of Saida (Lebanon), Warsaw and Cracow. In addition, clusters of communities have been studied in Johannesburg, Göteborg (Sweden) and Frankston (Australia).

In comparing the eight urban communities in the 1970s with the sixteen communities where research has been completed since 1995, some differences are evident. Participants spoke about crime, violence, drugs, environmental pollution, and racial and ethnic tension more often in the 1990s than in the 1970s. Although heavy traffic was already a problem in Toluca and the city centres of Cracow and Warsaw in the 1970s, it had become a much more pervasive danger and competitor for public space in the 1990s. Television, likewise, had become a more pervasive competitor for young people's time. In the 1990s, it was also not unusual for children to live in a single-parent family. Another difference was that in the 1970s, before the Convention on the Rights of the Child and its principle of children's right to participation, there were no questions asked about children's sense of political influence. In the 1990s, when this subject was explored, young people around the world, in well-established democracies as well as newly struggling ones, expressed a general sense of powerlessness and disbelief that adults would ever take their ideas seriously. As a 13-year-old boy in Northampton, England, expressed it: 'People like politicians and stuff don't really know what we want to do ... They just think, "Oh he's just a little kid, what does he know?"' (quoted in Percy-Smith 2002: 78).

Despite these differences in the project results in the 1970s and 1990s, there were many strong similarities in the ways that young people evaluated their cities then and now, as well as across locations. Lynch (1977) began GUIC with the assumption that comparative studies that would be accurate enough to inform policy decisions would need to be limited to single nations and cultures; but, in reviewing the eight urban locations that he co-ordinated, he conceded that 'the similarities we find in these disparate cases indicate the possibility of some human constants in the way children use their world' (Lynch 1977: 12). More extensive research in the 1990s reaffirmed the elements that bind children to their places with satisfaction and a sense of belonging or leave them frustrated and isolated.

Indicators of integration

In planning the revival of GUIC, in 1996 project directors from each country met for initial training in the project's principles and methods, and reconvened a year later to review their analyses of results. (For detailed case studies of each location see Chawla 2002.) From the beginning, people were encouraged to innovate by adding methods of particular use under local conditions; but a careful effort was also made to maintain a common core of methods across locations in order to make cross-site comparisons possible and to be able to compare project results in the 1990s with results in the 1970s. Based on this first phase of the project's revival, a set of child-based indicators was derived that summarised positive and negative community characteristics from children's perspectives. New project sites since this time have reaffirmed their relevance.

In their interviews, GUIC children talked about how well their environment functioned for them. They were asked to draw the area in which they lived and discuss their drawings. They were also asked: How would you describe the area where you live? Where do you best like to be in your area? Are there places where you don't like to go? Are there dangerous places? Are there any places that feel like your own? Are there places where you feel like an outsider? Has this area where you live changed in your memory? Has it got better or worse? If you could travel into the future, what do you think this place would be like in ten years time? If you could make changes in your place, what would they be? Ten years from now, where would you like to live? At most project sites, children also took photographs to illustrate positive and problematic features of their environment, and led researchers on neighbourhood walks to show the places they frequented and avoided. If most participants described their area in positive terms, identified many nearby places where they liked to go, believed that conditions were changing for the better and wanted to continue to live where they were, then the local environment was considered to satisfy children's own place priorities.

Places that children described in predominantly positive terms varied widely in geography. Although no place was without problems, young people frequently expressed contentment with their community in four out of the initial eight cities in the project revival: Bangalore, Buenos Aires, Warsaw and Trondheim. These locations included a self-built settlement for rural migrants in India and an old industrial river port district in Argentina, within economies of great disparity between rich and poor; a relatively poor district in the transitional economy of Poland; and two well-maintained old districts in the prosperous social-welfare state of Norway. According to the Human Development Index calculated by the United Nations Development Programme in 1997, when the project results were recorded, India, Poland, Argentina and Norway ranked respectively 138th, 58th, 36th and 3rd in terms of life expectancy, education and average incomes (UNDP 1997). The other four countries in the initial project revival, where participants expressed high levels of alienation, were South Africa, the United Kingdom, Australia and the United States: countries which ranked 90th, 15th, 14th and 4th in the Human Development Index. GUIC participants were evidently not evaluating their communities according to the standard economic and social indicators that adults use to measure well-being.

The positive qualities that these communities shared, according to their young people, are shown in the *Positive indicators* column in Table 8.1. In all five communities, young people felt accepted by adults and safe to move about, meet friends and take part in a variety of activities. Sathyanagar, the self-built settlement in Bangalore, had a clearly bounded village structure

Table 8.1 Indicators of community quality from children's perspectives

Positive indicators	Negative indicators
Social integration: Children feel welcome and valued in their community.	*Social exclusion*: Children feel unwelcome and harassed in their community.
Cohesive community identity: The community has clear geographic boundaries and a positive identity that is expressed through activities such as art and festivals.	*Stigma*: Residents feel stigmatised for living in a place associated with poverty and discrimination.
Tradition of self-help: Residents are building their community through mutual aid organisations and progressive local improvements.	*Violence and crime*: Owing to community violence and crime, children are afraid to move about outdoors. *Heavy traffic*: The streets are taken over by dangerous traffic.
Safety and free movement: Children feel that they can count on adult protection and range safely within their local area.	*Lack of gathering places*: Children lack places where they can safely meet and play with friends.
Peer gathering places: There are safe and accessible places where friends can meet.	*Lack of varied activity settings*: The environment is barren and isolating, with a lack of interesting places to visit and things to do.
Varied activity settings: Children can shop, explore, play sports and follow up other personal interests in the environment.	*Boredom*: Children express high levels of boredom and alienation.
Safe green spaces: Safe, clean green spaces with trees, whether formal or wild, extensive or small, are highly valued when available.	*Trash and litter*: Children read trash and litter in their environment as signs of adult neglect for where they live.
Provision for basic needs: Basic services are provided such as food, water, electricity, medical care and sanitation.	*Lack of provision for basic needs*: When basic services like clean water and sanitation are lacking, children feel these deprivations keenly.
Security of tenure: Family members have legal rights over the properties they inhabit through either ownership or secure rental agreements.	*Insecure tenure*: Children, like their parents, suffer anxiety from fear of eviction, which discourages investment in better living conditions. *Political powerlessness*: Children and their families feel powerless to improve conditions.

Source: adapted from Chawla (2002) and Swart Kruger (2001)

with dirt roads that were rarely entered by cars, where children moved through a supportive network of extended families. Families there had negotiated land tenure from the local government, which entitled them to invest securely in progressive home improvements. Boca-Barracas in Buenos Aires and Powisle in Warsaw also had clear boundaries with which their young people identified. In Boca Barracas, young people knew that they lived in the historic river port district of the city, which had launched the tango into the world, where famous artists and writers once gathered, and where there was still a vital local culture. Young people in Powisle considered their district more cheerful, peaceful, quiet and uncrowded than Warsaw at large, even if it was less interesting. There and in the two districts in Trondheim, the project sites bordered the old city centre, so that young people had access to a wide variety of shops and public places. These communities varied widely in the number of natural areas available for play; but when these areas were available, they were highly valued. These urban districts were not without dangers, but young people knew how to manoeuvre around the risks. In all five communities, young people had choices of places to go and things to do with friends.

These characteristics resonated with those that young people identified in the 1970s. Then, as now, young people appreciated living in localities with clear geographical boundaries that contained a variety of spaces for unprogrammed activities: local streets, courtyards and other hangouts where young adolescents could 'talk and meet and walk about together', 'play informal pick-up games' and 'mess around' (Lynch 1977: 13). In Powisle, which was revisited after a twenty-four-year interval, young people then, as now, appreciated being able to move back and forth between their more peaceful area and city-centre attractions. In the 1970s, the location with the most positive identity was Las Rosas, a well-defined community on the outskirts of Salta in northern Argentina. There children played important roles in an annual Christmas pageant and benefited from a tradition of self-help in the form of an active neighbourhood association and progressive family improvements to the small, standard houses. The area was described by its children as friendly, protected and fun, and gave 'the appearance of a hopeful and active community, however meager its means' (Lynch 1977: 30). The same terms applied to areas that children viewed positively in the 1990s.

Indicators of alienation

When GUIC participants described their area in negative terms, identified many disliked or dangerous places, felt that conditions were stagnant or getting worse and wanted to move away, the local environment was judged to fail children. When the project was revived in the 1990s, these were the predominant terms in which young people described their environments in a squatter camp in Johannesburg; in Braybrook, a peripheral suburb of Melbourne; in an old working-class area of Northampton; and in a low-income section of Oakland.

The characteristics of these areas were the converse of those that constituted good places in which to grow up. Rather than friendliness, young people told about bullies and adults who repeatedly told them to 'move on'. Rather than freedom of movement, they reported streets consumed by traffic or crime, and fear of leaving their home. Rather than a variety of interesting things to do, they reported barren, littered open spaces and a lack of affordable, accessible recreation places. Girls often expressed fear of sexual harassment. At the Johannesburg squatter camp, children also described the hardships and shame that they suffered because of insecure tenure and a lack of the most rudimentary services like running water and sanitation. In the middle of project work at this site, these children were evicted to empty veld on the periphery of the city. (See Table 8.1 for a summary of these negative indicators.)

These negative characteristics in the 1990s echoed project results in the 1970s. In the twenty-five years since Braybrook was first studied, little had changed in terms of young people's boredom and alienation in this Melbourne suburb. The geographic isolation that Johannesburg's squatter children faced after eviction in the 1990s was similar to the isolation expressed by children in Ecatepec, a self-built community on the edge of Mexico City, and by young residents of new high-rise housing estates on the edge of Cracow and Warsaw in the 1970s. Heavy traffic already restricted young people's movement at some sites in the 1970s. Problems that were more pronounced in the 1990s than in the 1970s were violence, pollution and ethnic tensions.

Whereas the qualities that characterised positive places enabled young people to move comfortably about their localities, meeting friends and finding interesting things to observe and do, these negative qualities severely restricted young people's lives: just at a time when these 10–15-year-olds were on the threshold of adulthood, with basic needs to socialise, try out different roles, observe a variety of adult roles, and prepare for community decision-making. In the terms of the Convention on the Rights of the Child, their environments thwarted their rights to play and recreation and to participate in the cultural life of their societies (Article 31), to freedom of association (Article 15), to seek and impart information and ideas through a variety of means (Article 13), and to express their views in matters that affected them (Article 12). At its most extreme, for the squatter children of Johannesburg, their environment endangered their basic survival and development (Article 6).

Measuring what matters to young people

According to a broad interpretation of the Convention on the Rights of the Child, the environment of children's everyday lives is a critical location for the fulfilment of basic rights. UNICEF, the United Nations agency for children, has advocated this broad interpretation. The community environment is repeatedly mentioned in the agency's *Implementation Handbook on the Convention of the Rights of the Child* (Hodgkin and Newell 1998), and the books *Cities for Children* (Bartlett *et al.* 1999) and *Urban Children in Distress* (Blanc 1994) explore the implications of the Convention for all aspects of urban policy – as do reports from a series of international conferences to develop the concept of 'child-friendly cities' (for example, Blanc *et al.* 1994). Every five years, governments that have ratified the Convention must submit to the United Nations Committee on the Rights of the Child a report on the measures that they have adopted to realise children's enjoyment of their rights (Article 44); and these reports need to include attention to the living environment.[3]

The indicators of life quality that governments typically gather undeniably relate to critical aspects of children's well-being, such as average purchasing power per capita, divorce rates, school enrolment and graduation rates, infant mortality rates, and access to clean water and health care. Survival, literacy and provisions for basic needs are essential aspects of healthy development. Much work needs to be done by governments to gather more reliable and accessible data of this kind, disaggregated by age, sex, ethnicity, socio-economic status and the geographic areas where families live (Bartlett *et al.* 1999). The results of GUIC suggest, however, that in addition to these familiar quantitative measures, governments need to understand how children themselves assess their well-being.

In terms of the sense of well-being in their communities that the 10–15-year-olds in GUIC expressed, the indicators that emerged from this research can be grouped according to four dimensions of community identity: whether the community was a place of *social stigma* or a place with a *hopeful positive identity*; whether it was a place of *fear* or *security*; whether it was a place of *isolation and alienation* or *social integration*; whether it was a place of *boredom* or *engagement*.

At the most basic level, some aspects of these indicators can be measured quantitatively. Data on sewerage, piped water, affordable housing and crime rates, for example, can be read as indirect measures of the squatter camp children's suffering from the stench and dirt in which they lived, for which neighbours taunted them, and their fears of crime and eviction. Sometimes, however, municipal data were misleading. City records for Northampton, England, and Braybrook, Australia, for example, showed generous acreage set aside for recreation space. What young people revealed was that these spaces were barren, littered, ruled by bullying gangs or criminals, or separated from housing by dangerous roads: in effect, truly empty space in terms of young people's needs. Other indicators that emerged from the project, such as boredom, engagement, alienation and integration, are fundamentally qualitative and require ethnographic methods to reveal how they are enacted in the everyday spaces of children's lives.

These indicators of urban quality through children's eyes can be interpreted as so many measures of social capital from children's perspectives. For what they describe is a socio-physical environment where the availability and physical quality of public places determine whether or not children have opportunities to be part of their larger society, at the same time as the quality of social relations determines whether or not public places appear open and inviting. At its best, the public realm affords young people occasions to develop the social networks, norms and interpersonal trust that are associated with social capital (Morrow 1999, 2001). These positive indicators are also similar to the environmental features associated with place attachment in middle childhood and adolescence (Chawla 1992).

The indicators that emerged from GUIC are not unique to this project. Other studies which have asked young people what they like and dislike about their urban environments have uncovered many of the same priorities. In surveys and interviews, school-aged children and young teens have repeatedly identified heavy traffic, violence, bullies, gangs, garbage, litter, pollution, and a lack of places to play and meet friends as the most serious problems they face (Buss 1995; Gosset 1996; Horelli 1998; International Save the Children Alliance 1996; Moore 1986; van Andel 1990, Woolley *et al.* 1999). Conversely, they particularly value nearby places to play with friends, nearby shops and recreation centres, safety, quiet and cleanliness. In these different studies, the value of natural areas depends on its context. Sometimes trees and flowers are appreciated for their beauty and green spaces are sought out for adventure play; but sometimes natural areas are perceived to be scary and dangerous. In a dramatic example of how young people evaluate places according to an overriding need for safety, 115 9–11-year-olds in crime-ridden Los Angeles almost unanimously rejected parks and other public spaces as the domain of gangs and 'bad people', although these were the spaces publicly designated for their recreation. Instead, they found freedom to move about in malls and other commercial places (Buss 1995). In a smaller, safer California city, older 14–18-year-olds particularly sought out natural areas where they could be alone or with friends in an informal, unsupervised way (Eubanks Owens 1988).

On the basis of interviews and participant observation with 13–17-year-olds in Lund, Sweden, Lieberg (1997) concluded that adolescents need to be able to move between *places of retreat* and *places of interaction*, which can also be thought of as *backstage* and *onstage* places. In backstage places of retreat, such as the home bedroom, friends' homes, close-to-home niches and hideouts, young people can be alone or with a few close friends with a minimum of adult supervision and control. Onstage places are locations to see and be seen, such as shopping centres or public squares, where adults and other youth groups serve as simultaneously spectacle and audience. Lieberg argues that both types of places are necessary for adolescents' construction of personal and collective identities. Similarly, Werner and Altman (1998) emphasise the importance of *secondary territories* beyond the home that are meaningful to the identities of the individuals and groups that use them, where children can simultaneously develop as independent individuals and learn to benefit from and contribute to social relationships and community activities.

It is necessary to qualify the results of these studies by age, sex, ethnicity and socio-economic level (Lieberg 1997; Malone and Hasluck 2002; O'Brien *et al.* 2000). The school-age children and adolescents in these studies are at an age when they are usually eager to move out to discover their world, meet friends and assume an increasing variety of roles in their society. In the words of Hugo at the beginning of this chapter, they are the 'sparrows' who move deftly through their city's streets and public spaces. When, that is, they are able to do so. When they are not girls in cultures that forbid them to leave the home or nearby spaces under a caretaker's eye, or in families that keep girls at home to care for younger siblings. When their out-of-school hours are not filled by programmed activities that their parents devise. When they do not live in areas that are so dangerous that they are never allowed outside alone. It is also important to qualify whether young people move through the city in search of play and pleasure, or whether the city pavements are where they labour and live (Boyden and Holden 1991; Swart 1990).

The qualitative character of many of young people's concerns, combined with the need to understand how these concerns are affected by age, sex, ethnicity and socio-economic status, means that many of the determinants of children's sense of well-being slip through the sieve of city statistics. This conclusion is doubly true when one considers that how well city districts function for their children has to be determined in the context of specific resources and risks. As Porter (1995) has observed, the very essence of the objectivity and credibility of government statistics is that numbers reflect impersonal standards, in contrast to personal, local knowledge. Children, however, live in the local. The quality of their lives is determined by local resources, dangers and deprivations. Therefore it is necessary to combine quantitative data on urban quality with processes that enable young people themselves to specify what works and doesn't work for them in the places where they live. The remainder of this chapter will focus on two case studies of ways in which city governments in Australia have attempted to open channels for young people to make this kind of input into municipal decision-making.

Research into action

The GUIC project was first introduced in Australia in 1972 under the direction of Peter Downton, a young urban planner (reported in Lynch 1977). Downton chose to work in Braybrook, a working-class suburb with a high proportion of public housing in the midst of industrial development, because it was typical of the low social and economic status that characterised the western side of Melbourne. Using photography and film as well as interviews, observations and 'walkabouts', Downton worked primarily with 14-year-olds to understand how they used and perceived their environment. What he found was that young people of both sexes overwhelmingly characterised their area as boring. He concluded that,

> The absence of creativity and invention in the thinking and use of time and space by these children is most noticeable, and the apparently unavoidable conclusion is that this is directly traceable to the lack of experiences, challenges and opportunities available in the social, physical and educational environments.
>
> (cited in Lynch 1977: 118)

On the basis of this study, Downton made a number of recommendations to the City Council to improve conditions for young people, but when

GUIC was reintroduced in Braybrook in 1996 under the direction of an environmental educator (and this chapter's second author), there was no evidence that the city had ever acted on any of the recommendations.

As a consequence, the contemporary version of GUIC in Australia began with a commitment to move from research to action. As child and youth researchers who support the rights of children, the people who lead GUIC projects in different countries consider it their responsibility somehow to change the world of children in the direction of greater democracy and justice. For this reason the GUIC project adopted a paradigm which has a change orientation: participatory action research.

Participatory action research, or PAR, is a dynamic process (Alderson 2000; Greenwood and Levin 1998). Its purpose is not to describe social reality by understanding *what is* but to transform reality by providing a vision of *what could be*. Generally PAR aims at three types of change:

- development of a critical consciousness in researchers, participants and the broader community
- improvement of the lives of those involved in the research, through democratic processes
- transformation of societal structures and relationships that marginalise or disadvantage individuals or groups.

Through a commitment to democratic processes, PAR with young people supports forms of social organisation in which silenced or marginalised children and young people have the opportunity to be heard. This commitment to democracy is a not a commitment to process alone. It is rooted in and informed by a moral agenda guided by a commitment to human dignity, social justice and liberation.

PAR with young people reconceptualises the role of the researcher, the researched and the research. Through the act of participation, writing in and about young people's lives, the research contributes directly to a change in young people's conditions.[4] It is based on the view that simply talking or writing *about* young people is a poor substitute for researchers working *with* young people to bring about change actively.

PAR with young people is an act to support their empowerment (Hart 1996). But, as Jennifer Gore points out, empowerment is more than just a process. It is a precursor to a shift in the distribution of power in the form of added social capital:

> Empowerment is not just a discourse or state of mind. Empowerment requires the *acquisition of the property of power* and its *exercise in the accomplishment of some vision or desired future condition*. That vision cannot simply be the condition of a text to be published. [emphasis added]
>
> (Gore cited in LeCompte 1993: 14)

Actual empowerment requires a translation of awareness to action. It requires the appropriation of power by young people beyond just knowledge of the source of their disempowerment to opportunities to engage in activities to change their situation. Young people are recognised as valid and valued contributors to social capital. Whereas one of the goals of PAR is to create environments where young people can develop the positive networks that are one ingredient of social capital, another goal is to give them direct experience with active citizenship, which is another essential ingredient (Schuller *et al.* 2000).

The intention of the PAR process discussed in the following case studies was embedded in ideologies of democratic empowerment and change that were sensitive to children's rights and civil liberties. It was a process which moved beyond naming or listening to the silenced lives of the marginalised young people who inhabited the neighbourhoods, to actively creating opportunities and opening up new spaces where they could contribute authentically to the ongoing policy development and social and physical planning of their cities.

Streetspace

'Teens stride on' is the caption accompanying a local newspaper article, and next to it is a picture of a group of smiling teenagers walking single file along the suburban street of Braybrook behind Maggie Fooke (a local environmental designer) and Tania Gadea (a schoolteacher from Braybrook Secondary College). Next to the picture, a quotation from the school principal states: 'If the students start to participate in their community and gain the confidence to become part of that society, they can become a pressure group with a say . . . They need to take responsibility for what happens, to reflect on what they have done and have some input into what happens in the future.'

The week before this story, the same newspaper ran an article on the high incidence of drug-related violence in Braybrook, and spoke of the need to deal with 'the menacing youth who congregate on the streets'.

What is the role of young people in communities? Villain or change agent? The following case study highlights the enormous capacity young people have to contribute to the planning and design of their neighbourhoods when they are given the opportunity to exercise power over the places where they live.

The streets are highly contested terrain in suburban neighbourhoods: They act as buffer zones between public and private domains; they are the connecting pathways and entry and exit points of neighbourhoods; and they can also be places to socialise, ride skateboards or play ball. For residents of Braybrook, the streets represented danger and oppression. Built in response to a slum clearance in the inner city of Melbourne, the 488-hectare fibro cement housing estate in the industrial outer west ring of the city was constructed from cheap building materials with a limited life expectancy. The estate quickly fell into disrepair and became, as did many estates of this era, a site of urban poverty. Empty streets, shuttered shop windows and the deserted treeless parks created an air of anxiety and fear. From behind closed doors and venetian blinds, residents surveyed the streets. Many of these residents were young people home alone, watching television or babysitting siblings while their parents attended to work or recreation outside the neighbourhood. For most young people, the quintessential experience of growing up in Braybrook, in the 1990s as well as in the 1970s, has been to feel alienated and disconnected from their physical and social surroundings.

Indicators emerging from the qualitative phase of the GUIC research showed that young people in this neighbourhood suffered from the social stigma of living in a neighbourhood that historically identified its residents as *underclass*. This stigma contributed to young people's feelings of isolation and alienation, due in part to the lack of planning and physical infrastructure provided by the City Council, and in part to their fear of public spaces, which was based on perception as much as fact. Additionally, young people recited stories of being regularly harassed and told to 'move on' by police when they ventured into the streets. The high incidence of needles from drug use that littered the streets also added to the evidence that the streets were a dangerous place. Owing to this fear of crime, many parents did not allow their children to move beyond the pavement outside their houses. For these reasons, it was not surprising that the issue of safety and security in the streets was identified as a priority by Braybrook youth. On a list developed by young people about 'what young people need to feel good about themselves', they included: *secure and safe corridors for moving around the urban environment without harassment, regulation and surveillance.* On this list they also identified the need for: *opportunities to engage in discussions with others about their concerns, needs and aspirations and have their views listened to and acted on.* These and another seven concerns, accompanied by a discussion paper explaining the process through which these issues had been identified, were presented on behalf of the young people to the local City Council and the local media. The report ignited a public outcry over the state of the physical environment, with local newspapers quoting many residents to the effect that over a long period of time the council had neglected their civil responsibility to provide a safe and secure environment for all residents.

Using the momentum these issues raised in public debate, the GUIC team collaborated with teachers from the local secondary school, young people, an environmental designer and members of the City Council to apply for funding to develop Streetspace, an environmental education and design research project which addressed these issues. The project received funding from Arts Victoria to employ designer Maggie Fooke as an in-residence artist. With the support of teachers, community members and the GUIC team, she implemented an environmental education and design programme with fifty seventh-year students at Braybrook Secondary College. For six months, the local neighbourhood became their outdoor classroom, as the young people took on the role of designers, educators and experts on young people's and community needs.

The purpose of Streetspace was to provide an opportunity for young people to be active participants in initiating community discussion and dialogue: to confront their historical powerlessness by reconstructing the identity created through the media and the myths which positioned them as intruders in the architecture of the streets. The objective was to 'take back' the streets in both a metaphorical and physical sense. During the project, young people were engaged in a number of structured activities:

- curriculum projects in social and environmental education
- model-making and design (including mosaics)
- walking tours of neighbourhood and community
- city bus tour to other neighbourhoods and parks throughout Melbourne metropolitan area
- photographic grid of neighbourhood
- email dialogue between students and project managers
- an excursion to a local play installation art design company
- guest speakers and guided tours of the landscape
- meetings with council officials and local community groups
- presentations to council officials and community members

As an outcome of this structured curriculum, the young people were invited by the City Council to plan and design a youth-specific space in Ash Reserve, a local open space. In small groups, young people designed the redevelopment of the park utilising data they had obtained through their curriculum activities. They worked alongside the resident designer to create three-dimensional models of their designs. At the culmination of the six-month project, the young people invited the local council and community members to Celebrating Streetspace, a public presentation that they had organised. The students reported on their findings, stating that they felt the City Council focused on the needs of young children in their playground designs without giving consideration to the needs of youth. For these reasons, the young people said 'they felt marginalised and when they occupied streets they were seen to be loitering'. The students particularly asked the council to consider 'providing safe passages around the neighborhood, including better lighting, street trees, seats and drinking fountains, so they felt welcome to move freely around'. Students also commented on the need to 'green up the neighborhood and have nature and art in the neighborhood to create an environment which showed people cared about each other and the neighborhood'. In the designs and models young people constructed for Ash Reserve, many included areas of greenery and water: places where people of all ages could sit quietly and reflect, engage in conversation with others, socialise and have barbecues. Many of the designs also included play zones or

Figure 8.1 Young people discuss their open space design during Celebrating Streetspace, a youth-organised presentation to city officials and local community members. Photo by Karen Malone

areas away from the quiet spaces, where young people could throw hoops or maybe even construct a skateboard half-ramp. All the designs presented an ideal that the reserve should be a shared space, and that it should encourage community members from all age groups to use it, even though their design brief from the City Council was to create a youth-specific space. Other elements included in the models were rose gardens, seats, pathways, community vegetable gardens, sculptures and artwork, bike tracks, a children's adventure playground, fences, and above all, an emphasis on places where everybody felt safe and secure.

Additionally, when the young people shared their designs with the community, they spoke about the importance of not seeing all young people negatively, because they were individuals with very different aspirations. They ended their presentation with a speech by two of the young women of the group, who reinforced the importance of engaging young people in authentic participatory action:

> Our local area desperately needs more facilities for young people. Streetspace allowed us the opportunity to design spaces for the youth of Braybrook. We only hope that the Council will now seriously think over our ideas and allow us to have more facilities and usable space. The Council and planners always think about facilities for toddlers such as

playgrounds, but now we would like them to think about facilities for older children and teenagers.

(Emma, 14 years old, Streetspace researcher)

Young people should have a say in what their area looks like. I think the council should listen to what young people have to say because they live in the area and they are future taxpayers.

(Amanda, 14 years old, Streetspace researcher)

At the conclusion of the project, a number of the young people sent email messages to thank the GUIC team for supporting their project. The following is an extract from one of the messages:

This term as part of Streetspace we made a model of Ash Reserve. We are trying to improve this open space. We've decided that many more trees should be planted and many students wanted to make it a fun and friendly place to be. When we presented our model we knew we had worked hard and put much effort into it – we hope the community realises that we have good ideas and we aren't all bad. Thanks for all your efforts in supporting us. We have learnt more about positive things we can do in future times and how to make things change when people don't listen.

(Justin, 13 years old, Streetspace researcher)

Streetspace was a student-focused project which allowed the GUIC team to initiate an action based on research findings. The proposed outcomes from the project were twofold: to create a context in which students could partic- ipate in social transformation through a democratic process; and to involve students in the planning, design and construction of a local landscape feature which would improve their quality of life, especially in the area of safe mobility. Did we achieve these goals? If not, why not? In respect to the first outcome, the project was successful. Students became very involved and committed to the project. Four years later, the team still has contact with a number of students who talk about the value of the 'process of involvement'. The second outcome was harder to achieve. Following are some reasons why we believe this was so, and why, when we started a new project site, we changed the dynamics of our relationship with the council.

First, because we had volunteered our services to the council in Braybrook, we were often viewed as less 'qualified' or 'significant' than those consultants who were charging high fees. This meant we were often marginalised, with less attention given to our concerns or needs. Marginalisation included not being informed of changes in meeting times and places, and restricted access to the Mayor and other high-ranking officials in the council. *Response*: Clearly articulate expectations and negotiate a role which can hold policy-makers accountable.

Secondly, the project was located in Community Services, an office which has the least amount of political power in the hierarchy of council departments and services. Therefore those who were supportive of the project didn't have much internal influence. *Response*: Position the project within a council group which has power, support and cross-sectoral influence.

Thirdly, because youth and children are seen as a less powerful group in local politics, who lack voting status, it was easy for council members to be supportive but not committed to the project, especially around election time. *Response*: Make youth problems be seen as community problems. Embed youth needs in the context of community needs instead of allowing them to be identified as youth-specific, and therefore last on the list or viewed as least significant.

Finally, presentations alone, even when given to high-level government officials, have limited scope. Long-term processes for accountability and follow-up need to be incorporated into final phases of the project – especially if the project is about *change now*, not just about providing students with experiences of democratic process in preparation for later life. *Response*: Construct timelines, infiltrate management groups and sit on committees which can follow through on young people's recommendations. Or, as in the case of our next project site, Frankston, take the young people a step further to infiltrate the council with their own management group that has been ratified by the Mayor and the city councillors as a key decision-making body in the council.

YSMT–Youth Safety Management Team

'I suppose I am guilty of judging young people – not being very tolerant', states Mary, Local Councillor for the Frankston City Council. 'It's just the way they look, hanging around in groups, untidy, smoking – they look like trouble. When I think about it though, I guess they aren't doing anything wrong – it's just that they look like they could.'

(Malone 2000: 141)

In Frankston, another Australian city where GUIC activities have been implemented, lack of tolerance in this city with a high population of young people from diverse social backgrounds and neighbourhoods has contributed to high levels of tension and conflict in public space. For many young people living in Frankston, boredom due to lack of facilities is a significant issue. Frankston, like many medium-sized cities that are outer suburbs of larger metropolitan areas in Australia, has a central business district surrounded by spreading suburban sprawl. Peripheral neighbourhoods, built in quick succession on reclaimed rural land, have meant an exploding population of young people who find their neighbourhoods hold little attraction. The lack of leisure and recreational opportunities in local neighbourhoods has meant that many young people congregate in the town centre, competing with other young people and adults for the limited facilities available there.

Figure 8.2 Young people gathering in the Frankston city centre. Photo by Karen Malone

The findings of the Growing Up In Frankston Youth Needs Assessment, conducted by the GUIC research team in conjunction with the Frankston City Council, identified clearly that young people felt marginalised and disadvantaged in a city where many adults viewed them with suspicion and distrust. The following extract from the executive summary of the final Growing Up In Frankston report identified these issues:

> Fundamentally, this research report provides some insight into what young people are thinking and feeling about their city, where they go and what they do. It also provides some suggestions of problems identified by young people as of particular concern to them in regard to their personal safety when moving in and around the city. They have provided us with a number of possibilities for change through their list of things they need to feel good about themselves. Such things as friends, high self-esteem, good parents, more activities, money, fun, and a good family rate high on their list of needs. In response we need programs which enhance young people's pride, encourage them to take ownership of their environment and to participate in developing its potential for themselves and other members of the community. There is evidence young people are doing this in neighbourhoods around the city – this needs to be encouraged, formalised and the experiences shared with other young people.
>
> (Malone 1999: 3)

To gather information to inform local policy recommendations, GUIC activities were carried out with 8–18-year-olds in eight Frankston neighbourhoods.

The final report identified eight key issues and recommendations, which were presented and ratified by the Frankston City Council and integrated into their Safer Cities Plan. The eight main issues were bullying and violence, traffic, drugs, access and safety when using public transport, skateboarding around the city, community facilities, youth facilities and community integration. The project team lobbied particularly around the issue of community integration, as it felt that the other specific issues could only be addressed once young people were given legitimate status in the community. The recommendation to the council read:

> *Community integration* is important for young people's sense of belonging, ownership and civic responsibility. Many young people spoke of the need for youth places and activities, which existed within rather than outside mainstream community life. Most young people said they felt their presence in shopping centres, community facilities or even in the streets was seen by many members of the public as a threat. *Recommendation: Public space and community planning programs should include input from young people and focus on ways of integrating young people into community life.*
> (Malone 1999: 44)

The mechanism suggested for addressing this issue was to develop a Youth Safety Management Team (YSMT) that would be embedded in the structure of the City Council. In keeping with the lessons that we learned in Braybrook, we also instructed the community safety officer that, instead of youth being treated as its own discrete category in the safety management plan, youth needs should be integrated with community needs and woven into the overall plan.

When the Mayor and the Community Safety Management Team launched the Community Safety Plan in late 2000, the development of the YSMT was included as one of four priorities for 2001: 'to contribute to the development and implementation of policies, programs and projects related to community safety and crime prevention' (Frankston City Council 2000). The YSMT had its first meeting in late December 2000. Membership in the group was through a call for nominations requested from each of the local secondary colleges, the local university and further education college, the Yellow Ribbon project group (a youth-run volunteer group supporting youth in crisis), InCYNC (a youth support group run by Council Youth services), and through public media.

Youth members of the team and the council YSMT administrator (Philippa) gave the following responses when asked about their participation in YSMT and its role.

> Adults stereotype young people too easily. They are only 'visible' when they do things that adults don't do. For example, young people enjoy hanging around with their friends, but that doesn't mean they are going

to break into a store or sell drugs. Most young people are doing fantastic things but adults don't see this, concentrating on a small group making trouble who'll probably grow out of it anyway. I hope to represent young people in my community while I am in the YSMT.

(Amy)

The purpose of this group was to provide a connection between young people living and working in Frankston with the local council. The YSMT can provide the council with a direct consultation link between young people and the council on a range of issues. I joined to gain a greater understanding of the decision making process and other community issues. I think youth participation is important. Young people eventually become 'old' people and will be responsible for such decisions. By involving them at an earlier age, you are providing them with the experiences and skills that they shall require later in life.

(Scott)

YSMT was developed as an action under the Community Safety Plan as a result of the Growing Up In Frankston work. I get to listen to people who think I'm really old and for some reason get to make other adults in the 'youth' fields feel really nervous/angry/threatened. This is probably a good sign! They're giving us a perspective that we didn't have before.

(Philippa)

At the time of this writing, the ten-member group has met four times. During that time they have conducted and published a survey on the concerns of young people who use the skate ramp facility in the city, and developed an action subcommittee to submit a proposal for a long-term facility management plan. The team is also in the process of developing a media release focusing on positive images of youth, to counteract the current plethora of negative portrayals of youth in local newspapers. Representatives of the group attend the monthly meetings of the City Council Community Safety Management Team and provide regular input on youth concerns.

I think we've achieved a lot. I like the 'equality' with adults I've experienced since joining the YSMT. We can tell the adults exactly what we want – exactly what is going on. It's a lot different when you are on the same level as adults. No one asked us before 'what do you think?' It's hard to have a voice in a community unless someone asks you.

(Emma)

Integrating children and youth into community life

The cross-national GUIC comparisons reviewed at the beginning of this chapter showed that, according to young people themselves, the major criterion that determined whether a locality functioned well or poorly was whether it integrated them into an accepting and secure community life or excluded and stigmatised them. Both integration and exclusion had many facets: adults who valued and welcomed young people, safety to move about, engaging places to visit, places to meet friends, provision for secure tenure and basic needs, and a positive and hopeful community identity, or the absence of these things. Research in Braybrook and Frankston revealed that their young citizens faced high levels of exclusion and responded with correspondingly high levels of boredom and alienation. Expressed in terms of the Convention on the Rights of the Child, their social and physical environment thwarted many of their basic rights, and failed to prepare them for active and informed citizenship.

The need for integration in their societies that young people at GUIC sites expressed can be related to the importance of 'places of interaction' and 'onstage places' that Lieberg (1997) observed during his research with Swedish teenagers, as well as the 'secondary territories' that Werner and Altman (1998) considered central to children's community attachment. These authors contend that opportunities for children and adolescents to develop confident and balanced individual and collective identities require public and semi-public places where young people can observe and experiment with a variety of roles.

The participatory processes illustrated by GUIC create opportunities for places of this kind in two ways. From the beginning, the participatory activities themselves are occasions of this kind. In the meeting rooms of the YSMT and during the Streetspace activities and final presentation, youth were interacting with others from around the city and with adults who represented many different professions and perspectives, and they had chances to present themselves in new contexts. Secondly, the proposals that they formulated through these processes aimed to create public places that would be more liveable and friendly for all ages even when, as in Braybrook, their brief was to create a 'youth-specific' space.

Eubanks Owens (2002), a landscape architect in California, has reported that she and her colleagues are frequently asked to 'design teens out' when they are given public commissions. Participatory processes like GUIC illustrate the alternative strategy of creating more inclusive societies by inviting children and youth to help design and manage public places. As this chapter goes to press, representatives of world governments will have met at the 'Habitat +5' Conference in 2001 to review international agreements to create more sustainable human settlements, and will be about to meet at the 'Rio +10' Conference in 2002 to review progress in creating societies that are both environmentally sustainable and socially just.[5] According to the rhetoric of both programmes of action, children and youth are vital contributors to these goals. GUIC in Braybrook and Frankston illustrate two of many possible ways to enlist their energies and ideas. It is up to municipal governments and their citizens to turn this rhetoric into action, bearing in mind that the exclusion of children and youth from the public life of their communities means the exclusion of hope and potential for the future.

Victor Hugo's metaphor of city and child as 'eagle' and 'sparrow' is ambiguous. The sparrow is denizen of the streets and other places of everyday life. The eagle is associated with soaring flight and distant vision, but it is also a bird of prey. To see humanely, those who hold power in cities need to combine long-term vision with attention to the voice of the sparrow, which reminds them about what is nearby and present, where the future in fact is growing.

Acknowledgements

Ongoing support for the co-ordination of Growing Up in Cities is provided by the MOST Programme of UNESCO. Growing Up in Cities initiatives in Australia, under the direction of Karen Malone, were made possible by contributions by: Lindsay Hasluck, Beau Beza, Maggie Fooke, the Braybrook Secondary College staff and students, AEDIS, the Australian Research Council and the Maribyrnong City Council, in Braybrook; and by Lindsay Hasluck, Sandrine Depeau, the young people of YSMT, and the Frankston City Council, in Frankston.

Notes

1 The term *children* is used here in the broad sense of the United Nations definition, which includes all people under the age of 18.
2 Growing Up in Cities began in the 1970s in Argentina, Australia, Mexico and Poland. It was revived in the 1990s in Argentina, Australia, Britain, India, Norway, Poland, South Africa and the United States. More recent locations include Sweden, Lebanon, Papua New Guinea, Vietnam and Venezuela. For updated project reports see www.unesco.org/most/growing.htm.
3 As of 2001, all member states of the United Nations have ratified the Convention on the Rights of the Child except for the United States and Somalia. For information on the Child Friendly Cities Programme of UNICEF, which focuses on monitoring and implementing these rights in urban areas see www.unicef-icdc.org.
4 See Johnson *et al.* (1998) for a number of case studies of PAR projects with children.
5 For information on these international meetings see www.unchs.org/Istanbul+5 and www.johannesburgsummit.org.

References

Aitken, S. C. and Ginsberg, S. P., 1988, 'Children's characterization of place'. *Association of Pacific Coast Geographers Yearbook*, 50, 69–86.
Alderson, P., 2000, 'Children as researchers'. In P. Christensen and A. James (eds), *Research with Children: Perspectives and Practices* (London: Falmer Press), 241–57.
Bartlett, S., Hart, R., Satterthwaite, D., De la Barra, X. and Missair, A., 1999, *Cities for Children: Children's Rights, Poverty and Urban Management* (New York and London: UNICEF/Earthscan Publications).

Blanc, C. S. (ed.), 1994, *Urban Children in Distress* (New York and Yverdon: UNICEF/ Gordon and Breach).

Blanc, C., Fonseca, L., Iacofano, D. and Hart, R., 1994, 'Children on the city agenda: report on the international meeting of mayors, urban planners and policy makers, Florence, Italy'. *Children's Environments*, 11 (1), 61–70.

Boyden, J. with Holden, P., 1991, *Children of the Cities* (London: Zed Books).

Buss, S., 1995, 'Urban Los Angeles from young people's angle of vision'. *Children's Environments*, 12 (3), 340–51.

Chawla, L., 1992, 'Childhood place attachments'. In I. Altman and S. Low (eds), *Place Attachment* (New York: Plenum Press), 63–87.

Chawla, L., 2001, 'Putting young old ideas into action: the relevance of Growing Up in Cities to Local Agenda 21'. *Local Environment*, 6 (1), 13–25.

Chawla, L. (ed.), 2002, *Growing Up in an Urbanising World* (Paris and London: UNESCO Publishing/Earthscan Publications).

Driskell, D., 2002, *Creating Better Cities with Children and Youth* (Paris and London: UNESCO Publishing/Earthscan Publications).

Eubanks Owens, P., 1988, 'Natural landscapes, gathering places, and prospect refuges: characteristics of outdoor places valued by teens'. *Children's Environments Quarterly*, 5 (2), 17–24.

Eubanks Owens, P., 2002, 'No teens allowed: the exclusion of adolescents from public spaces'. *Landscape Journal*, 21 (1).

Frankston City Council, 2000, *Community Safety Plan* (Frankston: Frankston City Council).

Gosset, C., 1996, 'Perception of environmental health by children in cities'. In C. Price and A. Tsouros (eds), *Our Cities, Our Future* (Copenhagen: WHO Healthy Cities Project Office), 178–85.

Greenwood, D. J. and Levin, M., 1998, *Introduction to Action Research: Social Research for Social Change* (Thousand Oaks, CA: Sage).

Hart, R. (1996) *Children's Participation in Sustainable Development: The Theory and Practice of Involving Young Citizens in Community Development and Environmental Care* (New York and London: UNICEF/Earthscan).

Hodgkin, R. and Newell, P., 1998, *Implementation Handbook on the Convention on the Rights of the Child* (New York: UNICEF).

Horelli, L. (1998) 'Creating child-friendly environments: case studies on children's participation in three European countries'. *Childhood*, 5 (2), 225–39.

International Save the Children Alliance, 1996, *Children on Their Housing* (Stockholm: International Save the Children Alliance).

Johnson, V., Ivan-Smith, E., Gordon, G., Pridmore, P. and Scott, P., 1998, *Stepping Forward: Children and Young People's Participation in the Development Process* (London: Intermediate Technology Publications).

LeCompte, M., 1993, 'A framework for hearing silence: what does telling stories mean when we are supposed to be doing science?' In D. McLaughlin and W. Tierney (eds), *Naming Silenced Lives*. (New York: Routledge), 9–27.

Lieberg, M., 1997, 'Youth in their local environment'. In R. Camstra (ed.), *Growing Up in a Changing Urban Landscape* (Assen, The Netherlands: Van Gorcum), 90–108.

Lynch, K. (ed.), 1977, *Growing Up in Cities* (Cambridge, MA: MIT Press).

Malone, K., 1999, *Growing Up in Frankston: Children and Youth Needs Assessment Executive Summary Report, Volume 1* (Frankston: Monash University).

Malone, K., 2000, 'Dangerous youth: youth geographies in a climate of fear'. In J. McLeod and K. Malone (eds), *Researching Youth* (Hobart: Australian Clearing-house for Youth), 135–48.

Malone, K. and Hasluck, L., 2002, 'Australian youth: aliens in a suburban environment'. In L. Chawla (ed.), *Growing Up in an Urbanising World* (Paris and London: UNESCO Publishing/Earthscan Publications), 81–109.

Moore, R. C., 1986, *Childhood's Domain* (Beckenham: Croom Helm).

Morrow, V., 1999, 'Conceptualising social capital in relation to the well-being of children and young people'. *The Sociological Review*, 47 (4), 744–65.

Morrow, V., 2001, *Networks and Neighbourhoods: Children's and Young People's Perspectives* (London: Health Development Agency).

O'Brien, M., Jones, D., Sloan, D. and Rustin, M., 2000, 'Children's independent spatial mobility in the urban public realm'. *Childhood*, 7 (3), 257–77.

Percy-Smith, B., 2002, 'Contested worlds: constraints and opportunities in an English Midlands city'. In L. Chawla (ed.), *Growing Up in an Urbanising World* (Paris and London: UNESCO Publishing/Earthscan Publications), 57–80.

Porter, T. M., 1995, *Trust in Numbers* (Princeton: Princeton University Press).

Schuller, T., Baron, S. and Field, J., 2000, 'Social capital: a review and critique'. In S. Baron, J. Field and T. Schuller (eds), *Social Capital* (Oxford: Oxford University Press), 1–38.

Swart, J., 1990, *Malunde: The Street Children of Hillbrow* (Johannesburg: Witwatersrand University Press).

Swart Kruger, J., 2001, *'We Know Something Someone Doesn't Know . . .' Children Speak Out on Local Conditions*. Unpublished report commissioned by the City Council of Johannesburg.

United Nations, 1992, *Agenda 21* (New York: United Nations).

United Nations Centre for Human Settlements (UNCHS), 1997, *The Istanbul Declaration and the Habitat Agenda* (Nairobi: UNCHS).

United Nations Development Programme (UNDP), 1997, *Human Development Report* (Oxford: Oxford University Press).

Van Andel, J., 1990, 'Places children like, dislike, and fear'. *Children's Environments Quarterly*, 7 (4), 24–31.

Ward, C., 1978, *The Child in the City* (London: Architectural Press).

Werner, C. and Altman, I., 1998, 'A dialectical/transactional framework of social relations: children in secondary territories'. In G. Görlitz, H. J. Harloff, G. Mey and J. Walsiner (eds), *Children, Cities and Psychological Theories* (Berlin: Walter de Gruyter), 123–54.

Woolley, H., Dunn, J., Spencer, C., Short, T. and Rowley, G., 1999, 'Children describe their experiences of the city centre'. *Landscape Research*, 24 (3), 287–301.

9 Regenerating children's neighbourhoods

What do children want?

Margaret O'Brien

The Childhood, Urban Space and Citizenship project team has been examining children's lives in contrasting neighbourhoods within London and a lower-density new town, Hatfield.[1] One of the objectives of the study was to explore and facilitate 'child-friendly' urban regeneration. We wanted to help promote sensitivity to the perspectives of children in the minds and plans of those involved in the complex task of reviving ailing cities. When the project was first thought about in the mid-1990s, there was, as there still is, intense debate about the declining quality of life in the large cities of Britain. Then, as now, rarely a day passed without a news item on gridlock traffic, inner-city crime or neighbourhood collapse. At the time children's voices were relatively quiet on these matters, despite the legacy of the pioneering work of Kevin Lynch in 1960s America (Lynch 1977) and its recent replication through the UNESCO Growing Up in Cities project led by Louise Chawla (Chawla and Malone, Chapter 8). However, in the mid-1990s British local authorities and city planners rarely incorporated children's perspectives, at least not in the self-conscious manner we see signs of now, with children's drawings and paintings adorning the many building sites of London.

We designed our study to gather systematic data on children's use of and views about their neighbourhood and also incorporated parental accounts, as we anticipated that parental beliefs and practices would be a significant influence on children's participation in the life of their neighbourhood. The study therefore involved a child and parent survey from which we selected a smaller sub-sample of families for in-depth case studies.[2] We wanted to compare patterns of urban living for different sorts of children living in diverse neighbourhoods (between affluent and poor children; between children living in inner London neighbourhoods and those in the suburbs or new towns, between boys and girls and diverse ethnic groups) and also to explore some of these patterns in more detail for a smaller number of cases through interview, observation and group discussion. For outer London two suburban neighbourhoods were chosen: the more professional and ethnically mixed borough of Harrow to the west of London and the more homogeneous white working-class borough of Barking and Dagenham to the east. Within the inner core of London we selected four case study sites: a poor, ethnically mixed social housing neighbourhood estate in Islington, a predominately poor Bengali neighbourhood in Tower Hamlets and two more materially mixed neighbourhoods within Camden and Brent which included a higher level of middle-class households.

This chapter focuses on what the children in our study said they wanted from their neighbourhoods, the children's representations of what has been described by Littman (2000) as their 'neighbourhood pulse'. I will examine how their views varied in relation to their local environment and personal circumstances and also contrast their views with that of their parents to uncover whether there is consensus between the generations on the apparent and desired quality of life in and around contemporary London. Whilst neighbourhood regeneration schemes are beginning to incorporate ideas about people as well as designs for building refurbishment into master planning, the child dimension is often overlooked. In this chapter I will argue for a generationally inclusive approach to revitalising cities, suggesting that making cities more attractive places for children and their parents is a vital aspect of improving urban life for all. Sensitivity to children's concerns about urban living also illuminates factors promoting suburban drift or urban sprawl that we have been witnessing in the UK and in many European cities since the 1980s, since it is often the arrival of children which provokes a family's move out of inner city centre (DETR 2000).[3] As Ward (1978: 66) noticed, the suburb is becoming 'the child-rearing sector of the city'.

The design of the study allowed the neighbourhood experience to be contextualised in terms of the everyday life of the children and their parents. For instance, when we interviewed children individually we structured the interview around the child's day from getting up, going to school and returning home. Children's sense of place and experiences of the neighbourhood were ascertained through a mixture of direct questions such as on what the area was like as a place to live, how they felt walking through their neighbourhood, their connection to local associations and amenities such as sports clubs, libraries and parks. When the interview was finished, children pointed out significant personal landmarks on a map of the neighbourhood, including friends' homes, favoured places and scary places in order to physically locate their sense of neighbourhood. In order to capture a visual representation of neighbourhood from the children's perspectives, some children took photographs of these places on a walk around their neighbourhood with the researchers, or in other cases we took photographs for the children. In this chapter I will present these photographs and interview accounts alongside findings from the survey.

Improving London? Children's perspectives

It should be noted at the outset that most children in the study appeared to be 'getting by' and 'making do' in the space that was available in the range of neighbourhoods in which they lived. Although there was some evidence for a slight decline in independent spatial mobility for the younger children, when compared to Hillman's data of the 1970s (fewer children walked to school and parental chaperonage had increased) only a small minority of children led very spatially restricted lives (Hillman *et al.* 1990; O'Brien *et al.* 2000).[4] However, for certain categories of children, notably girls, minority ethnic children and children in the more deprived neighbourhoods of London, there was a sense of struggle and low expectations about what was possible in terms of life outside the home.

In his book *London: The Biography*, Peter Ackroyd (2000: 2) argues that London 'is not civilised or graceful . . . but tortuous, inexact and oppressive . . . It is a city based on profit and speculation, not need and no mayor or sovereign could withstand its organic will.' For Ackroyd, London has a life of its own deeply embedded in its past. Its inhabitants struggle through, and indeed this theme resonated with many of the children of our study who lived in the poor neighbourhoods of London. It is notable that, whilst there has been a long tradition of inquiry into the decline of the quality of life in London, the focus of this commentary has tended to be on the adult activities and preoccupations. For example, Young's (1995: 51) insightful observations about the importance of preserving 'civility, tolerance, calm sociality and mutual enjoyment' in London are discussed in terms of adult citizens and not applied to the children and youth of the city.

In our survey both children and their parents were asked to 'name one thing that could be done to make your neighbourhood a better place for children'. This theme was explored in more depth during individual interviews and focus-group discussions. What did children think was the one change that would improve the quality of life for children in their neighbourhood and did parents want the same thing as their children?

As can be seen in Figure 9.1, there is some overlap between children and parents' most desired neighbourhood improvement but, as I will go on to show, there were differences in the ordering of their wishes. Four key areas were revealed in the data: more and better play spaces and places (e.g. better parks, play spaces near home, leisure centres for youth), greater security (e.g. cameras, heightened police presence, restriction of dangerous persons), traffic measures (e.g. traffic management or calming, including, for example, more zebra crossings, lollypop persons, speed bumps) and infrastructural maintenance (e.g. clearing up rubbish, graffiti and dog mess, washing down streets).

Children's most desired improvement was for more and better play places and spaces, as one girl argues:

> Stop building so many houses and ugly buildings, 'cos children want space to play and they can't be expected to stay indoors for the whole of their time – children have to have space.
>
> (White girl, 11 years old, New town)

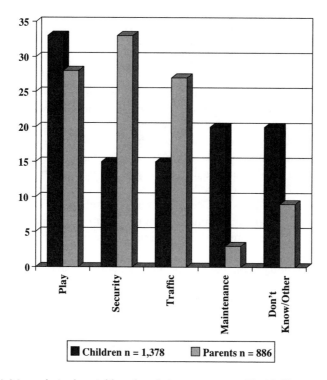

Figure 9.1 Most desired neighbourhood improvement, % (children and parents compared)

Making space for children was a complex and somewhat paradoxical process during the late nineteenth and twentieth centuries. Within developed urbanised countries the process has involved the loss of old spaces alongside the advent of new spaces. The loss of the street as a place to play and the loss of unstructured space free from regulation and supervision are significant transformations in children's lives. Reflecting on children's street play in the 1950s and 1960s, Iona and Peter Opie (1984: vi) for example noted that 'there is no town or city known to us where street games do not flourish'.

> When children play in the street they not only avail themselves of one of the oldest play-places in the world, they engage in some of the oldest and most interesting of games, for they are games tested and confirmed by centuries of children, who have played them and passed them on, as children continue to do, without reference to print, parliament, or adult propriety.

The speed at which street space for children's play has been lost is remarkable, although there is some debate about when the significant downturn actually happened. Even my childhood streets of the 1960s were certainly not 'teeming' with children in the way Anna Davin describes in her history of East London working-class childhood in the early part of the last century (Davin, 1996: 64). She argues that:

> The street offered a range of pleasures: the company of other children and all the regular street games, for example. Smooth paving stones were good for marbles and 'buttons' or hopscotch; ... If you could get a length of robe, you could fix swings from lamp-post to railing, or skip, or from the lamp-post bar twist two ropes tightly together and play 'swing-twist-'em', clinging dangerously as the ropes untwined.

Many of the street games she describes could be observed until the 1930s, when the municipal park became the more favoured space for such vigorous physical play, particularly for working-class children (Humphries *et al.* 1988).

Children's emphasis on their improving play and leisure space, found in our study, suggests that contemporary children are expressing a desire to be included in the neighbourhood, to have a public space for themselves. Whilst parents also wanted these leisure and play spaces for their children, ensuring security was uppermost in their minds. Clearly a balance needs to be struck between an enhanced provision of spaces for children in urban centres such as London and the development of a greater security framework, sensitive to parental anxieties, for children to be able to actually participate in this space.

The importance of asking children as well as parents about neighbourhood improvement is also shown by the unexpected difference in their preoccupation with improving the physical infrastructure of the neighbourhood. Interestingly, maintenance of the physical dimensions of the neighbourhood infrastructure emerges as much more significant to children than to their parents, as can be seen from Figure 9.1. As one of our case-study children, a Turkish boy living in inner London, put it:

> I'll say just all the street cleaning, the things they throw on the floor, people throw on the floor. I'll say that, clean the streets. Not clean but campaigns to people to learn not to do that, you know. Tell things, make up a group or something, you know, to do it. That's it, say that. That's it.

Many of the photographs of children's unfavoured places included rubbish on streets and corridors of apartment blocks and graffiti drawn on public walls (Figure 9.2). Children are keen observers of the crumbling infrastructure of their urban environment, and because of their size closer than adults to its more offensive features – the broken glass, the uncleared litter and dog dirt. As Colin Ward (1978) and others have remarked, the smaller size of children

Figure 9.2 Disliked graffiti

means they are more likely than adults to be closer to ground level and even want to lie on it (Figure 9.3). Uneven or 'lumpy' streets and pavements, as one of our respondents called them, really matter if you are small in size and riding a bike. In the inner London focus groups it was hard to get the children to think about positive aspects of their local living space, and comparisons were often made to other, seemingly better, areas: as one child in inner London said, 'the streets are cleaner in other European cities. Bin men are rubbish. Clean the area up. Make the place look better. More parks, more green. Clean up Islington.' The Prime Minister should 'come and see what we're living in'. London children living in less affluent areas ask for more maintenance of streets and buildings and better play spaces. Dissatisfaction with the general level of filth and drab buildings was high for these London children but less of an issue for children living outside London, where urban deterioration was not so striking.

Whilst the provision of play space and improvement of the local urban infrastructure were important for parents too, they were more likely to prioritise neighbourhood security and traffic management. For instance, a Harrow

Figure 9.3 At street level

case-study mother quoted below wanted to reduce the risk to children from residents being let out of psychiatric institutions, and other parents wanted to restrict what they saw as dangerous men's access to children in public spaces.

> I think people that have got problems you know whatever their problem is I think it's really important for the safety of all concerned that they are given more care, more support and kept a better eye on.
>
> (Harrow mother)

> Our direct area we want, and we're sort of campaigning for is a couple of speed bumps in the road to stop the cars because . . . we get young boys driving really, really fast down the lane. They use it as a racetrack late at night, and not even necessarily late at night.
>
> (Hatfield mother)

Several parents of girls and minority ethnic boys revealed high levels of parental anxiety about letting their children play out:

I: When you say you worry about him, in which way would you be worried?

F: Possibility of an accident, or being bullied on the way home, because his sister went through that once before, so I worry about that. Anything can happen. And especially at this time that there's darkness around 5 o'clock. I don't like him walking on his own in the dark because of the incidents that happen all the time around this area. It's not safe being in this area you know because of the pickpockets and the things we've witnessed around this area. You can see people fighting or you can see people being shot.

(Mother of 10-year-old boy, African, inner London)

Parental anxiety is amplified in poor, distressed urban environments such as this one. Indeed, in this context the parenting strategy of 'keeping him in' or 'keeping him close' is a legitimate, protective response.

Children's unsafe places

In the study we did ask children directly about whether there were any areas in their neighbourhood where they felt unsafe. Urban and new town dwellers alike had remarkably similar levels of perceived risk and danger: about one-third of children expressed anxieties about unsafe places in their neighbourhood. As shown in Figure 9.4, children universally disliked dark and dingy places but particularly children living in outer London and the new town.

Paradoxically, new town children found poorly lit underpasses, designed to help them cross the roads more safely, very frightening. Several new town case studies included photographs of these passageways and under passes in their 'scary' portfolio (Figure 9.5).

In terms of 'the street', inner London children were the most concerned about the safety of their streets. Perceiving 'the street' as unsafe was twice as likely for inner London children when compared to their outer London and new town peers (21, 12 and 11 per cent respectively).

Perceptions of risk were interwoven with avoidance of the streets, as only 18 per cent of inner London children reported that the street was their main location for playing out, in contrast to 28 per cent of outer London and 36 per cent of new town children. Concern about the safety of London's streets has heightened more recently, in the wake of rising levels of street crime involving theft of mobile phones (*Evening Standard* 2002).

For children living in social housing estates the building fabric itself was threatening, in particular lifts and stairwells (Figure 9.6). One focus group of six children from the Islington housing estate, containing three of our case-study children, centred their discussion around dangerous stories such as trolleys being thrown off high-rise flats, drinking and drug-taking, and fires being started in rubbish bins.

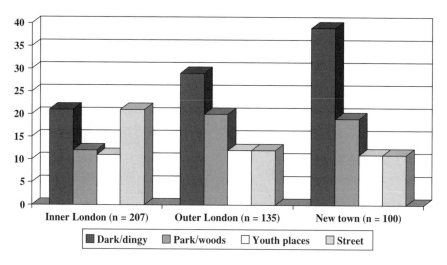

Figure 9.4 Children's unsafe places, %

Figure 9.5 New town underpass

M: Some of the flats lifts don't work and they should make some new lifts.
M: I don't like the big bins as they are always open.
F: People light fires in there.
M: Did you hear about the tenth floor they put broken trolleys?

Figure 9.6 Dark stairwell

F: Tesco trolleys?

M: Yeah, and they, I saw these boys and they go to the tenth floor and they try to throw something.

All: Waw.

M: And once it just missed a small girl.

M: Once someone threw a small mirror.

F: The most dangerous thing is like glass, if you throw glass you can get badly.

F: In my flat . . .

M: On the floor there's broken glass.

I: Which floor, sorry?

M: On the road there's always on the road. If you trip or fall then it goes into your hand and it really hurts and it's really sore.

M: I have a scar on my knee where a bit of broken glass went into my knee. It's on my knee. It went right into my knee and it came right out of the other end.

M: The other end?

M: Yeah, say it's like this then it came out like this.

M: Just round my flat when I get in, they go into the cupboards [there were large containers in the hallway] and smoke or take drugs. I don't like that. And the top bit they have a gate – they break that bit and all the boys can go up with all the girls and they take drugs. My friend the postman came up and he wanted to go into the flat to give his letter up but he couldn't as he had to go through the broken window to get there. To get into the flat.

M: These things are terrible, man.

F: That's the way life is. (all laugh)

M: You can't change it, can you?

M: Every area has good things and bad things. You can't have a really, really good area with no bad things.

'It's the way life is.' A one liner-thrown by one of the boys made all the children in the group burst into laughter, making them question: 'Does it have to be this way?' Can London, as Ackroyd (2000: 645) has recently intimated, only be 'reared and protected by the sacrifice of children'?

From the perspectives of the children participating in this study there were many ways of making their neighbourhoods more secure. When they were asked how their neighbourhood could be made a safer place, the themes of security, light and maintenance emerged as the most significant themes, as shown in Figure 9.7. There was some overlap with their parents' ideas, such as both parents and children stressing CCTVs and more police in the public domain, but also the children had other more distinctive wishes – for instance 'guards' outside shops and in parks. Our focus on security improvement in this question prompted children's own ideas about zoning - having special places and spaces for children, which would exclude specific categories of feared adults and other disruptive or violent children.

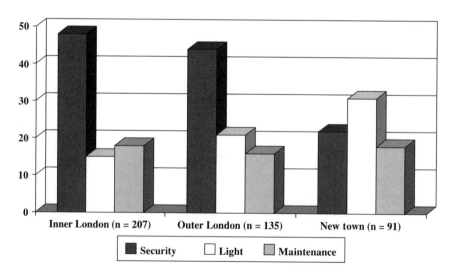

Figure 9.7 Making the neighbourhood a safer place, %

The theme of 'light' and the brightening up of streets and passageways was a particular concern of new town children for making neighbourhoods safer. Planning innovations such as the new town underpasses had unintended consequences for children which might have been avoided if children had been consulted. Holistic and flexible solutions, which attempt to meet children's desire for both self-determination and self-protection, could provide more successful child-sensitive neighbourhood revival strategies. Within inner London, increasing the power of street lights is an obvious practical solution. The illumination of public spaces is a relatively recent phenomenon, commencing in London towards the end of the seventeenth century, and although Oxford Street may shine powerfully and perpetually, paradoxically many residential streets still remain dimly lit. Weak night lighting systems contribute to children's sense of feeling unsafe even in places that in daylight are familiar.

Gardens, parks and urban amenities

Clearly one consequence of the high levels of population density in inner London is that they reduce children's pool of play spaces, in particular the garden. Within city centres such as London there are fewer green spaces and parks and fewer houses with attached gardens. The British, particularly the English, unlike many of their European partners, traditionally attach much significance to the garden ('the English country garden'), which is also typically an important outdoor play space for children. Indeed Valentine and McKendrick's (1997) work in north-west England suggests that 'the garden' has become synonymous with outdoor play for many children. Forty per cent of the parents in their study reported that most of their children's outside leisure play took place in gardens. Gardens provide a space to engage in a wide range of activities: playing with pets, playing ball, hanging out with friends and family, sunbathing, gardening, relaxing, cycling, barbecues, parties were all mentioned. Within our study, 30 per cent of inner London children had no garden, in comparison to 3 per cent in the suburbs and 1 per cent in the new town who were 'garden rich'.

Amongst 10- and 11-year-olds gardens were the favoured outside play area for the more affluent inner London neighbourhood, for children in Harrow and more generally for girls. The proportion of 'garden-poor' children rose to 48 per cent in the Tower Hamlets area, where children compensated with enhanced park usage: recent park attendance was also the highest in this neighbourhood – 72 per cent had visited a park in the last week in comparison to the inner London average of 45 per cent. Clearly parks still provide urban children with much valued play space, especially for those children with no access to a garden. In children's accounts parks gave lots of open space, opportunities to meet with friends and play games. For boys, parks were particularly appealing, with many using their local park space to play football. By contrast there was a tendency for girls not to bother with their parks (for example, only 35 per cent of inner-city girls had used them in the last week in comparison to 56 per cent of inner-city boys). Girls more generally perceived parks as unsafe or boring places. However, our data also suggested that when girls did use their parks they appeared to participate in a wider range of activities than boys. The favoured parks shone out, often close to home, 'small and cosy' in the new town, or multipurpose, welcoming, well-monitored and busy in London. Many children were also quite critical of and disappointed in their local park – poor maintenance, limited play apparatus, litter and dog waste were commonly mentioned as aspects of parks which were unattractive.

Whilst high density reduces the number of inner London's gardens and green spaces, it is fertile ground for easy access to a variety of consumer and leisure outlets. The range of consumer-oriented leisure spaces and their ease of access was liked by London's children – 'so many things to do' (and buy) if the finances were available.

I: So what's good about living around here?
F: Well there's lots and lots and lots of places to go, by bus or by tube. The tube is just down that road or just around that road. And there's one if you go round and up. There's lots of tube stations where you can get to and they're all different lines, which are really close. And there's buses that can go to places if you know the right bus to get on. That's really good 'cos there's lots of transport.
I: So that takes you to different places?
F: Yeah. Like if you want to go to the movies then you just go to the one down there or the one down there. Or if you want to go to a different one then you go to the one down there.
I: That sounds great.
F: And you can take the bus to the shopping centre. And there are video shops and things.
I: So there's some good things about living round here?
F: Yeah.
I: It's not all betting shops and pubs?
F: No. (both laugh)

So cities such as London can be exciting places for children because they offer a range of activities and facilities to participate in and consume, and the proximity of public transport can help children's mobility. One of the paradoxical aspects of the regulation of play for contemporary children is that it has led to the construction of many exciting dedicated areas and buildings for children within urban centres. Department stores such as IKEA and public houses now often have integrated play spaces for children within the building fabric (McKendrick *et al.* 2000). Many contemporary cities contain specialised theatres, museums, adventure playgrounds, city farms and leisure parks all designed with children in mind. London and other main cities are 'teeming' with cultural and leisure opportunities for children, as a glance at any *Kids Time Out* (a London magazine for children and parents) indicates. However, access to many of these new spaces, unlike the street, is dependent on children and their parents having money to spend. The continuing economic inequalities between children has meant that these significant cultural assets in London just pass by many children.

However, there are attractive aspects to living in London that do not cost money. The activity, business and noise of cities with the presence of other children, shops, roads, cars, Tubes and buses can create a buzz and immediacy for children in the urban centre lacking in less urbanised environments. A hankering after the excitement and diversity of city life emerged in one of the discussions amongst a group of new town children.

I: What's good about living here?
M: There are a lot of trees to climb and it's quiet.
M: I can't hear you as you have a pen in your mouth!
M: It's a peaceful place.
M: But it's boring!
M: Can I talk about Hollybank [local shopping centre] because . . .
M: Boring.
M: But I can walk to Hollybank and I go there a lot.
M: Boring!!
M: I can walk there though.
M: I know what's good. You can go to the woods at the top of the field.
M: You can ride your bike there and go through the woods. There are playing fields there as well.
F: It's really good as you can hide behind the fences as cars come by and you can scare cars as they come by.
F: Yeah and then we have to hide for fifteen minutes!! (all laugh)
F: We soaked the car with waterbombs and we soaked the driver. A 20-year-old.

These children living just on the edge of Hatfield, however, appeared to want the best of both worlds: that is, they wanted places that had the capacity to provide both solitude and the potential for excitement.

I: What would be your perfect city or place to live in?
M: A modern skyline and a big mega mall.
M: I want to live in Watford.
F: And it doesn't have any snobs.
F: I'd like to live in Watford.
F: 'Neighbourhood name' is wonderful.
M: Watford has a massive shopping centre and Megaworld.

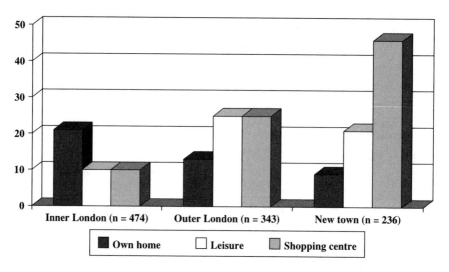

Figure 9.8 Children's liked buildings, %

M: Let's just go around in a circle and decide.
F: We've decided 'Hollybank' with a mega mall and a cinema.
M: A chippie and a mega mall.
I: So what does it feel to live in 'Hollybank'?
M: Boring.

Buildings and a sense of place: looking in, looking out?

Another way to explore children's neighbourhood pulse was through asking them about the favoured and least favoured buildings in their neighbourhood. Children's evaluations of the buildings in their neighbourhood suggested that the home itself may be a more salient element in inner London's children's representation of neighbourhood in comparison to their suburban and new town peers (Figure 9.8). Inner London children, particularly children in less affluent neighbourhoods, were more likely to choose their own home as their favoured building and to choose other estates or flats as their most unfavoured building. It may well be that high levels of attachment to home is but one of a range of adaptations children make to getting by in a more insecure urban locations. In this move 'inwards' and 'inside' into the private sphere children have the potential to shape their own personal places and identities within the home itself and in their movements between and perceptions of the inside and outside (see too Halldén, Chapter 3, above).

By contrast, the public buildings of leisure and shopping appear more salient in suburban and new town children's representations of neighbourhood:

Figure 9.9 The Galleria

46 per cent mentioned the Galleria (Figure 9.9), or a similar centre in a close-by town, as their favoured building – 'my fantasy' as one of our case-study new town girls described it (many also disliked the Galleria). It may be that the relative spatial freedom of the new town promoted an enhanced awareness of local public space and a sense of emotional connection, less possible in more anonymised contexts such as London. One new town girl who 'loved' the Galleria regularly cycled to it from home to shop but also just to stop by, look and gaze.

The case studies also revealed another important reason why some inner London children may favour their home most. For some children who experienced racial abuse in the public domain, for example in the street or at school, the domestic space served as a fortress or refuge against outside adversity. A complementarity appeared to develop whereby children's preference to stay indoors was supported by parental protection strategies. As one Afro-Caribbean mother of a self-defined indoor-orientated son reflected, 'I mean I'm here, whatever's going on out there [the local gangs and their "roughness"], that's their business.' The family lived their life in a style which attempted to block the outside world so that it did not infiltrate and pollute them further. Ward's (1978: 21) observation that disenfranchised urban children can be 'caught in a cage' aptly captures this family's existence.

In this movement 'inwards' and 'inside' into the private sphere children have the potential to shape their own personal places in the home, but this is a real choice only if all options for engagement in the public domain are equally available. Being home-based, chilling out, by choice in a materially rich spacious house is a world apart from exclusion in an over-crowded inner-city flat. Attention to differentiation in children's access to space in the public realm raises considerations about principles governing distributive justice and fairness in contemporary urban settings and their link to domestic space.

These data point to the growing importance of the home as a play space for children, whether by choice, parental constraint or other factors. The additional time that children spend in the home therefore puts pressure on the traditional layouts and space standards of conventional social housing. City planners will increasingly need to reconceptualise indoor as well as outdoor space requirements in the move towards child-friendly neighbourhoods.

Many factors identified in the study, such as varied access to the urban public realm, are unjust and unfair to children and could be ameliorated by some very practical and sometimes even simple interventions through which cities could be made more physically and emotionally available to all children. The suggestions made by children and parents participating in this study are summarised in Figure 9.11 opposite.

Figure 9.10 Fence surrounding a London park

- More powerful street lights that are closer to the ground
- Lighting up passageways
- Regular estate and street cleaning
- Walkabouts with different children prior to new developments
- Removal of child-unfriendly notices in parks e.g. 'no games'
- Consulting with girls to enhance parks' attractiveness to girls
- Sensitivity to materials used in defensive structures for parks and buildings (see Figure 9.10 taken by an 11-year old boy)
- Play areas close to home
- Regular neighbourhood-based and central 'free access for children's leisure events
- Designing in children's spaces within domestic dwellings

Figure 9.11 Child-friendly neighbourhood improvements

Conclusion

Making neighbourhoods good enough places for children and families is at the heart of the contemporary urban renaissance debate in Europe and North America. For some the renaissance is happening at too slow a pace for this generation of urban children, and these families are on the move. For other families, particularly those living in dual-earner or poor households, urban living remains the only viable economic or lifestyle option. The big question is: how can we organise and enhance the quality of life for both children and adults in our cities without pursuing an anti-urbanist stance?

Whilst it is the case that fear and loathing of inner-city traffic, pollution, crime, anonymity, density and poor public education have increased the attraction of out-of-town neighbourhoods for some parents, globally there is an inflow to cities because of the skills, jobs or knowledge nexus they contain. Moreover, as our data have shown, the close proximity of good transportation links and varied leisure and consumer outlets makes London highly attractive to many children. However, whilst the last twenty years have seen a burgeoning of dedicated places for children, many of these are expensive to access.

The recent arrival of a new Mayor and local government for London has created a significant shift towards a new public policy framework for advancing a child-centred urban regeneration programme. A concerted effort is being made to integrate a strategy to improve the position for London's children with a new spatial plan for the transformation of London's transport, building and neighbourhood developments (Mayor's Children's Strategy 2000).

A democratisation of our cities, such as that envisaged by the new London Mayor's Office, should include thinking about children in their everyday, nitty-gritty, ordinary life as well as in the grander projects. This chapter has included some examples of small and very practical steps, which would begin to enhance the quality of life for urban children and so help reduce divisions between children living in cities.

Notes

1 The Childhood, Urban Space and Citizenship: Child-sensitive Urban Regeneration project was part of the Economic and Social Research Council (ESRC) Research Programme on Children 5–15: Growing into the 21st Century, L12951039 (other team members were Jon Greenfield, Deborah Jones, David Sloan and Michael Rustin, to whom the author expresses many thanks).
2 The first stage of the study involved a child and parent school-based survey (n = 1,378) covering neighbourhood clusters in London and Hatfield, a first-generation British new town, situated some 60 miles north of London, built under the 1945 New Towns Act to house the overspill population from north and east London. The children were aged 10 years to 14 years. The second stage involved a sub-sample of twenty in-depth home-based case studies of 10–11-year-old children in their neighbourhood. Further details of the project are outlined in O'Brien *et al.* (1999).
3 In Britain there has been a tendency for people to move out of larger towns and cities into rural areas and smaller towns (DETR 2000). Rural areas tend to have settlements of fewer than ten thousand people and between 1981 and 1991 the rural share of postcode sectors in England increased by 7 per cent. Similarly, more people are moving from the inner cities to the suburbs. This trend is expected to continue despite projected population increases in London.
4 For instance, only 4 per cent of 10–11-year-olds did not play outside without adult supervision, were always accompanied to school and were never at home alone. By contrast just under one-quarter (23 per cent) of 10–11-year-olds were highly autonomous (played outside without adult supervision; were able to go to school unaccompanied and could be at home alone). The majority of children were situated in the middle range of the restricted–autonomous dimension.

References

Ackroyd, P., 2000, *London: The Biography* (London: Chatto and Windus).
Davin, A., 1996, *Growing Up Poor: Home, School and Street in London 1870–1914* (London: Rivers Oram Press).
Department of the Environment, Transport and the Regions (DETR), 2000, *Journey to School Project* (London: DETR).
Evening Standard, 2002, 14 February, 'Blunkett reads riot act on street crime'.
Hillman, M., Adams, J. and Whitelegg, J., 1990, *One False Move: A Study of Children's Independent Mobility* (London: PSI).
Humphries, S., Mack, J. and Perks, R., 1988, *A Century of Childhood* (London: Sidgwick & Jackson).
Littman, M., 2000, 'Gauging a neighbourhood pulse: measures for community research from The Aspen Institute'. *The Child Indicator*, 2 (1), 3–4.
Lynch, K., 1977, *Growing Up in Cities* (Cambridge, MA: MIT Press).
McKendrick, J., Bradford, M. and Fielder, A., 2000, 'Time for a party! Making sense of the commercialisation of leisure space for children'. In S. L. Holloway and

G. Valentine (eds), *Children's Geographies: Playing, Living and Learning* (London: Routledge).

Mayor's Children's Strategy, 2000, 'Issues paper'. Children's Strategy team. Available team@londonchildrenscommissioner.org.uk.

O'Brien, M., Rustin, M., and Greenfield, J., 1999, *End of ESRC Report Childhood, Urban Space and Citizenship: Child-sensitive Urban Regeneration*, L12951039, www.esrc.ac.uk.

O'Brien, M., Jones, D., Sloan, D. and Rustin, M., 2000, 'Children's independent spatial mobility in the urban public realm'. *Childhood*, 7 (3), 257–77.

Opie, I. and Opie, P., 1984, *Children's Games in Street and Playground* (Oxford: Oxford University Press).

Valentine, G. and McKendrick, J., 1997, 'Children's outdoor play: exploring parental concerns about children's safety and the changing nature of childhood'. *Geoforum*, 28, 2, 219–35.

Ward, C., 1978, *The Child in the City* (London: Architectural Press).

Young, K., 1995, 'Public space and civility in London'. In A. J. Halsey, R. Jowell and P. Taylor (eds) *The Quality of Life in London* (Hants: Dartmouth).

10 Improving the neighbourhood for children

Possibilities and limitations of 'social capital' discourses

Virginia Morrow

Background

The second half of the twentieth century saw increasing urbanisation and suburbanisation in the UK. The requirements of industry for increasing mobility of workers meant that housing was provided on a very large scale, and 'new towns', suburban sprawl and high-rise housing estates developed rapidly, particularly around parts of the south-east of England. Increased road building and corresponding volumes of road traffic have gradually changed the urban landscape in these areas. Children under 18 often constitute a disproportionately high section of the population of the suburbs and 'new towns' (Morrow 2001a). Local authority planning provision does not appear to have been able to keep up with changes in the structure of the population, nor changes in the physical structure of the landscape in terms of provision of leisure spaces, parks and places for children[1] to play in or to 'hang out' in (Morrow 2001a). However, renewed focus on the importance of neighbourhoods and communities in UK social policy has brought about a wave of social research that has explored lay people's concerns about their localities, and a consistent theme that emerges from this research (and policy concern) is anxiety about children and young people in neighbourhoods (SEU 2000).

The chapter draws on data collected in a research project conducted for the Health Education Authority[2] that explored the relevance of Putnam's (1993) concept of *social capital* in relation to children. Social capital consists of the following features: social and community networks; civic engagement or participation; community identity and sense of belonging; and norms of co-operation, reciprocity and trust of others within the community (Putnam 1993). The premise is that levels of social capital in a community have an important effect on people's well-being. Health behaviours and practices may superficially appear to be a private matter for the individual, but in reality health practices take place in a range of social arenas, which, for children, are constrained by everyday contexts, which will vary from school or institution (for previous research see Mayall 1994), family (see Backett 1992; Brannen *et al.* 1994; Christensen 1997) and peer group (see for example Christensen 1993; Michell 1997; Pavis *et al.* 1996, 1997). Neighbourhood health effects are less well documented in the UK, where health promotion research with children and young people has tended to focus on individual topics or risk behaviours (such as smoking, drug taking and alcohol consumption), and little is known about children's social networks, their views of their neighbourhoods, their levels of trust and community identity, and the implications of these for quality of life or well-being.

A critique of social capital in relation to children

Social capital is a concept that has been contested at a number of levels, conceputally, methodologically, and theoretically (see for example Fine 2000; Gamarnikow and Green 1999; Hawe and Shiell 2000; Labonte 1999) and much work still needs to be done to clarify how it can be used to formulate policy responses aimed at tackling health inequalities. Specifically, there are a number of conceptual problems inherent in trying to use social capital in relation to children. Firstly, it should be noted that Putnam did not intend the concept to incorporate young people, who are by definition excluded from civic participation by their very nature as 'children'. This is important, given the finding from previous research on the relationship between social capital and health in adults, that civic engagement appears to be more health-enhancing than other dimensions of social capital (Campbell *et al.* 1999). Secondly, there are definitional problems that relate to the meaning and measurement of the different components of the concept (Foley and Edwards 1999). In other words, what precisely is meant by concepts such as *trust, reciprocity, sense of belonging* and *community*, and how can these be measured in a meaningful way? Thirdly, previous research has tended to ignore economic and historical context (Portes and Landolt 1996), and, where the past is acknowledged, it tends to be romanticised (Levi 1996). Fourthly, the concept tends to be somewhat blind to gender differences (women's employment is seen negatively whether for community cohesion or for child outcomes) (Frazer and Lacey 1993); fifthly, it is not clear that the concept can be transported, and there are many obvious cultural differences between and within the UK and the USA (Rustin 1997); and finally, in much existing work on social capital, children are constructed as the passive recipients of culture, their agency is denied and there is no acknowledgement of how children actively generate, draw upon or negotiate their own social capital or even provide active support for parents (Morrow 1999).[3]

One of the problems of the recent wave of social capital research in the UK is that it was structured around Putnam's initial conceptualisation of social capital (Putnam 1993). Recent research on social capital has recognised that there are many forms of social capital. In his book on social capital in the USA, Putnam has emphasised the centrality of social networks to his definition of social capital, and played down the other elements. He has also suggested that there are two forms of social capital: bonding and bridging. Groups may have high levels of social capital that maintain group solidarity by bonding members together, but show very little of the kind of social capital that bridges other divisions such as gender, social class, ethnicity or generation (Putnam 2000). To further complicate the picture, others have suggested a third form, 'linking' social capital, in other words, social capital that bridges or links groups to influential others (Foley and Edwards 1999). For Putnam, social capital is essentially a community-level attribute that can be measured empirically. In policy terms it is then assumed that social capital can somehow be 'built' in order to counter social exclusion. This is in marked contrast to ideas about social capital found in Bourdieu's work, which provides a more complex and contextual account of differ-ent forms of capital – symbolic, economic, cultural and social – and their interrelationships. In *Distinction* (1984), and more explicitly in 'The forms of capital' (1986), Bourdieu distinguishes between cultural capital and social capital. Cultural capital can exist in various forms: institutional cultural capital (that is, academic qualifications); embodied cultural capital (part-icular styles, modes of presentation, including use of language, forms of social etiquette and competence, as well as a degree of confidence and self-assurance); and objectified cultural capital (material goods such as writings, paintings and so on). Social capital for Bourdieu consists of two key elements: firstly, social networks and connections: 'contacts and group member-ships which, through the accumulation of exchanges, obligations and shared identities, provide actual or potential support and access to valued resources' (Bourdieu 1993: 143); and secondly, sociability, in other words, how net-works are sustained, which requires necessary skill and disposition. Bourdieu is primarily concerned with how economic capital underpins these other 'disguised' forms, how these forms of capital interact with wider structures to reproduce social inequalities, and how the day-to-day activities of social actors draw upon and reproduce structural features of wider social systems.

For Bourdieu, the outcomes of possession of various forms of capital (sym-bolic, cultural, social) are reducible to the economic: but the processes that bring about these alternative forms of capital are not. Each has its own dynamic: the processes of conversion of these different forms of capital are 'character-ised by less transparency and more uncertainty'. Thus, exchanges involving social capital 'tend to be characterised by unspecified obligations, uncertain time horizons, and the possible violation of reciprocity expectations. But, by their very lack of clarity, these transactions can help disguise what otherwise would be plain market exchanges' (Portes 1998: 4). Elsewhere Bourdieu suggests that symbolic capital 'is the form in which the different forms of capital are perceived and recognised as legitimate' (Bourdieu 1985: 724). This interrelationship tends to be missing from the current debates about social capital that follow Putnam's conceptualisation.

Operationalisng 'social capital': methodology and methods

The research reported in this chapter utilised the sociology of childhood paradigm[4] and welfare research paradigm[5] to explore the following questions with children:

- social networks: what is the composition, durability, ease of access to and frequency of use of children's social networks? How are these networks defined and what do these networks provide, and how does this differ according to age and gender? What does friendship 'mean' to this age group?
- local identity: do children have a sense of belonging and identity with their neighbourhoods or communities?
- attitudes to institutions and facilities in the community: what physical spaces, such as parks, streets, leisure centres, clubs used for social interaction, are available to and used by children? Do children feel safe in their neighbourhoods?
- community and civic engagement: to what extent do children engage in local community activities? To what extent do they feel they participate in community and institutional decision-making?

The research explored 12–15-year-olds' subjective experiences of their neighbourhoods, their quality of life, the nature of their social networks and their participation in their communities (see Morrow 1999, 2000a, 2001b).[6] The research was carried out in two schools in relatively deprived wards in 'Springtown' (all names in this chapter are pseudonyms[7]). Springtown is about 30 miles from London, and has grown very rapidly. The population of the town was 172,000 in the 1991 census, and the 1996 mid-year estimate was 182,000. Almost one-third of the population of the town are under 20 years of age. Research was carried out in two parts of the town, 'West' and 'Hill'. 'West' consisted of 'suburban sprawl' on the outskirts of the town, with postwar housing and factories; 'Hill' consisted of a mixture of industrial development, and Victorian interwar and postwar housing development. Research was carried out in schools, and the sample comprised 101 boys and girls in two age bands: 12–13-year-olds and 14–15-year-olds, with a significant proportion from minority ethnic groups. In West School, three children were African-Caribbean, two South Asian and three white/African-Caribbean. In Hill School, there were children whose families originated in Greece, Turkey, Cyprus, South Asia, and the African-Caribbean. One or two children declined to describe themselves as being from a particular minority ethnic group.

The research used a variety of qualitative methods with the children:

- children's written accounts of out-of-school activities, their descriptions of people who were important to them and why; their 'brainstorm' responses to the questions 'what is a friend?' and 'what are friends for?', their future aspirations and whether or not they knew someone who was doing that kind of job; their descriptions of where they felt they 'belonged'

• visual methods, including map drawing and photography by the participants of 'places that are important to me' (see also Rasmussen and Smidt, Chapter 6, above). This generated seventeen maps or drawings and a hundred photos

• group discussions, exploring use of and perceptions of neighbourhoods, how they would improve their neighbourhoods, and their community and institutional participation. As a 'prompt' in group discussions, children were shown two newspaper cuttings: one depicting their town in negative terms, and one on 'child curfews' (see Morrow 2001b).

The research thus generated a range of qualitative data, and this chapter draws on some of these data to explore children's perspectives on their social networks and their neighbourhoods.

Friendship

Positive relationships with friends (and family members) appeared to provide the main source of a strong sense of belonging to children in this age group. Friends' houses featured in the maps and photos. As noted, they were asked to photograph places, not people, but children often found ways of incorporating friendship into these photos and maps.

'This road is the most important road because it leads to my *friend*'s house' (Tom, 14)

'My old school: I often play football there with my *friends*' (Bob, 14)

'This is our school playground, we hang around with our *friends* there' (Wendy, Leila, Chloe, West area)

'This is McDonald's. I always go there every week with my *friends*' (Jennifer, West area)

'Park. Where I used to go as a child and still go with my *friends* now' (Maggie, Hill area)

'School. Where we sit at lunch time' (Maria, Hill area)

'I took this photo of my *friend*'s house, because she is my next door neighbour, and I hang around in and outside her house' (Gemma, Hill area)

'Corner of a street where I meet my *friends*' (Mary, Hill area)

'[High Road] area. Lots of my *friends* live there' 'My *friend*'s house, I'm often in there, and there is a park behind the house' (Jagu, Hill area)

Children often spend more time with their friends than they do with their families, especially as they get older. As Veronica, 15, put it: 'Why are my friends important? Because, I spend nearly all of my time with them.' And Maria, 14, 'My friends are also very important to me because I spend so much of my life with them.' Their daily activities were often structured around encounters with friends:

> After school I often ring my friends and talk on the phone for quite a while as well ... After eating I will either go round a friend's house, go to a local youth club, the cinema, or just stay in. My weekends are usually spent in the town centre with different friends. I sometimes go to the cinema, or bowling, or just out.
>
> (Maria, 14)

In many cases, how children felt about where they live seemed to depend on proximity to friends:

> I love my house and my area, because there are three parks near me, the town is a five-minute walk away, the school is close and I can visit my friends without having to take a bus or walk miles. Most of my friends live in Hill Ward, or my area.
>
> (Maggie, age 15, Hill area)

Not having friends living nearby was a reason children gave for disliking their neighbourhoods, and this seemed to be more marked in West School, which, as noted above, was in a sprawling, suburban locality with few facilities for children. It seems likely therefore that density of population has implications for children's social networks and, as it was mostly girls who described this, it could reflect parental constraints on girls' mobility. For example, Olanda, 14, described how 'I'm fairly happy with where I live but would rather live in my old house ... this is because a lot of my close friends live up there. Usually I walk up there most days after school. It would be a lot less hassle if I lived up there near them.' Rebecca, 13, described how she doesn't like her neighbourhood:

> It's boring, there's not many people of my age living round there. Because my best friend moved away she only lives 10 minutes away, but it's too much to walk every day there. I've been *best friends* with her all my life, and I've never broken up with her once. We do a lot of things together.
>
> (Rebecca, 13)

Jody, 14, described how 'It's a bit awkward because I live two miles away from the school and my mates live quite far away. At least I still have my old mates who live near me and I always make time for them.' In Hill School, some children did comment that they don't see their friends as often as they like, for example, Tobi, 13, described how 'During the week I don't go out much because all my friends live up in [Hill Ward] and I live down town'; and Amanda, 13, who lives outside Hill Ward, described how 'There is nowhere around the area where I live to go in the evenings, and it is too far to go to my friend's house every night. So by the time I get there, I have to go soon after.' In a discussion when asked 'how would you improve your area?', Paris, 13, who lived in Hill Ward, said, 'Have all my friends live next door to me.'

Ethnicity was another important factor for understanding how children experienced their area. In a group discussion with younger boys in Hill area, two boys said how much they liked their neighbourhoods. Wassef (13, of Pakistani-Kashmiri origin) said: 'Yeah, but the thing is, he lives in a good place, in Hill Ward, because he's got all his mates there, it's got a community, and he [the other boy] lives just off town, he's got all the mates you can have, there, he's like the centre of attention where he lives.' Ajit, 15 (Indian), described how 'I don't like the area I live in, as many of my friends live far away from my area and I can't walk there, I would rather live in [another part of town] as more of my Indian friends live there.'

Children's accounts of where they feel they 'belong' similarly highlighted the importance of social relationships rather than geographical place: most children said they felt they 'belonged' at home, with their friends and family, and as one boy put it, 'I think I belong in a community where I am treated right, and a place that is warm and friendly' (Rock, 15, Jamaican/white background).

In terms of social capital, then, informal social networks of friendship were crucial to leisure activities and provided a source of security and trust (see also Zeiher, Chapter 5, above). Some children described having two homes and thus two sets of friendship groups, in the case of parental separation. Time spent at school was important because it was time to be with their friends: in this sense, school was a source of identity and belonging to the community. Family members (especially mothers) were described as a source of support and 'being there' when needed; and wider kin were also frequently mentioned, even though they lived in other parts of the country or abroad. In children's responses to questions about their future aspirations and whether or not they already knew someone doing the kind of job they aspired to, familial networks appeared to be the most likely source of information about jobs in the future, and these networks were not only locally based but spread widely.

How did the material circumstances of children's physical environments impact on their relationships with their friends? The rest of this chapter explores children's perspectives on these environmental settings, and highlights the contradictory nature of their experiences of communal areas. While friendships for the most part were perceived very positively, children's accounts of the practical problems they encounter in leading their social lives in their town and their neighbourhoods – for example the lack of appropriate places for them to go (especially as they become older) – were very negative. The chapter then explores children's suggestions for how their neighbourhoods might be improved (the *possibilities*); and finally it discusses their lack of participation in their communities (the *limitations*). Many writers have pointed to the importance for children to do things away from the gaze and control of adults. The lack of such opportunities is likely to have adverse effects upon children's social and emotional development as well as their quality of life in the here and now (Adams 1995; see also Davis and Jones 1996, 1997; Henderson 1995).

Children's perspectives on their neighbourhoods and public space

Generally, children described their town and neighbourhood environments negatively. Children who lived in a cul-de-sac in a suburban area, for example, mentioned that it was 'too quiet and boring', and children who lived on a busy street said 'There's too much traffic.' There were differences according to gender, ethnicity and age. None of the children participating in this study described themselves as a 'Springtonian'. They were well aware of the negative reputation of their town and of particular parts of the town. They also knew the areas that were safe and those that were not. Overall, children described a strong sense of exclusion on a number of levels related in particular to the lack of appropriate facilities for children and of 'places to go'; cost barriers; and the practical problems caused by traffic.

Facilities and activities

All children described 'not having enough to do' in terms of appropriate facilities, activities and places to go. Very few described involvement in organised voluntary activities: six boys mentioned being members of a formal sports team; and ten children mentioned using the local youth clubs. For most children, especially boys, their activities outside school centred around playing football, cricket and cycling, informally with friends in local parks and neighbourhood spaces. However, these parks were often not pleasant places to go for a number of reasons. Harry, 13, described how:

> there's a park where we live, we call it 'Motorway Field' because it's right by the motorway, and it's just covered in dogs' muck, you just don't like to go there, people let their dogs go anywhere, so we like to play football there, but 'cos you don't know where the dogs' muck is, you don't play because you don't want to get covered in it.

Dog mess was nearly always mentioned as a problem in the context of playing in local parks. Rock, 15, photographed a primary school playing field near where he lived, and described how he plays football there: 'It's good,

Figure 10.1 I play football here

because there are no dogs, and no adults screaming at you to stop'. See Figure 10.1.

Several younger children described a lack of wild places where they could play and 'make dens'. One girl in West area said 'We used to have a den, in the woods there, and me and my friend found loads of, like, drugs and stuff, packets and things, so we took them to the police'. One 12-year-old boy mentioned that he didn't like his area:

> 'cos it's so built up, there's not much to do, and like, where my sister lives, she lives in [another town], and just across the road there's a big forest, and my brother likes to go over there with their dog, and they'd be out for hours and hours, and that's what I like when I go there.

Older children perceived local youth clubs as being suitable only for younger children, and a few of the younger children did use them and liked them. Youth clubs were not particularly popular with girls, either, and some felt there was not enough for girls to do at the youth clubs: 'All they do is play football and basketball' (i.e. activities for boys). On the other hand, some of the boys in the same year group did use the youth club: Fred described how 'It's open three times a week, I go there most times, sports, play games, listen to music.' A lack of things to do and places to go was a general explanation by participants for their sometimes 'anti-social' behaviour: 'We're

Figure 10.2 No Ball Games

only getting into trouble because we're hanging around on the street because there's nothing for us to do.'

Many children mentioned 'No Ball Games' signs that prevented them from playing near their homes on patches of communal grass. The signs were photographed (see Figure 10.2) depicted on maps and discussed in groups by the children themselves: Isabelle, 15, explained her photograph: 'This is a sign that is on a piece of greenery on my road. It stops children from playing typical games, but little children need somewhere to play . . . they may not be allowed to go to the park.' In a later discussion she said

> They've got 'No ball games' signs all over our streets, and there are loads
> of little pieces of grass where kids could just play, and be fairly happy and
> fairly safe, but they put up 'No ball games' signs and then they can't play
> there, and it's like stopping them from . . . enjoying themselves.
>
> (Isabelle, 15)

Another girl, Katie, 13, included the sign on her map, and wrote underneath: 'not fair'.

Exclusion by cost

In both schools, the cost of activities was frequently mentioned as a barrier to participating fully in community life, and there appeared to be very few leisure opportunities for children in the town that did not involve spending money. A new leisure complex had recently been opened in the town centre, but all age groups in both sites complained about the cost. A group of younger children had the following discussion:

Cameron: If there was a swimming pool, or a cheaper cinema, we'd be there.
Dion: If they made more . . . like adventure centres, . . . and things like that, then we'll be down there nearly every weekend, and things like that, but since they don't have anything like that we wander about the streets and get in trouble for it.
Shannon: The most fun thing we can do, without our parents having to pay for it, is just go and walk round the shops in town.
Dion: Exactly.
Angelina: And we can't afford it, 'cos we can't get jobs at the moment.
Casey: It's hard, 'cos me mum don't get paid that much.

For children in both schools the town centre was an attraction. Older children described how 'I like town better, there's much more action'. However, children from West area, which was further away from the town centre than Hill area, complained that the bus fare would rise to an adult fare when they are 13 or 14 years old, but that they would not necessarily have much money to spend on the expensive entertainments in town. One girl in Hill area said: 'The thing that annoys me is that the police always moan that we're on the streets, so they build places like the new clubs and stuff, but we have to pay to get into that.' Further, when children went into the town centre, they felt they were regarded with suspicion by security guards and shopkeepers, who gave them 'dirty looks' because they thought the children would be shoplifting (Matthews *et al.* 2000; Morrow 2000a; Woolley *et al.* 1999).

Practical exclusion and the problem of road traffic

Road traffic was a major preoccupation in discussions particularly with the younger children. They described how it was often very difficult for them even simply to cross the road. Kellie described how in her neighbourhood there was 'nothing to do much, we live on a main road, it's quite busy, it's hard to cross the road'. Rebecca added: 'I don't like the person across the road, because we have to make sure when we cross the road, there's this man, that lives across the road, and he zooms round and he nearly hit my brother.' Others complained about motorbikes joyriding, or riding on pavements:

> We have motor bikes that come straight onto the mud track of the field, they go straight past the houses and down and you have little kids

walking sort of like on the path and that, and they have motorbikes that go down there. (Kerry)

In both schools, the issue of traffic led to long discussions and graphic descriptions of accidents and near-accidents:

Cameron: My brother got run over a couple of weeks ago, by a bus driver, and the bus driver just opened the window and swore at him, but . . . [my brother] was on his bike, and he gave way, because they come so fast round the corner, he hit him, and just started shouting at him, through the thing, and left him in the road . . .

Dion: it's getting worse, like now, 'cos like when it was in my mum's, and your time, it would have been safer, out on the streets, now it's even worse.

The traffic was also a problem for Casey, who described how when she is babysitting a little boy: 'I can't take 'em anywhere, because [the little boy] runs around the streets, and one time he was crossing the road . . . he was about that much away from getting knocked over.' A discussion among a group of 12- and 13-year-olds illustrated the everyday encounters with careless driving by children:

Sonia: Miss, there's traffic lights, you know down town there's that road, there was a car going by, there was a lot of traffic, the light was red, it just went past.

Charles: I was nearly run over outside school walking across the zebra crossing! A car speeded up and just missed me.

Iftikhar: When they're turning they should use the little yellow light [i.e. indicator] because they don't use it.

Busy roads formed a barrier to children's freedom of movement, and it seems likely that traffic may impinge on their social interactions in significant ways. Hillman's (1993) study showed how increased traffic was used by parents as a reason not to allow their children out on the streets on their own, and other recent research from elsewhere in the UK has shown that traffic may constrain neighbourhood activities for children (Davis and Jones 1996, 1997).

Improving the area: the possibilities

Children discussed ways that their neighbourhoods might be improved, and they made a range of practical suggestions. These can be clustered around the following themes: activities for their age group, and for older or younger children; suggestions about improving the traffic, and making the paths and shortcuts they used safer and cleaner; and finally, suggestions about the police.

Activities for children

Most of the children's suggestions for improvement centred on the provision of leisure facilities. One girl said: 'To make our neighbourhood better, I think they should do stuff for teenagers.' Others said 'they should have more facilities', 'make the parks better', 'just somewhere to go'. Other suggestions included better BMX tracks, more clubs, ballet and gymnastics and dance clubs, and so on. Bart, 13, who lived in West area, described how 'Motorway Field' 'is like a long strip, and at the end, there is this round bit, there's a few trees there, but it'd be nicer if . . . they planted more trees there, so it was like a little mini-forest where people can build dens, that won't be kicked in and stuff, so there's more variety of things to do.' As already noted, others expressed a strong view that if there were more facilities, they wouldn't undertake anti-social activities.

One notable feature of some suggestions was the concern expressed for other members of their communities. Several girls suggested there should be more facilities 'for little kids'. Cameron, a 13-year-old girl living in Hill area, described how disappointed her 9-year-old cousin was when she was finally allowed out on her own: 'My little cousin, she was so excited, she couldn't wait, her mum said right, "I'll let you out, you're allowed out to go to the park and whatever you want to do, call for your friends", and she was so excited, she got out, and she went, "Oh, is this it?"' In other words, her cousin was disappointed to find that, although she was now allowed to go to many new places in the neighbourhood, it did not offer her exciting activities. Cameron was also very bothered by 'joyriders'.[8] She had a well-formulated solution to this problem: 'Because most of the boys down our area are interested in cars, and motorbikes, if they could learn about mechanics, then maybe they would be off the streets, because at the moment, that's why they're breaking into them.'

Paths, routes and roads

Some children in both study sites complained about the difficulties encountered on the shortcuts and routes they took. One girl, in Hill area, said

> I hate walking through subways, I walk through two subways on the way to school, and I think 'Am I ever going to get to school?' 'Cos you don't know whether there's someone hanging around the corner, or whatever, or following you behind, no one would see you if you're under the subway, so . . . and I hate walking through.

A boy in West area described how 'There's this great big wind tunnel, and you can't see around it, and you can't see who's in there, and there's often quite a lot of people in there that are like . . . drunk.' Children had a number of suggestions for making these routes safer and cleaner. These included the installation of mirrors in subways, CCTV cameras, better street lighting, more bins for litter, and more signs telling dog owners to pick up dog mess. As we have already seen, road traffic was described as a problem, and children had many suggestions as to how to calm the traffic, including more traffic lights, parking on one side of the road to slow the cars down, more speed bumps and, not least, telling drivers to use their indicators.

Security, safety and fear

Many of the children in West area suggested that seeing more police officers on the street would make their neighbourhoods feel safer. As John said, 'I've only seen policemen in cars, I've never seen a bobby on the beat.' However, simply putting more policemen on the streets was not straightforwardly accepted by all children, and some young black men described how they felt under threat not only from other groups of young people but also from the local police. In Hill area, children felt as though they were specifically targeted by the police, as Asa May complained: 'The police go round our area, looking for my age playing about, but they don't do anything about all the ones who have left school, driving around in their cars, they don't worry about them. And when they're looking for us, they could be doing other things, instead of looking for kids playing.'

In summary, children were resourceful commentators on their environments, and they put forward many reasonable suggestions for improving their areas (see also Baraldi, Chapter 11, below). However, one of the problems for this age group, as the next section shows, is that there are no consistent channels for them to communicate these views about their environments.

Exclusion from participation: the limitations[9]

As noted, Putnam's emphasis on civic participation as a key aspect of social capital is obviously somewhat limited in the case of children, given that they are positioned outside of democratic structures by their very nature as 'minors'. Indeed, participation in community decision-making for children was extremely limited. Only one boy felt he could go to his local residents' association and make suggestions about his local area. If the council did ask about local facilities, they felt that their parents were consulted, not them. Amy said: 'They send questionnaires to our parents but it's not our parents who want to go to the Youth Club. It's us!! So they should ask us.' One girl said: 'I don't think people are really bothered about kids'; in another group a boy said: 'They just do things like little tiny parks for little kids . . . we don't want little parks.' One girl commented that she felt they should have a say in the community, 'because what happens does affect us as well as the adults and they don't seem to think about that when they're making decisions'. Although the town council has recently started a 'Youth Forum', the children were not aware of it. Furthermore, as Miranda's comment, below, suggests, some children will also be well aware of the limits of democratic participation and representation. In a group discussion three girls discussed the council's initiative in this way. This is an extract from their conversation.

Gemma: No one knows about it, if there is one.
Tamisha: I think there should be one, but . . .
Miranda: But they'd choose the people who do all the best in school, and everything, and they're not average people, are they?

   These data suggest that participation, in the sense of being actively involved in decisions that affect them in their neighbourhoods, appears to be virtually non-existent for children. Even where supposedly democratic structures such as school councils are in place, as was the case in one of the schools, children did not seem to feel they were experiencing 'participation' through them, and the exclusion they feel is likely to limit their sense of self-efficacy and control over their environments (see Morrow 2000b). One of the problems facing this age group is that they have no formal channels through which to communicate, or to convert their energy into a positive resource for their neighbourhoods. Youth forums are the most common way of facilitating children's views, but they do not necessarily work effectively (see Fitzpatrick *et al.* 1998).

Implications for social capital

In summary, this chapter has suggested that children's views of their physical environments were fairly negative. They did not appear to derive a strong sense of belonging from identifying with Springtown. Rather, social interaction with friends was, from their point of view, crucial for a sense of belonging. They described a range of practical issues that impinged on their social interactions with friends, such as traffic and lack of facilities. Hill area was perceived as particularly inadequate by the children participating in the study because of the lack of green spaces in which to play ball games. The town centre was a strong attraction for children, but often experienced negatively because of the 'dirty looks' children felt they got from security guards, shopkeepers and other adults. Further, visits to the town centre involved spending money, or the temptation to spend money, and their cash was often limited.
   In terms of possibilities for improving their neighbourhoods, as I have shown, children put forward and discussed many reasonable and practical suggestions. However, they were well aware that they had limited self-efficacy and participation in their neighbourhoods. As noted, in terms of civic participation, this is not really surprising, but the experiences they have *as children* may have implications for their perceptions of democratic institutions and structures later on when they do leave school, and this raises the question of whether or not a 'healthy scepticism' is learnt early on in life. They were frequently faced with situations that did not meet their perceived needs, and

sometimes children feel that the only forms of resistance available to them are 'anti-social' ones. Young people and children are rarely regarded as stakeholders in their communities, and their perspectives and views are not consistently elicited, as the data reported in this chapter study show (see also Speak 2000).

There were elements of children's social lives that fit the 'plural' forms of social capital discussed at the beginning of this chapter. However, these can work in contradictory ways. Bonding social capital derived from tight friendships and group membership does not necessarily contribute to social cohesion for children. On the contrary, the way that children go round in 'gangs' may have a negative effect upon social cohesion. At the individual level, children probably need both bonding social capital, for their experience of social support and emotional well-being in the here and now, and bridging social capital for the future, to help children to enter the labour market. Linking social capital, however – that is, enabling children to gain access to power structures and influential others – was clearly lacking for these children. However, the data gave rise to more complex forms of capital than merely well-defined forms of social capital, and thus, operationalising social capital in Putnam's sense in community-based empirical research is too limited. The chapter therefore concludes by discussing some of these limitations, clustered around methodological, conceptual and theoretical issues.

Methodological problems

Putnam's notion of social capital hinges upon being able to define community as a geographically circumscribed area, and for children this is problematic. This chapter has shown that community for children appears to be located in a sense of belonging that resides in relationships with other people, rather than in places. The study suggested that a number of different elements of social life comprise 'community' for children. Firstly, school is a community, in that it is an important site for social interaction with other children. Secondly, families and wider kin are communities, and family may be in more places than one, in the case of parental separation or migration. Thirdly, a child's neighbourhood may be experienced as a safe or hostile community. Fourthly, children may be members of a community of interest, for example participating a dance class located in a neighbouring area or a sports club in a different part of town. For children, then, community is more often a virtual community of friends based around school, town centre and street, friends' and relatives' houses, and sometimes having two homes, and thus two sets of friends in two different towns, rather than a tightly bound easily identifiable geographical location.

Elements of social capital may be experienced differently according to gender, age and cultural, religious, or ethnic background. The study highlighted how children are not a homogeneous category. Social capital needs to be able to accommodate a range of different social identities. For girls, for example, personal safety was a crucial issue, and sexual assault was perceived as a threat.

There were differences in children's accounts according to age: the needs of 12-year-olds, for example, for places to play and make dens differed from the needs of 15-year-olds, for example for places to socialise away from the sometimes hostile gaze of adults. Further, there were significant differences in priorities according to ethnic background, and several children experienced racial harassment. Such harassment is likely to lead to social and emotional exclusion, and this kind of hostility is likely to inhibit social cohesion at the neighbourhood level (see also O'Brien *et al.* 2000).

Conceptual problems

In this sense social capital is a woolly, catch-all category that incorporates a number of features, some of which have relevance to children's experiences of everyday life. For example, social cohesion may arise from knowing your neighbours simply because you've lived next door to them for a long time. But does this really constitute social capital? Further, a tool for analysis of social environments needs to be dynamic and able to accommodate the way families, children, friendships, social networks, institutions, norms and values change temporally (through the life course) and spatially (as neighbours come and go).

Theoretical limitations

There were a number of theoretical limitations to using social capital in the research. Firstly, children experienced a range of practical, environmental and economic constraints. These included the extent to which their ability to move around freely to participate in activities with their friends is likely to be constrained by the physical geography of the built environment, issues of community safety and traffic, and parental norms about when children may go out, as well as access to financial resources. These issues are usually neglected in studies of children's health behaviours. Furthermore, these constraints might be more usefully conceptualised as influencing children's access to social resources, rather than social capital per se. There is a danger that, in operationalising social capital in research based on Putnam's conceptualisation, other forms of capital (material, economic, symbolic) are overlooked, as the social is reified and separated out as a unit of analysis. It seems unlikely that merely adding different forms of social capital (bridging, linking, bonding) to the equation will help to address these limitations.

Secondly, Bourdieu's concept of sociability (the ability and disposition to sustain and use one's networks) as a component of social capital must be accounted for: actors need to recognise their networks as a resource in order for these networks to constitute social capital, in other words, there has to be some agency involved. Bourdieu's 'social capital' is conceptualised as the property of individuals or actors, or groups, but is not generalisable to 'geographical communities'. It was clear from the study that neither bonding nor bridging social capital was confined to the neighbourhood. Further, bonding social capital resides in friendship relationships and peer groups that provide a sense of belonging in the here and now, and symbolic capital was clearly related to this sense of belonging. Moreover, relationships that give rise to bonding social capital are not necessarily neighbourhood-based. Further, linking social capital (access to influential others and power structures) may be underpinned by the other forms of capital described by Bourdieu.

Thirdly, the term appears to be used in different ways. Social researchers may see social capital as a tool with which to explore the social world, while policy-makers seem to conceptualise it as a 'build'-able, measurable 'thing'. Putnam's social capital is being expected to carry a heavy burden as a theoretical basis upon which to develop social policy responses to social exclusion and deprivation, and there is a danger that social capital becomes a kind of deficit theory syndrome, yet another resource that unsuccessful communities or neighbourhoods lack. Some have argued that a focus on social capital facilitates a neo-liberal withdrawal of the welfare state (Fine 2000). In *The Weight of the World* (1999), Bourdieu draws attention to the ways in which government policy is often the cause of some of these effects, and this too is missing in the social capital debates. Rather than seeing social capital as a measurable outcome, it might be more helpful, I suggest, to use it as a heuristic device with which to explore processes and practices that are integral to social life, and to other forms of 'capital'.

More optimistically, there are undoubtedly advantages to using social capital as a research tool, and the social capital research in the UK has undoubtedly enabled social policy research to focus on the circumstances of people's everyday lives. In the study reported here, a focus on social capital as a community level attribute has allowed research to prioritise the social context of children's everyday lives, rather than their individual health behaviours. Children's subjective views and explanations of their social worlds, their neighbourhoods and networks, have been highlighted, and these offer perspectives that differ from adult-oriented preoccupations about the needs of this age group. These data show clearly that children are well able to articulate their views about their social environments. It is arguably necessary to understand whether children have a sense of belonging in their neighbourhoods if we want to bring children's views into the policy debates around public health (Davis and Jones 1996, 1997). Social capital is thus useful as a tool for exploring social processes and practices around children's experiences of their environments, and in doing so, it has highlighted children's social resources (or lack of them). The implication of this is that social capital needs to be conceptualised in relation to the other forms of capital that underpin it or are related to it. However, the relationship between the different forms of capital to each other, and to wider economic and political structures, and the attention to processes rather than outcomes, are missing from most debates about social capital. In exploring these issues in relation to children and young people this chapter has focused on one element of social life, that is, neighbourhood quality of life. There is a danger that, in doing so, broader questions may be overlooked, and the wider political responsibilities of central and local governments to ensure a good quality of life for children in environmental terms also need to be addressed.

Notes

1 For the purposes of this chapter, I am using the definition in the UN Convention on the Rights of the Child and will refer to all children and young people under the age of 18 as 'children'.
2 Then the health promotion arm of the England and Wales Department of Health; now the Health Development Agency, based in London.
3 It should also be noted that Putnam's formulation of social capital is derived partly from theoretical ideas developed in the USA by Coleman (1988), and an important strand of research has developed in the USA on parents' social capital and its impact on outcomes in children (see e.g. Furstenberg and Hughes (1995) for a useful critique).
4 Boyden and Ennew (1997), Christensen and James (2000), James and Prout (1997).
5 The emerging 'welfare research' paradigm seeks to incorporate social context into health research and to explore the importance of 'place', 'lay knowledge' and lay narratives into theories and research on health inequalities (Macintyre *et al.* 1993; Popay *et al.* 1998; Williams *et al.* 1999).
6 The research did not explore the direct effects of parents' or family social capital on children (see, for example Allatt 1993, 1996). Rather the intention was to explore the advantages and disadvantages of conceptualising social capital as a community level attribute in relation to children.
7 I have tended to anonymise both places and names in research I have conducted with children, for ethical reasons. In the study reported here, this was to assure those involved in the research process of the confidentiality of the research: the children themselves, the schools and representatives of the town council and the local health promotion agency who helped set up the research. Previous research in the same town had named the town, and everyone involved in this research appeared to be appreciative of the fact that the town would not be named in future research reports.
8 This term is used to describe someone taking a car without the owner's permission and driving it dangerously.
9 A further ethical point to note is that, in seeking consent, care was taken not to raise children's expectations about what the research might produce in the way of change in their environments. This was a serious concern for everyone involved in the research, was often raised by the children, and was discussed at length. Preliminary findings were fed back to the children in a leaflet and they were asked whether their views were represented fairly and accurately. Findings were also disseminated to the relevant agencies and the town council.

References

Adams, R., 1995, 'Places of childhood'. In P. Henderson (ed.), *Children and Communities* (London: Pluto Press).
Allatt, P., 1993, 'Becoming privileged: the role of family process'. In I. Bates and G. Riseborough (eds), *Youth and Inequality* (Buckingham: Open University Press).
Allatt, P., 1996, 'Consuming schooling: choice, commodity, gift and systems of exchange'. In S. Edgell, K. Hetherington and A. Warde (eds), *Consumption Matters:*

The Production and Experiences of Consumption (Oxford: Blackwell/The Sociological Review).

Backett, K., 1992, 'Taboos and excesses: lay health moralities in middle class families'. *Sociology of Health and Illness*, 14 (2), 255–74.

Bourdieu, P., 1984, *Distinction: A Social Critique of the Judgement of Taste* (London: Routledge).

Bourdieu, P., 1985, 'The social space and the genesis of groups'. *Theory and Society*, 14 (6), 723–44.

Bourdieu, P., 1986, 'The forms of capital'. In J. G. Richardson (ed.), *Handbook of Theory and Research for the Sociology of Education* (New York: Greenwood Press).

Bourdieu, P., 1993, *Sociology in Question* (London: Sage).

Bourdieu, P., 1999, *The Weight of the World Social Suffering in Contemporary Society* (Cambridge: Polity Press).

Boyden, J. and Ennew, J., 1997, *Children in Focus: A Manual for Participatory Research with Children* (Stockholm: Radda Barnen).

Brannen, J., Dodd, K., Oakley, A. and Storey, P., 1994, *Young People, Health and Family Life* (Milton Keynes: Open University Press).

Campbell, C., with Wood, R. and Kelly, M., 1999, *Social Capital and Health* (London: Health Education Authority).

Christensen, P., 1993, 'The social construction of help among Danish children: the intentional act and the actual content'. *Sociology of Health and Illness: A Journal of Medical Sociology*, 15 (4).

Christensen, P., 1997, 'Difference and similarity: how children are constituted in illness and its treatment'. In I. Hutchby and J. Moran-Ellis (eds), *Children and Social Competence: Arenas of Action* (London: Falmer Press).

Christensen, P. and James, A. (eds), 2000, *Research with Children: Perspectives and Practices* (London: Falmer Press).

Coleman, J. S., 1988, 'Social capital in the creation of human capital'. *American Journal of Sociology*, 94 (Supplement), 95–120.

Davis, A. and Jones, L., 1996, 'Children in the urban environment: an issue for the new public health agenda'. *Health and Place*, 2 (2), 107–13.

Davis, A. and Jones, L., 1997, 'Whose neighbourhood? Whose quality of life? Developing a new agenda for children's health in urban settings'. *Health Education Journal*, 56, 350–63.

Fine, B., 2000, *Social Capital versus Social Theory: Political Economy and Social Science at the Turn of the Millennium* (London: Routledge).

Fitzpatrick, S., Hastings, A. and Kintrea, K., 1998, *Including Young People in Urban Regeneration: A Lot to Learn?* (Bristol: The Policy Press).

Foley, M. and Edwards, B., 1999, 'Is it time to disinvest in social capital?' *Journal of Public Policy*, 19 (2), 141–73.

Frazer, E. and Lacey, N., 1993, *The Politics of Community: A Feminist Critique of the Liberal-communitarian Debate* (London: Harvester Wheatsheaf).

Furstenberg, F. R. and Hughes, M. E., 1995, 'Social capital and successful development among at-risk youth'. *Journal of Marriage and the Family*, 57, 580–92.

Gamarnikow, E., and Green, A., 1999, 'The Third Way and social capital: education action zones and a new agenda for education, parents and community?' *International Studies in Sociology of Education*, 9 (1), 3–22.

Hawe, P. and Shiell, P., 2000, 'Social capital and health promotion: a review'. *Social Science and Medicine*, 51, 871–85.

Henderson, P. (ed.), 1995, *Children and Communities* (London: Pluto Press).

Hillman, M. (ed.), 1993, *Children, Transport and the Quality of Life* (London: Policy Studies Institute).

James, A. and Prout, A. (eds), 1997, *Constructing and Reconstructing Childhood*, 2nd ed. (London: Falmer Press).

Labonte, R., 1999, 'Social capital and community development: practitioner emptor'. *Australian and New Zealand Journal of Public Health*, 23 (4), 430–3.

Levi, M., 1996, 'Social and unsocial capital: a review essay of Robert Putnam's *Making Democracy Work*'. *Politics and Society*, 24 (1), 45–55.

Macintyre, S., Maciver, S. and Sooman, A., 1993, 'Area, class and health: should we be focusing on places or people?' *Journal of Social Policy*, 22 (2), 213–34.

Matthews, H., Taylor, M., Percy-Smith, B. and Limb, M., 2000, 'The unacceptable *flaneur*: the shopping mall as a teenage hangout'. *Childhood*, 7 (3), 279–94.

Mayall, B., 1994, *Negotiating Health: Primary School Children at Home and School* (London: Cassell).

Michell, L., 1997, 'Pressure groups: young people's accounts of peer pressure to smoke'. *Social Sciences in Health*, 3 (1), 3–17.

Morrow, V., 1999, 'Conceptualising social capital in relation to the well-being of children and young people: a critical review'. *The Sociological Review*, 47 (4), 744–65.

Morrow, V., 2000a, '"Dirty looks" and "trampy places" in young people's accounts of community and neighbourhood: implications for health inequalities'. *Critical Public Health*, 10 (2), 141–52.

Morrow, V., 2000b, '"We get played for fools": young people's accounts of community and institutional participation'. In J. Bull and J. Ryan (eds), *Changing Families, Changing Communities: Researching Health and Well-being among Children and Young People* (London: Health Education Authority).

Morrow, V., 2001a, *Networks and Neighbourhoods: Children's and Young People's Perspectives: Social Capital for Health Series* (London: Health Development Agency).

Morrow, V., 2001b, 'Using qualitative methods to elicit young people's perspectives on their environments: implications for community health promotion initiatives'. *Health Education Research: Theory and Practice*, 16 (3), 255–68.

O'Brien, M., Jones, D., Sloan, D. and Rustin, M., 2000, 'Children's independent spatial mobility in the urban public realm'. *Childhood*, 7 (3), 257–77.

Pavis, S., Cunningham-Burley, S. and Amos, A., 1996, 'Young people and smoking: exploring meaning and social context'. *Social Sciences in Health*, 2 (4), 226–43.

Pavis, S., Cunningham-Burley, S. and Amos, A., 1997, 'Alcohol consumption and young people: exploring meaning and social context'. *Health Education Research: Theory and Practice*, 12 (3), 311–22.

Popay, J., Williams, G., Thomas, C. and Gatrell, T., 1998, 'Theorising inequalities in health: the place of lay knowledge'. *Sociology of Health and Illness*, 20 (5), 619–44.

Portes, A., 1998, 'Social capital: its origins and applications in modern sociology'. *Annual Review of Sociology*, 24, 1–24.

Portes, A. and Landolt, P., 1996, 'The downside of social capital'. *The American Prospect*, 26, 18–21.

Putnam, R. D., 1993, *Making Democracy Work: Civic Traditions in Modern Italy* (Princeton: Princeton University Press).

Putnam, R. D., 2000, *Bowling Alone: The Collapse and Revival of American Community* (New York: Simon and Schuster).

Rustin, M., 1997, 'Attachment in context'. In S. Kraemer and J. Roberts (eds), *The Politics of Attachment: Towards a Secure Society* (London: Free Association Books).

Social Exclusion Unit, Cabinet Office (SEU), 2000, *National Strategy for Neighbourhood Renewal: Consultation Paper* (London: Cabinet Office).

Speak, S., 2000, 'Children in urban regeneration: foundations for sustainable participation'. *Community Development Journal*, 35 (1), 31–40.

Williams, F., Popay, J. and Oakley, A., 1999, 'Changing paradigms of welfare'. In F. Williams, J. Popay and A. Oakley (eds), *Welfare Research: A Critical Review* (London: University College London Press).

Wolley, H., Spencer, C., Dunn, J., Short, T. and Rowley, G., 1999, 'The child as citizen: experiences of British town and city centres'. *Journal of Urban Design*, 4 (3), 255–82.

11 Planning childhood

Children's social participation in the town of adults

Claudio Baraldi

The Town of Children project: a sociological interpretation

The Town of Children project was created in 1991 in Fano, a small Italian coastal town, and was inspired by the Italian psychologist Francesco Tonucci (1997). Tonucci's starting point was a belief that everyday life in urban settings was becoming unsafe because of increases in traffic, and loss of places where people can walk, meet and enjoy public life. According to Tonucci, children are the main victims of this situation, being confined to their homes and educational institutional contexts, preventing them from autonomous action and movement. As a consequence of this restriction Tonucci suggested that children could be key active and conscious instruments for change in the future of the towns. In line with his ideas, the Town of Children project aimed at changing town life through children's empowerment in the processes of knowing, planning, advising, discussing, deciding and finally acting.

Since its inception the project has involved many children, mostly between the ages of 6 and 10 years old. Among its activities, three are particularly interesting and give a clear idea of the range of projects and their significance. The first is the *Children's Council*, where a group of children attending the fourth and fifth grade of primary schools discuss themes and political strategies for the town development, with the monitoring of an expert. Secondly, *Participated Planning*, where groups of children plan improvement of the urban environment, with the monitoring of a town planner and with teachers' help. Thirdly, *We Go to School by Ourselves*: promotion of children's autonomous movements from home to school, aimed at creating an urban and cultural environment supporting children's general autonomy.

Over the years, the Town of Children has become an important Italian project supporting children's citizenship rights and promoting children's social participation throughout the country. At present, about sixty towns have followed its example and about another 150 have implemented at least one of its main interventions. This success reflects a more general recent emphasis in Italy on the importance of public policies for children. The Town of Children project was influenced by wider global changes including the 1989 United Nations Convention on Children's Rights, which, among other things, insisted on children's social participation rights (Maggioni and Baraldi 1999). Social participation rights are at the core of the Town of Children project, as children are invited to participate in the town life as responsible persons in society.

However, high levels of participation in public life by children are still unusual in Italian contemporary society, and, according to some sociologists, they are rare in other western countries too. As both Jenks (1996) and Qvortrup (1995) have observed, in the contemporary western culture of childhood children are invited to be both autonomous and dependent. Adults tend to seclude children in protected places where they can both play and learn under adult control; towns therefore remain mysterious for children. Innovations such as the Town of Children project openly conflict with this way of thinking, promoting instead an autonomous discourse of childhood in the town. The approach of the project links directly with the new sociological approach to childhood, stressing children as competent social actors or persons, which arose in the same decade (see, for example, Alanen 1988; Ambert 1995; Chisholm *et al.* 1995; Corsaro 1997; Frønes 1997; James, Jenks and Prout 1998; James and Prout 1997; Jenks 1996; Maggioni and Baraldi 1997).

The Town of Children project adopts a perspective which is coherent with our concept of personalisation (Baraldi 1997, 1999), whose roots are in this new emphasis on the autonomous personhood of children (Jenks 1996). Personalisation may be considered as a social process constructing the meaning of individuals as unique and autonomous: in some social systems (interpersonal systems), individuals are directly considered persons, while in other social systems (impersonal systems), their personalised characteristics are considered necessary premises for participation. In each of these social situations, personalised individuals must demonstrate autonomy and sense of responsibility in their choices.

This social construction rose inside modern functionally differentiated societies (Luhmann and De Giorgi 1992), when individuals lost their primary status as members of groups. Instead individuals came to be conceived as responsible for personal choices through participation in highly differentiated social systems, for example through choices of educational and economical career, juridical conformity or deviance, political vote, interpersonal engagement and family formation, safe behaviours and so on. In the last century, the social expectations for personalised choices and responsibilities in normative, cognitive and affective situations continuously increased, leading many to argue for the existence of a 'post modern' society, where grand narratives and unchangeable normative structures are no longer possible and where instability due to individual interacting and contingent choices is maximised. Personalisation processes do not create the conditions for social identities: individuals are socialised into autonomous choices because society creates the structural conditions for their construction as unique and specific beings, excluding them from a primary condition of belonging or dependency.

According to developmental approaches (Clausen 1968; Parsons and Bales 1955; Zigler *et al.* 1982), children are a considerable exception in respect of these general social processes: they are considered incomplete persons because of their age status and are consequently submitted to an educational regime, aimed at creating personalisation for the future. According to the Town of Children project, children are personalised in the present, in spite of their age, that is they 'are who they are' (James *et al.* 1998: 14). Starting from this interpretative framework, the Town of Children project aimed at promoting children's social participation.

Town of Children and promotion of social participation

Social participation can be observed only in communication processes. Adapting a social system theory (Luhmann 1984, 1986), communication can be defined as the co-ordination between action and understanding, thus creating information (Baraldi 1993, 1999). Although individuals participate in communication by both acting and understanding, the idea of social participation specifically implies that they are active: participation in communication may also mean understanding, but it is socially visible only through action. Further, the idea of social participation implies that this action is 'public', that is, it must be visible in the whole society (or community), not only in particular interactive systems (such as families or classes). To sum up, social participation is *visible action in public (societal) contexts*. For this reason, social participation is a clear manifestation of citizenship.

Promotion is the creation of external opportunities for a (social or individual) system's autonomous enhancement. The necessary conditions of promotion are: (1) complete respect for other systems' autonomous operations and (2) renunciation of attempts to change other systems' structures or perspectives from outside. Promotion of children's social participation is thus the creation of opportunities for children's active and visible action in towns, meant as a spatial metaphor for society. Promotion tries to empower children's autonomous social practices, through affective, cognitive or normative forms of communication (Baraldi 1999). Specifically, the Town of Children project tries to create opportunities for children to plan the urban environment (*Participated Planning*), to advise the adult Town Council (*Children's Council*), and to move autonomously in town (*We Go to School by Ourselves*).

The relevance of these ideas can be understood if compared to a previous important intervention, internationally influential, the infant school movement in Reggio Emilia (Edwards *et al.* 1993). This innovation changed the concept of children's schooling, from an emphasis on the externally driven formation of personhood, based on adult control, towards an approach which promoted children's autonomous abilities without didactic teaching and control. Traditionally, while education aims at changing children's experience through adult's action, promotion aims at changing adults' experience through children's action. However, this approach tried to change schooling, seeing education as a form of communication.

Promotion of social participation is not based on an educational form of communication: instead, it makes use of *testimony* (Baraldi 1997). The testimonial form of communication is based on affective expectations, and deals with children as unique and specific persons, maintaining the primary value of respect and renouncing any attempt to change them. The testimonial form is different from the educational form because it refrains from dictating adult perspectives favouring instead an *affective attunment* with children (Haft and Slade 1989): children can 'tune in' to a form of communication which creates the meanings of emotional co-ordination and reciprocity, that is affective confirmation.

The promotion of children's social participation can enhance new cultural orientations that have an important impact on the whole society. To explain the meaning of these orientations, we can use the concept of social representations, in order to indicate 'the outcome of an unceasing babble and a permanent dialogue between individuals' (Moscovici 1984: 95). The culture of childhood and children's culture are made of social representations, and it is very important to understand in which way the promotion of children's social participation can affect them.

The research on *Participated Planning*

The Town of Children project offers a very well defined and theoretically supported programme of activities. However, the effectiveness of the practices supported by this project needed to be examined through empirical research, as the theoretical plans were not necessarily followed through in social practice. Many different variables can contribute to creating a gap between theory and practice, including weakly or vaguely shared basic ideas, difficulties in communication with children, unpredictable obstacles in the social context, underestimation of organisational deficits, political and technical relationship difficulties and so on. An excessive trust in the passage from project idea to actual intervention can create unanticipated problems and even lead to failure (Baraldi and Ramella 1999). In order to understand this passage, the Childhood and Adolescence Laboratory, at the University of Urbino, investigated the Town of Children project activities (Baraldi and Maggioni 2000). In this chapter I will focus primarily on the *Participated Planning* dimension involving children aged between 6 and 10 years of age.

Participated Planning activities consist of a series of workshops involving skilled adults and groups of children, aimed at promoting children's production of a variety of urban projects concerning an area of the town (a square, a school, a park, a street and so on). Children were invited to create plastic models or drawings of this area, illustrating their proposals for a new urban plan. The project co-ordinator was a skilled town planner who also trained teachers to facilitate the workshops. Over time, as the number of participant children increased, teacher-led workshops became more common, creating tensions between the adults: the teachers claimed that the town planner did not give them sufficient help, and the town planner complained that the teachers were insufficiently sensitive to the ideas behind the project.

In order to understand, explain and evaluate this intervention, a complex research methodology was used, including: (1) interviewing the town planner co-ordinating the activities, the teachers involved in them, and the politicians who promoted them; (2) videotaping the children's group workshops with the town planner and their teachers; (3) creating participatory group interviews with the children (including pre-adolescents who had been involved in past activities).

In this way, the researchers compared the adults' perspectives, the children's perspectives and the videotaped communication processes, producing an analysis of: (1) forms of communication between children and adults, encouraging or not encouraging children's social participation; (2) children's social representations of adults' social world and adults' social representations of children's experience and action, including a positive or negative evaluation of the promotion of social participation; (3) the relationship between forms of communication and social representations, through a comparative analysis.

Forms of *Participated Planning*

Over the years, the *Participated Planning* activities produced a great number of plastic models and drawings, concerning schools, squares, roads, parks, suggesting how these places could change and be adapted through the perspectives of children (Figures 11.1–11.3). Children were able to transform their individual ideas in a group-work context and then in final-quality products. The high quality of these products demonstrated both the children's abilities and the efficacy of the group work co-ordinated by adults. These products are grounded in the form of communication between children and these adults.

On one hand, the teachers felt that the *Participated Planning* activities presented an educational methodology, in the double meaning of specific technical training (in relation to the way of planning) and the construction of a global personality (in relation to children's responsibility towards the town). The teachers considered education as the basis for activities.

On the other hand, the town planner openly declared his reluctance to assume an educational role and to use educational methodologies. Like the teachers, the town planner observed the effects of planning activities on children's development: he emphasised the growth of children's participation competence, their sense of responsibility and their competence in claiming their own rights. However, he placed greater emphasis on other issues. In his opinion, whilst the *Participated Planning* necessarily included training for technical aspects of town planning, 'it is not a didactic instrument, it does not have the purpose of teaching something to the children' (town planner,

Figure 11.1 Fano – a town model by children

Figure 11.2 Fano – a town model by children

Figure 11.3 Fano – a town model by children

interview). According to him, the primary purpose of the activities was not education but the promotion of social participation, through the construction of a logic of planning. Through stimulating the children's creativity and discussing planning problems (based on 'brainstorming' and personalised explanations and decisions), the co-ordinating town planner tried to implement a methodology which explicitly rejected teaching.

The *Participated Planning* methodology is based on testimony, focusing on listening, understanding and discussing the children's perspectives, giving voice to personal creativity, without evaluation, without interfering with the children's ideas and without directing the children's activities. The town planner linked the cognitive expectations implicit in the activities (the result had to be a change in the town's image) to non-educational forms of communication, giving relevance to social processes which were different from those appreciated by the teachers.

The testimonial form of communication between the town planner and the children was clear in the videotaped workshops, which presented the following general characteristics: (1) the rules were defined spontaneously, without any imposition, while silence and respect were created thanks to the interest in the activity and the methodology (normative testimony); (2) the town planner encouraged all the children's voices, including those of generally silent and shy children (cognitive testimony); (3) the town planner made use of his own body in communication, getting closer to the children, stooping to their height, using an affective tone, searching for sympathy (affective testimony).

The dominant form of communication was cognitive testimony, supported by respect for and closeness to children as persons, with the adult playing an active and personalised role. The planner always discussed with the children and invited them to express their wishes, encouraging them to produce ideas and transform them in technical projects, as illustrated in the following extracts from conversations between the town planner and groups of children.

The town planner (*TP*) is joking with the children (*CH*) about a word written on the blackboard: Piu Piu . . .

TP: So we said that we want a lake with a swimming pool in it.
All: Football pitch, swimming pool . . .
TP: Hold on, lake, swimming pool . . . you're thinking of a super school! You'll never want to go home.
CH1:   Let's stay here for ever . . .
(The other children laugh, there's a lot of confusion, everybody is talking at the same time.)
TP (to the child who is writing on the blackboard):   Draw the dashes, tennis . . . court.
CH1:   How do you spell 'tennis'?
TP: It's T-E-N-N-I-S. Then what?
CH2:   Bookshop.
TP: OK, a library, and then?
CH3:   If we are going to stay here, we'll need beds . . .
All: What?
CH2:   And then our mothers . . .
(The children talk, while TP helps the child at the blackboard who is in difficulty with the word 'library')
TP: We said we want classrooms with computers, video cameras, stereo sets, television . . . what do you call a classroom where you have all these things? Do you know?
CH: No.
TP: It's a . . . multimedia room, which means it contains all these things (he turns to a child who is writing and dictates the word 'multimedia'

to him). . . And with one word we say them all. Can you remember
the meaning of multimedia? What's in there?

CH: Computer, stereo, computer, projector . . .

TP: So all the classrooms must be multimedia. And then we said there
         must be a big aquarium.

CH1 (to the child at the blackboard):   An aquarium, Davide.

(Another boy corrects the child at the blackboard who has made a spelling
mistake. The children make fun of him, but TP defends him gently.)

TP: It's OK, it's still a 'Q'.

The generally respectful pattern of communication evident here derives
from the attention shown by the town planner to the children, for example
to those who had problems in expressing themselves.

The town planner called the children's attention to the different topics,
without guiding them along a pre-defined path: knowledge was constructed
through an articulated communicative action which implied the children's
active participation, without either evaluation of their performances or guiding of their paths.

TP: In your opinion, who makes the school? (He kneels down to the
         children's height)

CH1:   Builders!

TP: Builders! But who pays them? (The child points at him) Me? No,
         I'm not going to pay them.

CH2:   The headmaster!

TP: No, he is not going to pay. Who do you think is paying for it?

CH3:   The president!

CH4:   Our parents!

TP: Well, more or less! But that's not totally true.

CH5:   The teacher.

TP: He's got to pay for everything? (Smiling) Who decides what's right
         or wrong for our town?

CH2 (shouting):   The Town Council!

TP: That's it! The Town Council pays for it.

CH2 (making a gesture of satisfaction):   Yeeeas!

TP: Yes, but who pays the Town Council?

CH3:   If we want to use the roads . . . From the taxes they receive . . . we
         pay taxes to be allowed to use the roads . . . and with that money
         they build schools . . .

Sometimes this testimonial form shifted towards a moderate educational
form, specifically oriented to the children's learning of technical abilities. In
these cases, the strategic and educational promotion of children's learning
process prevailed, as in Reggio Emilia's infant schools, without teaching and
evaluating. The town planner promoted the children's learning of democratic

rules, through a methodology including (1) questions about the children's opinions, (2) the children's answers and (3) a final consensual (or majority) decision.

TP: The canteen in the garden?
CH1:   Yellow.
CH2:   Green.
TP: Who thinks it would be easy to build a canteen in the garden? (A boy raises his hand)
CH3:   No, yellow!
TP: It's difficult to build it.
CH3:   Yeah, that's true!
TP: Then, automatic caretakers.
CH4:   Green, green.
TP: What colour do you think they should be?
CH5:   Red.
CH6:   Yellow.
CH3:   How can we do that?
TP: Do you think it would be easy?
CH1:   Well, it's quite a job . . . ten million [lire] per caretaker . . . gosh . . .
TP: So you think that ten million per caretaker . . .
CH1:   No, it's not enough! (They discuss among themselves)
TP: Who thinks it would be easy to make automatic caretakers?
CH1:   If you have the money . . . (Some clap their hands ironically)
TP: Now, what colour shall we give it?
CH6:   Yellow.
CH (most of them):   Red, red.
TP: OK, then it's red. Do you think automatic caretakers are essential?
CH: Nooo!
TP: Who thinks they are? (They raise their hands)
CH4:   At least they work.
CH7:   Bravo!
TP: Who thinks they're not necessary? (They raise their hands) So, if they are not essential, we abolish them, because we have to start to see what we can do.
CH1:   Yes, that's true!

This communicative process openly intended to educate children to democratic discussion methodologies. The use of this method led to person-centred cognitive education, based on the expectation of encouraging cognitive progress in the children. This implies an orientation to the distinction between what is correct and what is not in their performance while remaining close to them and keeping listening to their points of view. This generates expectations in terms of learning and technical competence and highlights listening to the children. The town planner asked the questions, the children answered and he drew the conclusions.

The children declared a great liking for the *Participated Planning* activities and appreciated the town planner's approach much more than the usual scholastic methodology: 'Here we have fun'; 'At school, we write and we get bored' (children, participatory group interviews). In a similar manner to what happened in Reggio's infant schools (Edwards *et al.* 1993), the children could explicitly observe that they were learning without teaching: 'You also learn playing'; 'We made all the operations, like in maths, but with more fun'; 'The things done at school are more theoretical, while here you have immediately a practice and you have more fun, and you are able to produce more'; 'The *Planning* involves you. For example, you plan an area near your house, that is, you live there. At school, it is not interesting for you, personally' (children, focus groups).

The children clearly differentiated the form of communication with the town planner from the educational forms, because they could see in this form of communication the prevailing value of the basic intention (changing not children through education, but town and education through children). In our view, the moderate person-centred cognitive form of education was observed as very close to the testimonial form, due to its high promotional content. The children also appreciated some changes in communication with teachers, thanks to the participated planning: 'It is better, because in the normal lessons you can see that children are inferior to adults'; 'Normally we ask the teachers if we can do something . . . with this project the teachers ask us'; 'During the normal lessons, the teachers decide everything, during the children's project they listen to your opinions and you decide what you want to do' (children, participatory group interviews).

The children observed the possibility that teachers listened to them and allowed them to participate in their own learning, deciding and acting. However, this possibility was only sometimes transformed into reality, as teachers were often absorbed in their traditional roles. In many videotaped teacher-led planning groups the primary form of communication was educational, with low levels of affective attunment (Haft and Slade 1989).

In some situations, the educational form paid attention to the children's personhood: the teachers tried to give order to the children's tasks and to guide them, without forgetting an affective orientation to their persons, useful for the success of activities. In these cases, communication between the teachers and the children was very similar to communication between the town planner and the children, though the affective attunment was lower. This similarity encouraged the children's learning of techniques and participation values.

Teacher (T):	The flags in the football pitch are as high as the goals.
CH:	The goal is too small.
T:	It doesn't matter, that's OK. Do you understand Enrico? It's a good job, like Chiara's, but now (speaking to Chiara) why don't you go and draw with Federico?

Chiara:	May I draw a little football player?
T:	Yes . . . no, not a football player, because they are all there. Do you really want to draw it?
Chiara:	On the bench.
T:	Good, on the bench . . . But if you keep stumbling over the lamp-post, it will fall down again. OK, Chiara?
Chiara:	And this?
T:	We don't need it any more, you can take it home if you like.
Chiara:	Yes. (Chiara withdraws to do her job, but then attracted by the model she gets closer and touches it)
T:	Chiara, watch out. (The model of the lamp-post falls down)
T:	(She sounds sorry) Oh no . . . (she pretends she's crying and then puts the lamp-post back)
CH1:	Chiara, what have you done?
Chiara:	It won't stand up . . .
CH1 (joking):	Next time I'll bring some chains to tie you up.
Chiara:	Oh, yeah? I'll tie *you* up.

Children were free to work in the way they preferred, they walked around the classroom, they talked and helped one another, and were seldom told to be quiet or orderly. The teachers sometimes intervened when someone was in trouble, but most of the times they let the children decide freely. When the children finished a task, they showed it to their teacher who kindly corrected them or praised them.

In other situations, education was impersonal, directive and authoritative, the affective attunement was completely absent, and the expectations of learning notions and technical competence were evident. In these contexts children's personal identities were not in the foreground, primarily because: (1) the teachers' main purpose was clearly the achievement of good results and performances; (2) the teachers intervened in the children's task and the children felt insecure, continuously asking for an acknowledgement of their results; (3) there were few rewards and many reprimands; (4) the children talked little and in a low voice; (5) each of them had her or his own task and the teacher gave instructions as to what had to be done; (6) there were no affective gestures.

Teacher (T):	There's a mistake here, there's a mistake here . . . (She corrects the drawing using a pencil and a ruler) . . . because this part can't be . . . pass me the ruler . . . attached to the school, can it? Here, you see, there's a part that should be . . . where we should put the floor . . . on what? What's this? At the moment, before changing it, there are the offices. So, we have put the computer room upstairs and there are the offices downstairs, so this is where we are going to start . . . I'm not sure we'll do . . . here's

the tree, draw more leaves. And what colour shall we paint the school walls? Yellow?

CH1:   Orange.

T: But . . . we've done a red roof!

T: We can't stick the drawings to the photos yet, don't move them with your hands . . . go on with the trees . . . Sure, now you can colour everything, let's remove the tape, but keep thinking about the rooms inside; I mean, here we are behind the school and we have . . . What did we say we would put there? Can you remember?

T: No, you're moving everything, come on children, we need to put a little piece of tape back. Don't move it, don't move it. Copy the tree here: brown branches and green leaves . . . Wait, because it's all going to be stuck on a big sheet . . . Don't make a mess, or we'll have to start again. Today is the last day, we haven't got any more time.

(The girls speak in a low voice and move shyly. They stand for a while in front of the drawing without doing anything. The teacher moves to another group)

T: So, let's have another look at the rooms. This is the west side, no, the east side, so there should be . . . the girl is playing the piano, so it's the music room, and this should be the computer. Why has it got balloons?

CH2 (intimidated, in a low voice and slowly):   I didn't draw that.

T: Who did the east part of the school?

(After a while, two children arrive. The teacher's intimidating tone leads the children to try to blame someone else for the possible mistake)

CH2:   I did it too, teacher, but they did half the computer . . . (pointing at the other children)

T: This is the computer room.

(At a certain point, the teacher sees that the sky has not been evenly coloured)

T: Who did this sky?

CH1:   I didn't.

CH2:   Neither did I.

T: I didn't ask who did not do it. I asked who did it, because here, either you do the sky or . . . here it's no good . . . Come on Judi, fill the sky using the light blue marker. And here, you do the sky, colour all around here, together with him. How is this group doing? No more trees now, add some leaves, like this. Because the other children spoiled it, drawing the tops. Look how high this one is and look how far you went.

During the activities, these teachers indicated some standards that the children had to reach and the children followed their instructions. The teacher's continuous interventions concerned both the general behaviour and the specific planning activity: the teachers underlined as mistakes the personal and unexpected nature of children's productions (a particular way of observing a tree, the sky, the school building). In these situations, communication had as primary forms direction, correction, reprimand, shown in phrases such as 'someone has wrecked it', 'don't make a mess', 'don't scribble on the drawings', 'if these children paid more attention'. These forms prevented children from social participation and created expectations of normative direction and punishment. In some cases, these forms also created evident behavioural problems. The children went 'out of control' and the communication took an impersonal normative form, through which regulations ('speak in a low voice', 'sit down', 'finish your job', 'pay attention') were imposed under menace of punishment. In one videotaped interaction, the children shouted and ran across the classroom and the teacher continuously asked for silence; then, she lost her temper and shouted louder and louder. The request of respect for norms ended up in a final punishment, through which the hierarchical relationship became effective.

Teacher (T):	Eleonora, hush! . . . The labels are all ready. (Several children speak to the teacher at the same time, the situation is quite chaotic)
T:	Now, I need the . . .
Pasquale:	10 . . . 11 . . . 7 . . . (tries to put the labels that have to be stuck on the poster in order)
T:	So the number should be . . .
Pasquale:	. . . the small one.
T:	They are all numbered on the back, eh Elisa, there are the marks too . . . Pasquale? Pasquale, listen! Come on, Pasquale! (She goes nearer and takes his hand to make her call more effective) Are you listening to me? Look for them, first try to put all the numbers in sequence . . .
CH1:	Miss, it doesn't fit in . . .
T:	Look at them, see if there is a mark, check where it goes . . . Oh! You've got it?
CH2:	Yes. (There is a lot of confusion. The teacher goes from group to group, speaking in a loud voice, unsmiling. Some girls imitate her, telling their friends off)
T:	So, just a moment (The noise continues, her voice is louder) One minute! How many have got the brush? (Children raise their hands) Well, those three. (She shouts) I told you to stop sticking labels on the poster, I told you to go to the other desk.
Lisa:	Exactly! (She tells the child off, too)

T: Ale, come here, I need you! (She turns to another boy) I told
            you not to work on the desk with the poster on it, go down
            there! Alessandro what are you doing there? Come on! Davide,
            sit down. Come on!
            (The children get really wild, some of them fight, some run
            around in the classroom)

T: Hold on a second, don't stay near the posters because . . . (She
            speaks as she gets closer to the poster and sees it has been
            spoiled. Suddenly she shouts) Look at this! What's happened
            here? Very well, are we going to the gym today? I don't think
            so, I guess Davide is going to remain in the classroom and
            work. Go on, sit down!

This situation showed that the distance created between the children and
the teacher is connected to the failure of cognitive expectations: the children
did not participate in verbal communication, but remained silent, passively
working or running and shouting around the classroom. The gap between
cognitive expectations and results is evident and the consequence is an *impersonal normative education*.

When the children watched these videotaped sessions during the focus
groups, they clearly outlined the differences between the educational and the
testimonial form of communication: 'The teacher teaches the children, he
does not. He is an architect, he is not interested in teaching . . . he does not
follow us' (children, participatory group interview). They accepted the teaching role during the school lessons and evaluated the specific teaching abilities
positively, but they refused this role during the *Participated Planning*: 'If the
teachers are the only ones to contribute, it is no more an ideal project for
children; it is an ideal project for teachers'; 'This is the Town of Children,
and yet the teacher wants a perfect drawing!' (children, participatory group
interviews).

The children appreciated the adults' help and generally they expected
it. However, they claimed that this help was not a substitute for their competence and participation and that adults had to be sensitive to children's
autonomous choices and abilities. The general opinion was that 'children
must be free to do things as they know; if they imagine the sky with birds,
the teacher can not tell them to draw the sky with the sun' (boy, 10). If,
on the contrary, teachers do so then the promotion of social participation
fails.

The consequences for children's personalisation

The children participating in promotional activities expressed a positive
judgement of their experience and considered it suitable for their peers.
They found their experience of new activities, places and persons amusing
and interesting. They appreciated the opportunity to express their opinions

about interesting themes. Finally, they appreciated the collective dimension of the experience (group activity) and the community life which developed.

From children's perspective, both social participation in town life and learning techniques of planning were important results of their involvement in the activities. This project stimulated a strong interest in the town life: the children observed new communication and action possibilities in their social context. Thus, the project promoted their personalisation.

It is easy to observe that the testimonial form of communication enhanced satisfaction with activities and satisfaction with activities enhanced the children's interest in social participation, empowering their personal autonomy, sense of responsibility and request for respect. The children appreciated adults' help, but they asked for autonomy in choices and expressions, and for adults' listening to their opinions and proposals. In this way, the children's planning activity created new expectations among the children about communication with adults and appreciation for promotion through testimony.

However, there was also a widespread disappointment of expectations. Most of the children were critical about the lack of practical results emerging from the *Participated Planning*. As a matter of fact, some modest project ideas were transformed into real urban interventions (including a statue in a cloister and an artificial vista point in a park near the seaside), while the most challenging projects were ignored.

The children observed an 'objective' difficulty in the adults' decisional process about these projects: the adults could not perform the children's plans because they were unfeasible.

> Maybe we want too many things in our school, and then where are we going to put all those things?
>
> We could never make it because it's too difficult.
>
> I think they won't build it because the builders can't do so many things in two weeks.
>
> Children's imagination has no limits, so maybe they didn't build it because it wasn't possible.
>
> Now I understand it was impossible to make.
>
> I thought they could make it, but now I see things differently and I even laugh because I understand it was impossible.
>
> It was like wonderland, it was really too much. (children, focus groups)

In this way, children gained a 'realistic' way of assessing and evaluating the feasibility of plans. On the other hand, however, the children made a clear negative attribution to these adults' will: they did not want to perform the children's plans.

> I think the Town Council worries about important things; but these things [that is, the ideas and projects created by the children] are important too.

> They actually do the necessary things, but not really all of them, especially [not] things that are important to children. (children, participatory group interviews)

In this way, the children started to be sceptical about the adults' intentions and 'real' motivations. This result may be considered a negative one for the intervention, as it has the potential to create a lack of confidence and a sense of betrayal towards adult society. Indeed some local politicians and teachers were concerned by these issues and criticised the naivety of the project. It should be noted that Tonucci himself claimed that it is better if adults do not start activities which produce only disappointment (Tonucci 1997).

However, the experience of disappointment can have productive consequences for children. It has the potential to create a more autonomous and reflexive stance: children can consider their perspective as both different from adults' perspective and as valuable as adults' perspective. Combining the two disappointment consequences (realism and scepticism), pre-adolescents showed a particular competence in differentiating themselves from children (thanks to realism) and adults (thanks to scepticism): disappointment improved the children's cognitive personalisation process.

To sum up, the children's social representations of their social participation and of their persons arose both from satisfaction and from disappointment. On one side, satisfaction created appreciation for the values and the practices of social participation. On the other side, disappointment enhanced cognitive expectations about social participation. Both processes improved the children's personalisation process.

Resistance of the traditional culture of childhood

In this section I will review how adults reacted to *Participated Planning* and how the innovation affected social representations of childhood in society.

The teachers shared the opinion that society must give relevance to children's proposals, observing them as creative and active components. They openly stated that it is possible and right to listen to children's proposals, and that children have the right to give expression to their own ideas. Consequently, they showed appreciation for a form of education focused on children's persons, under the guide of competent adults: in this perspective, the activities of the *Participated Planning* were particularly supported and appreciated. Thus, these activities were appreciated only because they were thought to educate: first of all, they educate children in dialogue, friendship and participation; besides, they stimulate knowledge and interest in the town problems; thirdly, they enhance interdisciplinary knowledge about notions and techniques. Teachers appreciated the learning of organisational and collaborative abilities, of autonomy in group work management, of relational and critical competence and of the respect for common rules.

In appreciating these activities, the teachers clearly underlined their preference for educational forms of communication. They observed the advantage given by the guidance of an expert adult who is able to transmit useful knowledge. Their approval was conditioned by the activities' adaptation to the school system: they expected the activities to contribute to the children's formation, coherently with school functions. The teachers' perspective is clearly different from the cultural orientation of the Town of Children project: the teachers did not give any political meaning to the activities.

It is apparently more surprising that this educational interpretation was shared by politicians who were in the position to understand better and support the political meanings of promotion of children's social participation. The research demonstrated that most of the politicians were glad to give educational relevance to the project, but they did not accept the idea of children as planners. This sounded absurd because it was denied that children could achieve rational planning results: they cannot be compared to adults in thinking and planning the town and it is necessary to prevent children from thinking that they are *really* planning. An influential politician expressed this position very clearly:

> I give a positive evaluation of this intervention. Maybe, the achievements were not too many, but the Town Council made some choices, taking into account people's mobility seriously. Fano wants to give some liveability and some power to children, pedestrians, cyclists. However a fast change is difficult. We need to take into consideration children, elder people, businessmen. Politicians must avoid the creation of obstacles and they must find solutions for everybody, for example, cycle paths, pedestrian areas, game areas, respecting the existing facilities. When a child makes a good experience, it is a positive experience; it becomes negative when the child is frustrated, because she/he thinks that she/he was not considered in her/his merits. This is a wrong way to see the project: it is necessary to explain to her/him that she/he has done her/his best, she/he has received education. (politician, interview)

Also most of the parents interviewed about other activities shared the representation of the Town of Children as education. The parents of the children involved in the *Children's Council* activities observed this experience as very useful for their children's psychological and social growth. They thought that the experience could develop children's critical, decisional and creative competence, enhancing their understanding of the value of democracy. In their perspective, after this experience, children paid more attention to social problems and their rights, read newspapers, gave more expression to their ideas, were interested in facing problems and responsibilities and related to peers and adults more easily. However, parents were less enthusiastic about implementing the *We Go to School by Ourselves* element of the project.

The percentage of children who went to school on their own was quite low: replies from parents indicated that 23 per cent of children went to school on their own (29 per cent including those who were accompanied by their older siblings).[1] Yet, 84 per cent of the families agreed with the project, and so did a large majority of the parents who did not let their children go to school on their own (80 per cent). Moreover, almost all the parents (87 per cent) thought that the initiative had advantageous results, such as favouring the children's autonomy, increasing their ability to face danger and getting adults used to children being present in the streets. This discrepancy between principles and practice was mainly justified by the insufficient support of the local administration. The most important problem expressed by parents involved in the experiment was lack of safety (91 per cent), strictly linked to the fears of the parents (79 per cent). The meaning of 'lack of safety' consisted of a combination of deficiencies in the state of the roads, dangers related to traffic and the risk of meeting dangerous people. Failure, therefore, was related to the child's lack of safety on their way to school: this means that the lack of guiding adults was fatal to the project.

In our view, the failure of the overall project can be explained by a stress on the primacy of adult guidance, a cultural preference for education and the domination of a developmental theory approach. In Italy, the mainstream culture of childhood clearly follows the traditional developmental theory. Using social psychologist Serge Moscovici's theory (Moscovici 1984), we can say that developmental theory has been transformed into a widespread social representation of childhood and age status. This social representation has its roots in the apparent 'growth process' and in the psychological and behavioural differences between children and adults. Linked to this social representation is the fear for dangers and risks. Although the idea of a personalised child is becoming increasingly popular in society, the older and more traditional vision of a 'dyonisian child' who is systematically at risk (Jenks 1996) has not disappeared yet: our society is mainly concerned with children's weakness (Baraldi 1999), and the child's 'hybrid body' (Prout 2000) seems to confirm the main social representation. This social representation is continuously fed by mass media reports of children in danger or dangerous children. Consequently, it is very difficult to convince adults (above all parents and teachers) that children can be autonomous and active in society.

In this cultural context, an active minority (Moscovici 1976) of adults is more receptive to the idea of children as complete and autonomous persons, able to contribute to the political change of the town. However, for this minority it is not easy to challenge the mainstream culture. Experts themselves leave their educational prejudice with great reluctance, often asserting that social participation can be promoted only through educational forms of communication. In this way, education maintains its character of being an absolute necessity in society and alternative forms of communication between adults and children are ignored or condemned. Does this preference make some problems in society? Obviously, it depends on the observer's standpoint. Certainly, as we have seen, if social participation remains subordinate to education, the Town of Children project fails, although almost nobody will admit it.

Ambiguities: new cultures and old traditions

To sum up, we can observe that the Town of Children project has resulted in three new cultural approaches which can be added to the traditional culture of childhood: (1) adults' minority culture of promotion of children's social participation; (2) children's culture of a new way of communicating with adults and acting in society; (3) children's more sceptical and realistic culture of the social world.

In our view the promotion of children's social participation improves children's trust in the adult world only if and when children can observe a testimonial form of communication, that is, when adults show themselves to be persons who encourage and help children respecting children's perspectives, listening to their desires and needs, but also participating autonomously and technically with children. Through participation in the Town of Children project, children gave meaning to the difference between testimony and education, which enhanced their distinction between adults' help and adults' guidance. A testimonial approach works on changing the town rather than the child whilst an educational approach tends to focus on changing the child's personality.

In public opinion the educational approach to childhood continues to prevail and consequently children are seen as persons in progress, who are not able to make their own proposals without adult educational guidance. These difficulties are imported from the theoretical foundations of our culture of childhood: when we need to explain the way children are personalised, traditional socialisation theories based on developmental ideas (for example, Berger and Luckmann 1966; Clausen 1968; Denzin 1979; Parsons and Bales 1955; Zigler *et al.* 1982) always emerge beside new theories of social actors. It seems very difficult to avoid the idea that children *become* not only citizens, but also competent persons.

We can expect that in present society an effective support of children's social participation will be coupled with a largely ineffective attempt to change the mainstream culture of childhood. The Town of Children project promotes a contradiction between two different images inside this culture: children's competence and children's development. This contradiction becomes evident when, as we have found in this project, politicians hesitate about allowing children's social participation, teachers support only activities with a clear and high educational value, and parents refuse to adhere to activities which do not have a clearly certified educational value. These difficulties create a further contradiction between children's culture of society and adults' culture of childhood, feeding scepticism and realism among children.

We can conclude that our society is not able to choose between a developmental and a participatory interpretation of childhood. Thus, it is not clear whether the Town of Children project itself is currently either promoting competent planning children or planning children's development.

Note

1 This percentage was calculated out of 403 children from 6 to 10 years old, attending two schools in Fano which participated in the experiment.

References

Alanen L., 1988, 'Rethinking childhood'. *Acta Sociologica*, 31, 1, 53–67.

Ambert, A.-M., 1995, 'Sociological theorizing on children: concluding thoughts'. *Sociological Studies on Children*, 8 (Stamford: Jay Press), 247–56.

Baraldi, C., 1993, 'Structural coupling: simultaneity and difference between communication and thought'. *Communication Theory*, 3, 112–29.

Baraldi, C., 1997, 'Forms of education in infant schools: a sociological approach'. In F. Mouritsen and J. Qvortrup (eds), *Childhood and Children's Culture* (Odense: South Jutland University Centre and Odense University), 1–15.

Baraldi, C., 1999, *Il disagio della società* [*The Society's Discomfort*] (Milan: FrancoAngeli).

Baraldi, C. and Maggioni, G., 2000, *Una città con i bambini: progetti ed esperienze del Laboratorio di Fano* [*A Town with Children: Projects and Experiences in Fano*] (Rome: Donzelli).

Baraldi, C. and Ramella, F., 1999, *Politiche per i giovani: il caso delle Marche* [*Policies for Youth: The Case of Marche*] (Rome: Donzelli).

Berger, P. and Luckmann, T., 1966, *The Social Construction of Reality* (Garden City: Doubleday).

Chisholm, L., Büchner, P., Krüger, H. and Du Bois-Reymond, M. (eds), 1995, *Growing Up in Europe: Contemporary Horizons in Childhood and Youth Studies* (Berlin and New York: De Gruyter).

Clausen, J. (ed.), 1968, *Socialisation and Society* (Boston: Little, Brown and Co.).

Corsaro, W., 1997, *The Sociology of Childhood* (Thousands Oak: Pine Forge Press).

Edwards, C., Gandini, L. and Forman, G. (eds), 1993, *One Hundred Languages of Children* (Norwood: Ablex Publishing Corporation).

Denzin, N. K., 1979, *Childhood Socialisation* (San Francisco: Jossey-Bass).

Frønes, I., 1997, 'Childhood and social theory'. *Childhood*, 4 (3), 259–63.

Haft, W. L. and Slade, A., 1989, 'Affect attunment and maternal attachment: a pilot study'. *Infant Mental Health Journal*, 10 (3), 157–72.

James, A., Jenks, C. and Prout, A., 1998, *Theorizing Childhood* (Oxford: Polity Press).

James, A. and Prout A. (eds), 1997, *Constructing and Reconstructing Childhood*, 2nd ed. (London: Falmer Press).

Jenks, C., 1996, *Childhood* (London and New York: Routledge).

Luhmann, N., 1984, *Soziale Systeme* (Frankfurt am Main: Suhrkamp).

Luhmann, N., 1986, 'The autopoiesis of social systems'. In F. Geyer and Van der Zouwen (eds), *Sociocybernetic Paradoxes: Observation, Control and Evolution of Self-steering Systems* (London and Beverly Hills: Sage), 172–92.

Luhmann, N. and De Giorgi, R., 1992, *Teoria della società* [*Theory of Society*] (Milan: FrancoAngeli).

Maggioni, G. and Baraldi, C., 1997, *Cittadinanza dei bambini e costruzioni sociali dell'infanzia* [*Children's Citizenship and Social Constructions of Childhood*] (Urbino: QuattroVenti).

Maggioni, G. and Baraldi, C., 1999, 'Children's rights and contemporary sociological perspectives of childhood'. In F. Van Loon and K. Van Aeken (eds), *60 maal recht en 1 maal wijn* [*Sociology of Law, Social Problems and Legal Policy*] (Leuven: Acco), 63–74.

Moscovici, S., 1976, *Social Influence and Social Change* (London: Academic Press).

Moscovici, S., 1984, 'The phenomenon of social representations'. In R. Farr and S. Moscovici (eds), *Social Representations* (Cambridge: Cambridge University Press), 3–69.

Parsons, T. and Bales, R., 1955, *Socialisation and Interaction Process* (New York: Free Press).

Qvortrup, J., 1995, 'Childhood in Europe: a new field of social research'. In L. Chisholm, P. Büchner, H. H. Krüger and M. du Bois-Reymond (eds), *Growing Up in Europe: Contemporary Horizons in Childhood and Youth Studies* (Berlin and New York: De Gruyter), 7–19.

Prout, A. (ed.), 2000, *The Body, Childhood and Society* (Basingstake: Macmillan).

Tonucci, F., 1997, *La città dei bambini* [*The Town of Children*] (Rome: Laterza).

Zigler, E. F., Lamb, M. E. and Child, I. L., 1982, *Socialisation and Personality Development* (Oxford and New York: Oxford University Press).

Index

Note: page numbers followed by 'n' refer to notes.